Edexcel GCSE
Music

edexcel
advancing learning, changing lives

John Arkell • Jonny Martin

A PEARSON COMPANY

Published by Pearson Education Limited, a company incorporated in England and Wales, having its registered office at Edinburgh Gate, Harlow, Essex, CM20 2JE. Registered company number: 872828

www.heinemann.co.uk

Edexcel is a registered trade mark of Edexcel Limited

Text © Pearson Education Limited 2009
First published 2009

13 12
10 9 8

British Library Cataloguing in Publication Data
A catalogue record for this book is available from the British Library

ISBN 978 1 846904 03 5

Edited by Janice Baiton
Designed by Wooden Ark Studios
Typeset by Tek-Art, Crawley Down, West Sussex
Original illustrations © Pearson Education Ltd
Picture research by Elena Wright and Lindsay Lewis
Cover photo/illustration © iStockphoto/Titelio
Printed in Great Britain by Ashford Colour Press Ltd

Acknowledgements
We would like to thank Lucy Curzon for her kind permission to reproduce her story in the Exam Zone.

The authors and publisher would like to thank the following individuals and organisations for permission to reproduce photographs:

P7 Lebrecht Music and Arts Photo Library/Alamy; P18 iStockphoto/Steven Wynn; P20 The Print Collector/Alamy; P35 Lebrecht Music and Arts Photo Library/Alamy; P38 Photolibrary; P50 Photos 12/Alamy; P52 The Print Collector/Alamy; P53 Pictorial Press Ltd/Alamy; P63 Patrick Riviere/ Getty Images; P65 Alfred Eisenstaedt/Time & Life Pictures/Getty Images; P67 Pictorial Press Ltd/ Alamy; P76 Lee Campbell/Getty Images; P77 Ebet Roberts/Redferns; P84 L Shutterstock.com/ dan ionut popescu; P84 R iStockphoto/sabrina dei nobili; P86 Suzanne Long/Alamy; P88 Robert Holmes/Alamy; P90 Lebrecht Music and Arts Photo Library/Alamy; P104 Bob Berg/Getty Images; P114 Photolibrary; P126 Stan Kujawa/Alamy; P128 TL Eyewire; P128 BL Lebrecht Music and Arts Photo Library/Alamy; P128 BR Eyewire; P128 TR Ted Foxx/Alamy; P130 Stephen Power/Alamy; P135 ArkReligion.com/Alamy; P138 Photolibrary; P139 Photos.com; P143 Bruno De Hogues/Getty Images; P144 Photodisc/C Squared Studios/Tony Gable; P146 Images of Africa Photobank/Alamy; P168 Stockphoto4u/iStockphotos.

Every effort has been made to contact copyright holders of material reproduced in this book. Any omissions will be rectified in subsequent printings if notice is given to the publishers.

Disclaimer
This Edexcel publication offers high-quality support for the delivery of Edexcel qualifications.

Edexcel endorsement does not mean that this material is essential to achieve any Edexcel qualification, nor does it mean that this is the only suitable material available to support any Edexcel qualification. No endorsed material will be used verbatim in setting any Edexcel examination/assessment and any resource lists produced by Edexcel shall include this and other appropriate texts.

Copies of official specifications for all Edexcel qualifications may be found on the Edexcel website – www.edexcel.com

Contents

Introduction

This series is designed to help you succeed in your study of Edexcel GCSE Music. It contains all the information you need on the 12 set works that form the basis of the listening and appraising examination, including biographical information on the composers and a detailed analysis of all of the set works. It covers the requirements of the new specification as published by Edexcel (for first teaching in 2009).

The full set of resources that comprise the Edexcel GCSE Music series includes:

◆ this student book
◆ a teacher guide
◆ an anthology containing printed scores of all the set works
◆ a set of two audio CDs containing recordings of the set works.

The Student Book

The student book follows the structure of the new Edexcel GCSE Music specification with all of the topics arranged into four Areas of Study. Each Area of Study in the student book contains:

◆ contextual information on the period, style, movement or culture in which the set works were composed
◆ biographical information on the composers of the set works
◆ a detailed analysis of the set works, including bar numbers and CD timings
◆ listening and appraising tasks based on the set works to prepare you for the exam
◆ performing and composing tasks so you develop the full range of musical skills
◆ glossary definitions of any technical terms and musical vocabulary that you may be unfamiliar with
◆ Results Plus progress features, providing guidance on any areas in which students have struggled in the past and how to avoid these common mistakes.

The student book also contains a section on understanding music, as well as sections on preparing your coursework and a dedicated 'ExamZone' that will help you prepare for the exam.

There are various icons used throughout the student book, which signify the following:

 This signifies a track on one of the CDs, showing both the CD and track number.

 This signifies a listening task.

 This signifies a composing task.

This signifies a performing task.

 This signifies close analysis of a set work.

The Teacher Guide

The teacher guide contains foundation and extension composing tasks and understanding music worksheets. It also contains the answers to the listening activities that appear in the student book, as well as further information for your teacher.

Anthology and Audio CDs

The anthology contains written scores of all of the set works in one volume. This includes graphic scores of those set works where traditional music scores are not available elsewhere. You should use the anthology in conjunction with the analysis of the set works in the student book.

The audio CDs contain the recordings of all 12 set works and should be used in conjunction with the anthology and the student book in order to develop a full understanding of the musical features of the set works. It is not essential that you follow the book through from start to finish – you can choose the order in which you attempt each Area of Study. It is recommended that you read the 'Understanding music' chapter first so you can be sure that you have grasped the fundamentals of music theory.

The chapter entitled 'Preparing your coursework' provides invaluable information on what the examiners are looking for in composition and performance coursework. It is packed with useful advice on how to attempt your compositions and performances, as well as what pitfalls to avoid. You should read this chapter before you start any work that might be submitted as coursework for your GCSE.

This Edexcel GCSE Music course will introduce you to many different musical styles and cultures, some of which you will already be familiar with and others that will be quite new to you. The study of the 12 set works will help you to see how music is constructed and how different styles are achieved through the individual use of melody, harmony, rhythm, instrumentation, texture and tone. Linked to this, there are many practical opportunities to compose and create your own music as well as to perform as a soloist and in a group.

By the end of the course, you will have gained a broad knowledge of both classical and popular musical styles as well as music from around the world. This course will provide you with a solid foundation for further study of Music at AS and A level if you so desire.

Area of Study 1:

Western classical music 1600–1899

This first Area of Study takes in just under three hundred years of music history, during which time musical styles and conventions changed radically.

In the course of this period, the invention and evolution of instruments took place along with the formation of standard musical ensembles such as the orchestra, string quartet and so on. Large-scale musical structures, such as the orchestral symphony, the solo sonata, concerto for soloist and orchestra – as well as several large-scale vocal forms of opera, oratorio and cantata – all became standard.

Set works

The three set works you will study are in different musical forms, each one drawn from one of the three principal musical periods of:

The Baroque era (c.1600–1750)
Set work 1 – Chorus: 'And the Glory of the Lord' from the oratorio *Messiah* by G.F. Handel (1685–1759)

The Classical era (c.1750–1830)
Set work 2 – 1st movement from Symphony No. 40 in G minor by W.A. Mozart (1756–91)

The Romantic era (c.1800–1900)
Set work 3 – Prelude No. 15 in D flat major, Op. 28 by F. Chopin (1810–49)

G.F. Handel: Chorus: 'And the Glory of the Lord' from the oratorio Messiah (1742)

In the study of this set work you will learn about:
◆ the Baroque period and the main hallmarks of the style
◆ some background to the life and works of G.F. Handel
◆ the oratorio and the background to *Messiah*
◆ how the set chorus 'And the Glory of the Lord' is constructed through an analysis of the music
◆ the key features in the music.

The Baroque era (c.1600–1750)

This period in history witnessed a new exploration of ideas and innovations in the arts, literature and philosophy. Italy was at the hub of new culture and led the way when it came to exploring new ideas and fashions.

The word 'baroque' comes from the Portuguese for 'pearl' and was used in reference to the ornate architecture and elaborate gilded paintings, frescoes and designs that covered the interior walls and ceilings of German and Italian churches of the period. One particular aspect of this style that made its way into the music was the emphasis on an ornamented or 'decorative' melody line.

The most well-known composers of the Baroque period were Johann Sebastian Bach (1685–1750), George Frideric Handel (1685–1759), Henry Purcell (c.1659–95) and Antonio Vivaldi (1678–1741). There were many others too, but let us briefly look at the life of George Frideric Handel, who is the composer of the first set work.

George Frideric Handel (1685-1759)

Handel was born in Germany in 1685 and from the age of 18 devoted his life to music. In 1707 Handel's first serious opera – *Rodrigo* – was performed. Success followed and in 1710 he returned to Hanover to be appointed Kapellmeister to the Elector. As part of this role, he was given permission to take up a year's leave in London, England. He spent the rest of his life in this country and it was during this time that he wrote some of his finest instrumental works, especially the overtures and concerti grossi. When his employer, the Elector of Hanover, succeeded the childless Queen Anne and became George I of England, Handel became his Royal Composer. He wrote the *Water Music* (1717) to accompany the king's triumphant procession up the River Thames. Towards the end of his life his sight failed him and he died in 1759 and was buried in Westminster Abbey.

Features of the Baroque style of music

Before focusing on the set work, it is important to familiarise yourself with some of the basic 'hallmarks' or features of music composed during the Baroque period. Some general features and developments include:

◆ the use of ornamented **melodic** parts
◆ the establishment of the major/minor key system, replacing the old system of modes
◆ the use of the **diatonic** chords of I, IV, V, II and VI
◆ 'basso continuo' (literally continuous bass). The adoption of the ever constant keyboard instrument (harpsichord or organ) playing a chordal support with the bass line usually played by the cello
◆ different musical textures, such as **monophonic**, **homophonic** and **polyphonic**
◆ the use of the Baroque orchestra, based on the newly invented members of the string family with the harpsichord supplying the harmonies. Trumpets, horns and timpani drums were used. However, the use of woodwind instruments at this time was not standard and varied from piece to piece
◆ the prevalence of one '**affection**' or mood
◆ the contrasting of dynamics on two levels – loud and soft (called terraced dynamics).

Glossary

affection the mood of a piece of music. It was customary in Baroque music for a single mood to prevail in a movement

diatonic notes or chords belonging to or literally 'of the key'

homophonic a musical texture comprising a melody part and accompaniment

melodic refers to the melody line

monophonic a musical texture of a single melodic line with no accompaniment

polyphonic a musical texture featuring two or more parts, each having a melody line and sounding together

What is an oratorio?

An **oratorio** is a musical work based on words and stories from the bible. This form developed at roughly the same time as opera. It took its name from St Philip Neri's oratory or 'hall of prayer' situated in Rome, where the first oratorios were performed. These works were essentially made of operatic forms such as the recitative, aria and chorus and acted out with scenery and in full costume dress. The key difference between the opera and oratorio was that the oratorio used only texts for the story taken from the bible. By the time of Handel however, the 'acting' element to the oratorio had ceased.

Glossary

oratorio large-scale musical setting for chorus, soloists and orchestra of a biblical text. Designed for concert performance. *Messiah* by G.F. Handel is one of the most famous examples of an oratorio

Messiah

Messiah is arguably the most well known and loved of all oratorios. The **libretto** is in three main parts telling the story of the birth, death and resurrection of Jesus Christ.

◆ Part 1 consists of prophecies foretelling the annunciation (or coming of the Messiah) with texts taken from the Old Testament as well as the story of His birth from the New Testament.
◆ Part 2 is the passion music of the suffering and crucifixion of Jesus, set mainly to words from the Old Testament.
◆ Part 3 tells of Jesus' resurrection from the dead.

Glossary

libretto the text/words of a musical work such as an opera or oratorio

Structure of the oratorio in *Messiah*

In this structure, the oratorio closely follows the forms of Italian opera through the use of **recitatives**, **arias** and choruses. 'And the Glory of the Lord' is the fourth movement of the whole work and is the first chorus, scored for a four-part SATB (**s**oprano, **a**lto, **t**enor, **b**ass) choir plus orchestral accompaniment. Handel gave great importance to the chorus to comment on the action of the drama, more so than in opera where an aria would have served the purpose. It follows the opening instrumental overture, then two solo movements for tenor voice – a recitative '*Comfort ye my people*', and an aria '*Ev'ry valley*'. In these opening movements we have an example of each of the main musical forms used in the oratorio.

Recitative

In the recitative, the fundamental idea is to concentrate on getting the words of the narration over with a minimal use of music. In *Messiah*, the scene is set and we are told of the coming of the Lord in the words '*prepare ye the way of the Lord, make straight in the desert a highway for our God*'.

Aria

The aria is essentially a solo song which often reflects on a mood or emotion. The music is much more elaborate to display the vocal qualities and expertise of the singer to the full. The mood here is uplifting and joyful: '*Ev'ry valley shall be exalted*'.

Chorus

The aria leads directly into the first main chorus, 'And the Glory of the Lord'. The chorus has the function of summing up the action of the story at that particular point in the drama. At this point in *Messiah* not much has happened yet in the unfolding of this great story, so the chorus simply consolidates the positivity of the mood in the preceding two movements and the looking forward to the coming of the Lord. The text of the chorus sums up this mood: '*And the Glory of the Lord shall be revealed and all flesh shall see it together, for the mouth of the Lord hath spoken it.*'

The choruses in *Messiah* are powerful and contribute to the drama of the story. They are similar to the choruses of Greek drama, with the emphasis on the group or crowd commenting in a communal fashion. Handel had been influenced by his early experience of German Lutheran choral music and had also been impressed with the English choral tradition and ensured that the chorus featured prominently in his oratorios.

Glossary

aria a solo vocal piece with instrumental accompaniment

recitative a style used in operas, oratorios and cantatas in which the text is 'declaimed' (told) in the rhythm of natural speech

Further listening

Of Handel's many religious works in this form, the most well known are *Saul* (1739), *Israel in Egypt* (1739), *Judas Maccabeus* (1747) and *Jephtha* (1752).

Background to *Messiah*

Up until 1741, Handel had written many Italian operas in London, but these were now becoming unpopular with audiences. The idea of a sacred opera in English proved to be a popular substitute. As the Church forbade biblical stories to be acted out in the theatre, Handel produced oratorios for concert performance instead.

It was in the summer of 1741 that Handel composed his famous oratorio *Messiah* over an incredibly short period of only twenty-four days. It was first performed in Dublin in 1742. The first performance in England took place at the Covent Garden Theatre in 1743, but did not make a favourable impression on the London audience!

The piece itself, despite the religious nature of the subject matter, was intended for performance in the concert hall rather than the church. The original accompaniment was just strings and continuo with trumpets and timpani drums used in several of the uplifting movements, such as the famous 'Hallelujah Chorus'. Subsequently, Handel went on to add parts for oboes and bassoon, although they are not given solo roles but rather double the existing string parts and in places the voice parts too.

Key ideas in 'And the Glory of the Lord'

This chorus, like most of the other choruses in *Messiah*, is built on a series of musical ideas each relating to a separate line of the text. Handel's practice was to state each idea as a single line, then to develop the idea in various ways. In this chorus, we can identify *four* ideas:

Idea 1: *'And the glory of the Lord'*

This short theme has two characteristic features. The first three notes outline a triad (A major) and the second feature is a stepwise scale ending. The setting of the words is mainly syllabic (one note per syllable).

Idea 2: *'Shall be revealed'*

This idea is built up using two one-bar descending sequences and is a melismatic (several notes to a syllable) setting of the word 'revealed'.

Idea 3: *'And all flesh shall see it together'*

This is a repetitive idea consisting of three statements of the descending fourth idea. Because it is repeated like this, it gives the impression of a firm statement!

Idea 4: *'For the mouth of the Lord has spoken it'*

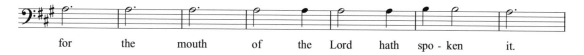

The fourth idea is characterised by long (dotted minim) repeated notes. These notes serve to emphasise the conviction *'the Lord hath spoken it'*. To achieve the strength of the statement, Handel doubles the part with tenors and basses.

All four of these short ideas are contrasted, so that when Handel combines them together, each 'melody' with its own character and shape can be clearly heard.

The whole movement conveys the joyful words through the sprightly triple time metre (3/4) and Allegro tempo marking. The key is A major with modulations to the **dominant** key of E major and dominant of the dominant key of B major. Minor keys are avoided, as the words dictate the prevailing joyful mood or 'affection' of the music. It was customary in Baroque music for a single mood to prevail in a movement and in this case the 'affection' is clearly one of glorification and praise.

Now that we have established the musical ideas upon which the chorus 'And the Glory of the Lord' is built, let us now look more closely at the set work.

Glossary

dominant fifth note of the scale or key – the strongest note after the tonic

CD1:1 Close analysis of Chorus: 'And the Glory of the Lord' from *Messiah* by G.F. Handel

Listen to the recording on the audio CD and use your Anthology to follow the analysis below. Then answer the questions that follow on page 15.

Bar numbers and timing	Analysis	Keys used

1–11	• Orchestral introduction in which the first two melodic ideas are stated. The lively triple time dance tempo gives the feeling of one in a bar. There are several features to note in the introduction:
	  ○ examples of a one-bar descending sequence at bars 5–6 (top part) and 7–8 (middle part).
	  ○ **hemiola** rhythms at bars 9–10. This was a very common practice at the approach to a **cadence** as is the case here.
	  ○ suspensions at bars 9–10.
	• The introduction ends with a **perfect cadence** (chord V followed by chord I) in the **tonic** key of A major at bars 10–11. The **harmonic rhythm** (that is how many times the chords change per bar) is either one chord per bar (e.g. bars 1, 4, 6 etc) or 2+1 (e.g. bar 2 beats 1 and 2 are E major (chord 5), then beat 3 is A major (chord 1)). This is the basic pattern, but occasionally we have three chords per bar, e.g. bar 3 (D/B minor/E).
	• Note that, in terms of the role and function of the orchestral accompaniment throughout the whole extract, the instruments double the voice parts. The music throughout the extract too is driven on through regular on-beat crotchet rhythms. Just look at the bass line!
		A major (tonic key)

11–14 (beat 1)	• Alto entry with melody 1 (*mf*). The setting of these words is mainly syllabic (one note per syllable). • Perfect cadence in A major at bars 13 (beat 3)–14 (beat 1).	A major
14–17	• *Forte* chordal response by the sopranos, tenors and basses. • Texture is **homophonic** and the melody (bars 11–14) is now heard in the bass part. • It is often the case that the bass has the melody in the chordal (homophonic) sections. • Perfect cadence at bars 16 (beat 3)–17 (beat 1) Vb–I.	A major
17–22 (beat 1)	• **Imitative** entries of melody 2 stated first by the tenor (bar 17), then bass (bar 19) and then soprano (bar 20). This musical idea is built on two one-bar descending sequences on the word '*revealed*'.	A major **modulating** at bars 21–22 to E major using chords **Vb**–I (dominant)
22 (beat 2)–33 (beat 1)	• At this point the first idea '*and the glory*' is combined with the second idea '*shall be revealed*'. • The tenor (bar 22) and soprano (bar 25) have the first idea (an octave apart) and the alto (bar 25) and tenor (bar 28) have the second idea. The result is one of two-part counterpoint (i.e. tune against tune). • Handel is clever to contrast the vocal textures so that we have variety, e.g. lower two parts (bass and tenor) at bars 22–25, then top parts (soprano and alto) at bars 25–28 followed by middle (alto and tenor) parts at bars 28–31. To the ear, this provides interest and is a feature of the whole movement.	E major Several perfect cadences in the dominant key in this section (e.g. bars 24 (beat 3)–25 (beat 1), bars 27 (beat 3)–28 (beat 1) and bars 32 (beat 3)–33 beat 1).

33 (beat 2)–38	• Strong, four-part homophonic rendition of idea 1 in E major. • Notice that the melody again appears in the bass part and that *'shall be revealed'* is tagged on to the end.	E major
38–43 (beat 1)	• Orchestral link using idea 2 *'shall be revealed'*. • Features include sequences (bars 38–39), hemiola rhythms (bars 41–42) and a suspension (bar 42). These features were also found in the opening introduction.	E major ends with a perfect cadence at bars 42–43
43 (beat 2)–50	• Idea 3 *'and all flesh shall see it together'*. As at bar 11, Handel gives the alto the first statement, followed by the tenor at bars 47–50. • Notice again that the texture now is contrasted with just one line at a time – i.e. a thin vocal texture compared to the four-part homophonic sections. • At the start of this section we move straight back to A major. • Look at the strong crotchet E–C♯–A bass of the accompaniment at bars 43–45. • A major is confirmed by the perfect cadence in this key at bars 46–47.	A major
51–57	• The tenor and bass parts introduce idea 4 *'for the mouth…'*. These strong dotted minims add weight and gravitas to the statement. • These repeated notes also act as a pedal (in this case, a tonic **pedal**) as it is the note A (the tonic note!). • This two-part texture becomes four part as above this, at bars 53–57, the sopranos and altos sing idea 3 *'and all flesh'* in sixths (to start with). • A perfect cadence (**V7c**–I) ends this section. • Notice the suspension between the alto and bass at bar 56. This is a 7–6 suspension as the interval (the distance between two notes) from the bass B to alto A is a seventh. This resolves to a G♯ (sixth on the second beat of bar 56).	A major
58–73	• Sopranos launch off with idea 4 *'for the mouth…'* on the note E, which is a dominant pedal (an inverted pedal, so called as it is at the top of the musical texture). • Alto, tenor and bass come in at bar 59 with idea 3. This small section ends with a **plagal cadence** (chord IV followed by chord I) at bar 63. We then have imitative entries in the order alto, tenor, alto during which time the music modulates to E major (see the D♯ in the tenor part at bar 65 beat 1) then to B major at bar 68 (see the A♯ last beat of bar 67 in the alto). • The strong Bs of the tenors and bass at bar 68 with idea 4 are joined with idea 3 in the sopranos and altos one bar later. As before (bar 53 onwards) these top parts are in sixths. This short section ends with a perfect cadence in B major (V7c–I).	A major modulating to E major (dominant) at bars 66–67 and swiftly then to B major (dominant of the dominant) at bars 67–68
74–83 (beat 2)	• A short orchestral link based on idea 1 takes us to a four-part homophonic rendition of idea 1 in B major. • Note again, the original melody in the bass part. This is then followed by idea 3, this time arranged in a new texture, i.e. alto/tenor together joined a bar's length later by soprano/bass. • However, fittingly all parts come together in strong homophony on the word *'together'*! This is merely a pause for breath as the cadence at bars 82–83 is imperfect (it ends on chord V, which sounds incomplete) and momentum is carried on immediately with the sopranos.	B major

Bar numbers and timing	Analysis	Keys used
83 (beat 3)–102 (beat 1)	• The section dovetailing with the last hears the sopranos sing idea 4 on top F♯. Notice how each time this idea comes back the **pitch** is higher. The first time was on A, then E in the soprano and now F♯. • Over the next dozen bars, Handel brings all four musical ideas together. • At bar 84, the altos sing the first idea *'and the glory'* followed by the second idea *'shall be revealed'*. • There is a sense of descending pitch achieved at bars 87–91, as first the alto, then the tenor and finally the bass sing short melodies. • Notice how idea 3 is shortened to one bar at bars 89–92. The feeling of a breaking down of texture is short lived as Handel brings all four voices in at 93–4. • From this point (bars 93–102) Handel uses ideas 1, 2 and 4 in different parts. The sopranos and altos sing idea 4 (starting at bars 93 and 96 respectively) whilst the tenor and bass have ideas 1 and 2 *'and the glory'*, *'shall be revealed'*. • During this section the music modulates back to the dominant key of E major (bars 93–94 is a perfect cadence in E major). The section ends with another perfect cadence in E major (bars 101–102), at which point we return straightaway to the tonic key of A major and the music stays in this key until the end of the movement.	B major until bar 94 where the music returns to E major (dominant)
102 (beat 2)–124 (beat 1)	• Altos lead with idea 3, although this is fragmented to one bar echoes in the tenor and bass parts of *'and all flesh'*. This is to reduce texture down to the minimum (albeit briefly) before the final section starts. • Parts are added quickly at bars 105–106 reaffirming the words *'shall see it together'*. • Over this the sopranos launch off with idea 1, reaching the climax of the movement on the top A at bar 110 on the word *'Lord'*. • This is answered by the three lower parts, again with the bass assigned the tune! • Imitative entries follow in the alto, tenor and bass parts. • At bars 118 (alto), 119 (soprano) and 119 (tenor) idea 3 is heard. This is underpinned with idea 4 in the basses on the note E (dominant pedal). • The section ends with an imperfect cadence (I–V) at bars 123–124.	A major
124 (beat 2)–134 (beat 2)	• The last section starts with the sopranos again on the note taking over idea 4 from the basses. • The other parts answer *'for the mouth of the Lord hath spoken it'*. • Again, insisting to the end, we hear another statement of idea 4 this time firmly on the tonic note (A). • This section i.e. bars 129–134 has already been heard at bars 51–55, except that the sopranos/altos and tenors/basses have swapped parts on this repeat. This is known as invertible counterpoint. • The three accompanying parts march onwards with *'for the mouth...'* etc before coming to a dramatic and sudden halt at bar 133. This is particularly effective and is something Handel often does just before the last few bars of a chorus (another good example like this can be found at the end of the 'Hallelujah' chorus).	A major
134 (beat 3)–138	• A dramatic three-beat rest in all four voice parts leads to the final grand (and slow 'Adagio') plagal cadence in glorious four-part homophony adding emphasis to the final words *'hath spoken it'*.	A major

Summary of the main choral styles in Chorus: 'And the Glory of the Lord'

The following styles can be found in this chorus:

Choral style	Example
Single-line writing (monophonic)	Bars 11–13
Four-part choir (homophonic)	Bars 33 (beat 3)–38
Simple imitation	Bars 17 (beat 3) onwards
Two ideas together	Bars 110–113
Doubling of parts	Bar 51 onwards *'for the mouth'*

CD1:1

Listening and appraising questions: 'And the Glory of the Lord'

Now that you have listened to 'And the Glory of the Lord' and studied the analysis on pages 12–14, answer the listening and appraising questions that follow.

1 How is the joyful mood or 'affection' of this chorus achieved by Handel?

2 Name three different types of musical texture that feature in this chorus.

3 Name the four voice parts that perform this chorus.

4 What instruments accompany the singers?

5 How many different melodies are used by Handel in the chorus?

6 Identify two ways in which the last three bars of the extracts ('*hath spoken it*') are given a dramatic setting.

7 Give bar numbers where you can hear:
  a One voice part
  b Two voice parts
  c Three voice parts
  d All four voice parts together.

8 In general, how are the words set to the music?

9 How is the word '*revealed*' treated throughout the piece?

Further listening

In addition to this set work, try to listen to other examples of a chorus movement found in *Messiah* by G.F. Handel, for example:

- 'And he shall purify'
- 'For unto us a Child is born'
- 'Glory to God'
- 'Surely he hath borne our griefs'
- 'He trusted in God'
- 'Hallelujah Chorus'
- 'Worthy is the Lamb'.

Glossary

cadence two chords at the end of a musical phrase. There are four main types of cadence: perfect, imperfect, interrupted and plagal

harmonic rhythm the number of times the chords change per bar

hemiola in triple time, this is a rhythmic device often used towards a cadence point, in which notes are grouped in two beat units, e.g.

homophonic common musical texture comprising a melody part and accompaniment

imitative literally separate parts copying or imitating each other. If the imitation is note for note the same, this will then be a canon

modulating when the music changes key

pedal a sustained note usually in the lowest bass part. In the middle of a musical texture it is called an inner pedal and if at the top, an inverted pedal

perfect cadence chord V followed by chord I

pitch how high or low a note sounds

plagal cadence chord IV followed by chord I

tonic the first degree of a scale, the keynote, e.g. in C major the note C is the tonic note

Vb dominant chord (V) in first inversion (b)

V7c dominant 7th chord (V7) in second inversion (c)

ResultsPlus
Watch out!

When listening and appraising pieces of music, it is important to give enough detail in your response.

■ Typically, weak answers lack in real musical detail. For example:

Question: Describe the texture of the music at the start of the extract.

Answer: It is thin then becomes thicker.

This just tells us that the texture changes. A better answer would be:

▲ At the start of the extract there is only a solo flute playing pianissimo (creating a monophonic texture). A few bars later the texture and dynamics increase as the strings enter providing an accompaniment to the flute creating a fuller homophonic texture.

W.A. Mozart: 1st movement from Symphony No. 40 in G minor (1788)

In the study of this set work you will learn about:

◆ the Classical period and the main hallmarks of the style

◆ some background to the life and works of W.A. Mozart

◆ the development of the symphony and the structure of sonata form

◆ the evolution of the Classical orchestra

◆ how the first movement of Mozart's Symphony No. 40 in G minor is constructed through a detailed analysis of the music

◆ the key features in the music.

The Classical era (c.1750–1830)

The Classical era saw a deliberate move away from the flamboyant and ornate Baroque ideals. Classical architecture and art reflected a new interest in a more restrained style inspired by the ancient world of the Greeks and Romans. Music from this era echoes the architecture in that it uses a clear-cut and balanced structure (which, like the architecture, has symmetry in its design). Simplicity and clarity of line also became a feature of the music in the emphasis placed on a graceful and regularly phrased melodic line.

These new stylistic Classical traits of clarity, order and balance were to be found in the Classical symphony, string quartet, concerto and solo sonata. The period was dominated by three Viennese composers: Wolfgang Amadeus Mozart (1756–91), Franz Joseph Haydn (1732–1809) and Ludwig van Beethoven (1770–1827). Beethoven in fact spanned two musical periods. His early music was firmly in the Classical style, whereas the music written around the turn of the century until his death in 1827 was very much Romantic in spirit.

There were of course other composers too, but let us look briefly at the life of Wolfgang Amadeus Mozart, whose work the 1st movement from Symphony No. 40 in G minor is the next set work.

Wolfgang Amadeus Mozart (1756–91)

Mozart was born in Salzburg on 27 January 1756. His father, Leopold, was court composer at the archiepiscopal court and a gifted violinist too. From the age of four, Mozart began to study keyboard and composition from his father. Leopold was quick to recognise his son's immense musical genius and, from an early age, Mozart and his talented elder sister Nannerl were taken on a series of tours around the courts of Europe to play before princes and emperors. As such, Mozart became famous from a very young age. Following employment in Salzburg as *Konzertmeister* to the archbishop, Mozart moved to Vienna in 1781 where he spent the rest of his life as a composer and performer.

Despite his relatively short life of thirty-five years, his musical output was vast and included famous operas such as *Le Nozze di Figaro* (1786), *Don Giovanni* (1787), *Cosi fan tutte* (1790) and *Die Zauberflote* (1791). He produced twenty-one piano concertos, five violin concertos, four horn concertos, concertos for clarinet and other wind instruments, forty-one symphonies, twenty-seven string quartets, six string quintets and seventeen Masses, including his last work, the incomplete Requiem Mass of 1791. The work was completed after his death by Franz Sussmayr, one of his pupils. Mozart died in Vienna on 5 December 1791.

The orchestra, the symphony and sonata form

In order to understand this next set work in the context of the Classical period, it is important to know something about the evolution of the Classical orchestra, as well as the most important of all Classical genres – the **symphony**. It is also crucial to focus in on the large-scale musical structure used to compose first (and sometimes fourth) movements of symphonic works – **sonata form**.

The orchestra

We have already seen how the orchestra began to take shape during the Baroque period (page 8), formed from a nucleus of string instruments and harpsichord continuo. During the early Classical period, the harpsichord was still used, but as the orchestra grew and came to include a standard woodwind and brass section, the harpsichord became redundant and gradually fell out of use. Its primary function – to provide a chordal support – was effectively taken over by the wind instruments.

Glossary

sonata form a large-scale form invented in the Classical era comprising three sections – exposition, development and recapitulation

symphony a large-scale genre for orchestra in three or four movements. Sonata form was often used for the first and last movements in symphonies

At the start of the Classical period, the orchestra was still small – strings plus two horns with either flutes or oboes (either one or two of each). However, it soon began to grow with the addition of the wind instruments complete with the bass instrument of the family – the bassoon. By the end of the 18th century, the newly invented clarinet joined the woodwind ranks. The brass section used two trumpets and two horns with percussion provided by the timpani drums.

The standard classical orchestra with its four families of instruments was born.

Strings	Woodwind	Brass	Percussion
Violins	Flutes (2)	Trumpets (2)	Timpani
Violas	Oboes (2)	French horns (2)	
Cellos	Clarinets (2)		
Double basses	Bassoons (2)		

Symphony

The symphony was one of the most important and popular large-scale genres invented during the Classical era. It continued to develop throughout the 19th and 20th centuries and up to the present day.

The word 'symphony' itself is derived from the Italian for 'sounding together'. This is appropriate given the formation of the Classical orchestra sounding together its complete four families of instruments. Early examples of symphonies can be traced to the Italian three-section **sinfonias** for strings and continuo. These were arranged in a fast–slow–fast structure. This idea of **tempo** contrast translated to the early Classical symphony of three movements, although as the period progressed another movement, the **minuet and trio** (a Baroque dance form), was placed between the second and third movements, making four in total. The usual plan was:

First movement	Second movement	Third movement	Fourth movement
Fast tempo and usually written in sonata form (often called 'first movement' form).	Slow tempo. Various forms used, including **ternary, theme and variations.**	Minuet and trio (or scherzo and trio).	Fast. Written in either **rondo**, sonata form (sometimes even a combination of the two: sonata rondo form) or even a set of variations.

Glossary

minuet and trio a ternary form structure, performed as minuet–trio–minuet. The minuet is a stately dance in triple time and the contrasting middle section (trio) usually features a reduction in instrumental parts. Often used as the third movement in a Classical symphony

rondo Classical form comprising a series of rondo sections interspersed with contrasting episodes. The simple rondo was structured as ABACA, where A is the rondo theme, and B and C are the episodes

sinfonia an Italian form in origin, these were works in three sections for strings and continuo

tempo speed of the music

ternary a three-part structure in ABA form in which the opening section is repeated and section B provides contrast

theme and variations a theme (melody) followed by a series of variations on the original theme

Further listening

The two greatest contributions to the symphony in the Classical period are the 104 symphonies of F.J. Haydn (often referred to as 'the father of the symphony') and the 41 works by W.A. Mozart.

Characteristics of sonata form

The set work focuses on the first movement of Mozart's Symphony No. 40 in G minor, which is written in sonata form. It is therefore important to have an overview of the main characteristics of this important Classical structure.

The word 'sonata' comes from the Latin *sonare* meaning 'to sound' and thus refers to instrumental as opposed to vocal music. Sonata form is used to structure a *single movement* of a work and does not refer to a complete work, be it a symphony, string quartet, concerto or solo sonata.

The two fundamental ideas expressed in sonata form (which in fact is also true of most music) are:

◆ repetition
◆ contrast.

The structure developed from the two-section binary form, except that sonata form includes a repeat (recapitulation) of the first section. The three sections are called:

◆ exposition
◆ development
◆ recapitulation.

This provided a pleasing symmetry to the form, rather like an arch shape with the exposition balanced with the recapitulation. There is also a neat parallel here to the typical structure of a five-act Shakespearian play.

Act 1 Exposition	The dramatis personae or contrasting 'characters' (musical themes) are 'exposed' or introduced to the audience.
Acts 2–4 Development	The unfolding of the drama (musical and literary). The characters (musical themes) from the exposition act out the story. Expect to witness conflict and unrest (just as in the music of this section).
Act 5 Recapitulation	The original characters return for the resolution to the literary (and musical) drama. This resolution, of course, can end in a gloom of tragedy or a 'happily ever after' scenario!

Act 5, Scene 3 from Shakespeare's Romeo and Juliet. *In musical terms, this is the 'recapitulation' of the play.*

The Classical composers, in the spirit of the time, wrote graceful melodies that were well balanced and characterful, often with defining rhythms and moods. Sonata form allowed for a contrast of melodies as well as development and then a return (repetition) of the main melodic ideas in the recapitulation.

The musical details of a typical sonata form structure represented in this Classical arch plan would be:

Development

In this central section, the composer 'develops' one or both ideas from the exposition. This development can be based on the complete melody or a fragment (motif) from it. Sometimes the composer will use several motifs and combine them in different ways, thus creating new variants of the original subjects. The section features various keys, but deliberately avoids the tonic and dominant keys. The music of this section is often adventurous as the drama unfolds and is constantly changing and restless because of the exploration of different keys.

Sonata Form Structure

Exposition

In this first section the main themes are presented or 'exposed'.

The first theme – called the **first subject** – is always in the tonic or home key. This theme is usually the most lively and rhythmic. There follows a short linking section called the **bridge passage** during which the music modulates (changes key) at which point we reach the contrasted **second subject**. The contrast will be both the mood and key of the music. The new key will be related to the tonic key of the music, such as the relative major (minor) or the dominant key. The whole of the exposition section is then often repeated so that the listener becomes familiar with the two subjects before the development occurs.

Recapitulation

This final section balances with the opening exposition. The composer recaps the first subject in the tonic key. The bridge section then follows to balance with the opening section, but does not modulate as the second subject is now heard in the tonic key as the work is drawing to a close. The work can conclude with a short rounding-off section called the coda.

Features of the Classical style

Before focusing on the set work, it is important to familiarise yourself with some of the basic hallmarks or features of music composed during the Classical period. Some general features and developments include:

◆ an emphasis on well-proportioned and graceful melody lines written in regular phrases of often eight-bars duration (four bars as a question, answered by four) – this is called periodic or regular phrasing
◆ linked to this, a melody-dominated **texture** became popular (melody-dominated homophony), although polyphony was also used

Glossary

bridge passage a linking passage often used to change the key of the music (modulate) in preparation for the second subject

first subject the first theme or melody

second subject the second theme or melody

texture the number of parts in a piece of music and how they relate to one another

- the musical structures employed had a sense of symmetry and balance (sonata form is a good example of this)
- structures were defined by clear-cut key schemes with regular cadences
- harmony was functional, i.e. chords were used for structural purposes (based on chords I, IV, V, II and VI)
- ideas of contrast in terms of key, melodies and more varied dynamics
- the orchestra was established as a standard instrumental ensemble during this period and the harpsichord became redundant
- new instrumental musical genres emerged – sonata for a solo instrument, concerto, symphony, string quartet.

We will be able to discover most of these musical features as we study in detail the next set work, Mozart's Symphony No. 40 in G minor (1st movement).

Background to Symphony No. 40 in G minor

This great symphony is written in the key of G minor and the melancholy feel of this key pervades the first movement, although the other movements are lighter in mood. Try listening to the work as a whole to get a feeling of the differing emotions conveyed.

The work comprises the usual four movements, but what is slightly unusual is that Mozart uses sonata form to structure the first, second and fourth movements. The third movement is the usual minuet and trio. Each movement is varied in terms of tempo, as shown below.

Movement	Tempo
I	Molto allegro (very fast)
II	Andante (at a moderate walking pace)
III	Allegretto (slightly slower than allegro)
IV	Allegro assai (very fast indeed)

The instrumentation

Mozart originally scored the work without the recently invented clarinets, although he later wrote another version which included two clarinets – it is this later version that you will study. Another interesting fact is that Mozart is modest in the instrumentation that he uses in this work, which only requires seven woodwind players (one flute, two oboes, two clarinets and two bassoons) and from the brass section, two horns – one in B♭ and one in G. This is to give him the notes G–B♭–D (G minor tonic chord) and B♭–D–F (B♭ major tonic chord). Of more significant note is the fact that Mozart does not use trumpets or drums! Compare this orchestration to the standard Classical orchestra of the time.

Listen to the recording on the audio CD and use your Anthology to follow the analysis below.

The first movement is a fast Molto allegro and is in 4/4 time. Let us now examine the work section by section.

The first point to note is that there is *no introduction*. After just three crotchet beats, the first and second violins playing in octaves (eight notes apart) state the first subject. This is marked with the soft dynamic *piano*, a rarity in symphonies up to this point in time. Quaver accompaniment is supplied by *divisi* (divided) violas and on-beat crotchet bass notes from the basses.

FIRST SUBJECT (bars 1–20)

Bar numbers	Analysis
1–5	• Bars 1–3: repeated idea (the first three notes become an important motif used throughout the movement) with an upward leap of a sixth balanced by bars 3 (last crotchet)–5 a descending stepwise pattern (two quavers/crotchet).
5 (last crotchet)–9	• This is a sequence (down one tone) of bars 1–4.
9 (last crotchet)–20	• Second part of theme – a repeated crotchet idea outlining chords V (bars 10 and 12) and chord I and Ib (bars 11 and 13 respectively). • Bars 14–16: woodwind enter playing a two-bar continuation in octaves (no oboes). • Bars 16–20: strong repeated woodwind chords with strings playing D octaves, which forms a dominant pedal. Following this point of repose on chord V (dominant) the first subject is repeated, but modified as we start the bridge passage.

BRIDGE PASSAGE (bars 20–44)

Bar numbers	Analysis
20–27	• First subject repeated but altered at bars 24–27 to modulate to the relative major (B♭). Notice the lack of F♯s. • Oboes and bassoons provide sustained wind chords as 'harmonic filling' to the texture. • There is a perfect cadence in the key of B♭ (bars 27–28).
28–44	• This is a robust *forte* passage in the relative major key of B♭ for full orchestra (see opposite). • Horns enter for the first time at bar 28. There is a bold theme in the violins outlining triads in the key of B♭. For most of this passage the bassoon doubles the string basses.
30–33	• Bars 30–33: good example of one-bar descending sequences in the violins.

| 34–43 | • Bars 34–37: strong *sforzando* chords for full orchestra which leads to
• Bars 38–43: five bars of dominant pedal (F) (see above). This dominant harmony prepares for the second subject at 44. This entry is dramatically heralded by a one-bar rest! |

SECOND SUBJECT (bars 44–72)

Bar numbers	Analysis
44–51	• This theme in the relative major is shared between the strings and woodwind. It is much more relaxed (notice the piano dynamics) and reduced instrumentation (see opposite). • The use of **semitones** is a characteristic of the graceful ***pathétique*** mood of second subject (see bars 44–5 and 48–9). • The falling figures at bars 44–45 and 48–51 help to conjure up the mood of sighing. Chromatic descent was always used to feature grief and sadness in music. See the bass part to the aria 'When I am laid in earth' by Purcell or the lute song 'Fall my tears' by John Dowland as two examples.
50–51	• Perfect cadence in B♭ major followed by a one-bar link (bar 51) before the theme is repeated.
52–58	• This time the string and woodwind (without oboes) parts change round as they play the theme.
58–66	• The theme is extended by a series of one-bar sequences at bars 58–61. • The harmony here is a dominant 7th chord in the key of A♭ major, although we never reach this key as the music surges and crescendos as the bass moves up **chromatically** so that we have chords Ic–V7–I in B♭ major at bars 64–66.

66–72	• A new six-bar idea is heard in unison violins (see below). It is made up of chromatically ascending quavers and a rhythmic element at bars 68–69 and a scalic descent from bars 70–72. This feature is used later in the movement and can be thought of as a second part of the second subject. The section ends with a perfect cadence in B♭ major (bars 71–72)

CODETTA (bars 73–100)

Bar numbers	Analysis
Throughout	• This section is based on the opening three notes of the first subject.
73–88	• The idea is passed from clarinet to bassoon. During this passage, the upper strings (violins) have just the first two notes of this idea in minims (doubling or more the original note values is called **augmentation**) in canon with the lower strings (violas, cellos and basses). • Following a perfect cadence in B♭ at bars 79–80, this is then repeated, except that the bassoon comes in first. This ends at bar 88.

88–100	• These last few bars are one long extended perfect cadence in B♭ (see bars 90–91, 94–95, 95–96, 96–97 etc).
	• This is also a good example of homophonic texture.
	• Bar 100: a dominant 7th chord in G minor is used as a pivot to link back to bar 1 for a repeat of the exposition. The repeat ensures that:
	  a the section balances in terms of bars with the final recapitulation section
	  b the listener is familiar with the two main subjects of the work.

DEVELOPMENT (bars 101–164)

Bar numbers	Analysis
Throughout	• The music of the whole development section is based entirely on the opening figure of the first subject.
101–114	• Bars 101–105: following a single G minor chord, a chromatic chord G♯–B–D–F (diminished 7th) chord leads to a woodwind chordal and scalic descent in the remote key of F♯ minor during which the theme enters in the violins. • Bars 103–114: first four bars of first subject is played three times in octaves in the violins. Each time the melody is heard at a lower pitch (descending sequences). The essential difference is that the harmony is now chromatic. Look at the descending chromatic chords in the bassoons (bars 107–114) for example.

114–138	• At bars 114–115 the music resolves into the key of E minor (V–I) and now the violas, cellos and bassoons enter with the theme, whilst at the same time the upper strings play a new quaver tune called a counter-melody. This simply means a melody that fits with another at the same time. 'Counter' literally means against, so it is tune against tune! Notice how this new melody is *staccato* to help make it stand out against the *legato* theme. • The role of the woodwind (except bassoons) is to provide chordal harmonic support during this long passage up to bar 132. The horns add sustained semibreves and minims at points when the woodwind enter to thicken the musical texture. • At bar 118, the music modulates to A minor and the melodies switch around with the counter melody now in the violas, cellos and bassoon with the theme in octaves in the violins. • D minor is reached at bar 120. A further switch around happens at 122, now in G minor (last crotchet), then to C major at bar 124 and then again parts switch at bar 126 (last crotchet) now in F major. B♭ major is reached at bar 128. • Notice how many times the music changes key and that each time we go up in a rising sequence by four notes, Em–Am–Dm–Gm–C–F–B♭! *Constant exploration of different keys is a major feature of the development section.* • Bars 134–138: repeated A in bassoons violas and cellos form a dominant pedal (in D minor). The repeated As in the violins add to the effect.
139–164	• In this section, texture is reduced as the three notes of the first subject are used as a motif (a short melodic idea of just a few notes) that is passed around between the woodwind and strings creating a dialogue effect. • During this passage various pedals are used, such as F (dominant of B♭ minor) at bars 140–142, G (dominant of C minor) at bar 143 and D (dominant of G minor the tonic key) in the horns at bars 153–160 where it is taken on by the bassoons up to the start of the recapitulation. • The section from bar 153 to 160 is a strong *forte* passage with powerful dialogue based on the three-note motif between upper and lower strings, whereas the following bars up to the start of the recapitulation are hushed and expectant. • Tension is provided by the dominant pedal D, which finally resolves to a tonic G at bar 166.

RECAPITULATION (bars 164–299)

Bar numbers	Analysis
Throughout	• The recapitulation is not just a direct repeat of the exposition. The bridge passage is extended and the coda is far more developed as we shall see.
164–184 (first subject)	• First subject in tonic key of G minor. This is exactly the same as in the exposition at bars 1–20. See notes above.
184–227 (bridge passage)	• This is much extended into a passage of some 51 bars, as opposed to 24 bars in the exposition. • The purpose of the bridge section in the exposition is to take the music from the tonic to dominant key in preparation for the second subject. This is not necessary here as the *second subject will be in the tonic key*. So, Mozart indulges in some further development of the thematic material. The bridge is needed to provide structural *balance* to the form as a whole – a Classical ideal! • Bars 184–191: the theme starts the same but almost immediately modulates to the key of E♭ major. Look at the A♭s appearing from bar 185. A perfect cadence in that key can be seen at bars 190–191. • Bars 191–227: during this section for full orchestra we hear the strong forte idea heard in the exposition. • We hear the theme spilt between upper and lower strings in alternating passages.

- Unlike at bar 28 onwards of the exposition, we now have added a quaver bass counter melody to go against the theme. Look at bars 191–197 and you can see the theme in the violins with the counter melody in bassoons, violas and cellos.
- Bars 198–211: the parts swap over. The theme is now in violas, cellos and bassoon, with the counter melody in violins. Music modulates throughout this short passage to F minor (bar 198), E♭ major (bar 205) and reaching the home key at bar 211.
- Bars 211–227 are like bars 28–43 of the exposition, except of course that we remain in the tonic key for the entry of the second subject at bar 227.
- Bars 221–225: dominant pedal note of D sounding in the cellos, horns and bassoons in anticipation of the second subject.
- The one bar rest at 226 adds to the drama of expectation!

227–260 (second subject)	• Bars 227–241: the second subject is now stated in the tonic key of G minor. The theme here (as in the exposition) is shared between the woodwind and strings. As before, the musical texture and dynamics are reduced. • Bars 241–245: this short section is an extension in which the music modulates to E♭ major. Notice the dominant pedal in this key (B♭) at bars 241–245 in the cellos and horns. • Bars 245–251: rising one-bar sequences. Look at the bass notes: B♭–B♮–C–D♭–D♮–E♭–E♮! • Bars 252–254: perfect cadence of Ic–V–I in G minor leads to • Bars 254–260: the rising form of the theme heard at bars 66–72 in the exposition, but now in G minor.

CODA (bars 260–299)

This is similar to the codetta from the exposition except that it is longer and therefore is a coda!

Bar numbers	Analysis
260–276	• The three-note motif from the first subject is passed between the clarinet, bassoon and flute, whilst the first violins exchange the first two notes of the motif in augmentation with the violas and cellos. • This section is rounded off with a perfect cadence in G minor at bars 275–276.
276–299	• This starts off as a scalic flourish building to the expected final cadence. • However this *forte* passage is suddenly interrupted with some piano woodwind chords at bar 285 during which we hear glimpses of the first subject in the second violins, then first violins at bar 287, violas at bar 289, then flute, clarinets and bassoons at bar 291.
293–299	• The final 'tutti' homophonic reiteration of a series of chords I and V in G minor ending with four emphatic full stops (G minor chords). • This last section of six bars corresponds to the last six bars of the exposition!

Glossary

augmentation doubling (or more) of the original note values

chromatically moving by semitones up or down

pathétique literally 'pathetic', refers to a melancholy mood

semitone half a tone – the distance between a white note and an adjacent black note on a keyboard

CD1:2 Listening and appraising questions: 1st movement from Symphony No. 40 in G minor

Now that you have listened to the 1st movement from Symphony No. 40 in G minor and studied the analysis on pages 23–32, answer the listening and appraising questions that follow.

1 What is unusual about the orchestra that Mozart uses in this symphony compared to the standard Classical orchestra of the time?

2 Describe two ways in which the first and second subjects differ in the exposition section of this movement.

3 Mention two features of the development section.

4 What is the purpose of the bridge section in the exposition?

5 What key is the second subject in during the recapitulation section, and why?

6 The final section is the coda. What does Mozart develop further during this final part of the piece?

7 How would you describe the mood of the first movement as a whole? Give three musical reasons to back up your argument

8 What is the role of the two horns in this piece and why is one in the key of G minor and one in B♭ major?

9 Name two different types of musical texture to be found in this work.

10 How many other movements are there in the rest of the symphony?

ResultsPlus

Watch out!

Question: This chorus was composed in the Baroque period of Western classical music. State **four** key features of music from the Baroque period. (4 marks)

As a starting point, remember that you will need to make **four different points** in your response, and these points must be about the features of Baroque music. For example, if you say 'it was written in the Baroque period' or 'Handel was the composer so it is Baroque' then you will not score any marks because these responses are not features of Baroque music.

Here are some sample answers.

■ A basic answer might include responses such as:

• The music uses lots of extra twiddly notes.
• There is a keyboard instrument playing.
• The instruments used in *Messiah* are made up of strings, harpsichord, trumpets and timpani.
• Voice parts copy each other as well as playing together.

▲ An excellent answer based on the above would be:

• The music of the period was characterised by ornamented melodic lines including trills, mordents and turns.
• The harpsichord and cello play throughout the music providing a chordal support. This is called the basso continuo.
• The Baroque orchestra in *Messiah* was built on a nucleus of strings with harpsichord continuo, trumpets and timpani.
• A common musical texture of the period was imitation or polyphonic writing. This chorus also has sections that are sung together in homophony.

F. Chopin: Piano Prelude No. 15 in D flat major, Op. 28 (1838)

In the study of this set work you will learn about:

◆ the Romantic era and the main hallmarks of the style

◆ some background to the life and works of F. Chopin

◆ the development of the piano and the rise of the virtuoso performer in the 19th century

◆ Chopin's pianistic style

◆ how Piano Prelude No. 15 in D flat major, Op. 28 is constructed through a detailed analysis of the music

◆ the key features in the music.

The Romantic era (c.1800–1900)

The 19th century was the age of **Romanticism**. Music was influenced by other art forms that dealt with the expression of intense but ordinary human emotions such as love, grief, joy, death and the beauty to be found in the natural world. Artists such as J.M.W. Turner painted landscapes that depicted both the beauty and the ruggedness of the natural world. Writers such as Lord Byron, William Wordsworth and Percy Bysshe Shelley compared human emotions and feelings with dramatic scenes from nature in their works.

Music followed suit. Romantic composers strove for freedom in order to write expressive music that responded to a wide range of emotions and also to nature. Beethoven's Symphony No. 6 (Pastoral) depicts a scene from nature in each movement. The elements of magic, mystery and the supernatural were also explored in Romantic art forms. Composers often wrote programmatic works that told a story through the music, such as the macabre tale of 'The Water Goblin' by Dvořák.

It is from this period that the next set work derives, namely Piano Prelude No. 15 in D flat major (known as the 'Raindrop') by Frédéric Chopin.

Glossary

Romanticism an artistic movement in Europe, between c. 1800–1900, in which the artist was more concerned with feelings and emotions than with form

Frédéric Chopin (1810–49)

Chopin was born in Zelazowa Wola, near Warsaw, Poland to a Polish mother and French father. His musical talents were recognised from an early age and he was playing piano concertos at the age of eight! Following school, Chopin attended the Warsaw Conservatoire of Music to study as a performer and composer. After graduation, Chopin decided to travel. In Vienna, Chopin made a name for himself as both a virtuoso pianist and a composer. In 1832 he travelled to Paris and became a sought-after teacher and performer. Chopin moved in influential social circles in Paris including such composers as Liszt and Berlioz, the writers Heinrich Heine and Honore de Balzac, and the artist Eugene Delacroix. After a succession of love affairs, Chopin met the authoress Aurore Dudevant (known as Georges Sand) with whom he had a nine-year relationship. During this period, he composed many of his finest piano works.

His piano music reflects his love of his homeland of Poland in its use of Polish folk melodies and dance rhythms (such as the mazurka and polonaise) that permeate the music. It was the modal nature of the folk melodies and the complex harmonies of the authentic Polish music that inspired him and can be found in evidence in the music he composed. We shall look at this in more detail in our study of the set work.

Towards the end of his life, Chopin suffered poor health and he became desperately ill with tuberculosis, which eventually killed him. In 1838, in an attempt to improve his condition in a warmer climate, he went to Majorca. However, as the local inhabitants feared they would catch the disease, Chopin and his lover were forced to seek exile in an isolated and derelict monastery in Valldemossa. It was here that Chopin composed the 'Raindrop' Prelude and completed the set of 24 preludes as well as the famous C♯ minor Scherzo. A year later, he had sadly split up from his lover and died at home in Paris on 17 October 1849.

Features of the Romantic style of music

Before focusing on the set work, it is important to familiarise yourself with the main features of music composed during the Romantic period. These include:

◆ an emphasis on expressing a wide range of feelings and emotions in music
◆ melody lines becoming longer and far more developed
◆ more freedom for the composer in the use of form and structure of the music
◆ the use of extended vocabulary of chords to create 7ths, 9ths,11ths. The **dominant 13th** was the epitome of the Romantic chord! Other romantic chords included the **diminished 7th**, **augmented 6th chord**, **neopolitan 6th**, etc
◆ the harmony is often chromatic and discordant to portray strong emotions such as grief and anguish
◆ inclusion of strong and varied dynamic contrasts (*pppp–ffff*)
◆ links to other art forms (art and literature) through the medium of programme music
◆ an increased level of technical demand in the music and the related rise of the **virtuoso performer**
◆ the rise of Nationalism (for example, Chopin's use of Polish folk melodies and dance rhythms in his piano music)
◆ the significant expansion of the orchestra with enlarged sections and new instruments
◆ the development of the piano.

The virtuoso performer

The Romantic idea of the struggle of the individual in the Romantic era led to the rise of the 'heroic' soloist as a virtuoso performer. Nineteenth-century composers such as Chopin, Brahms and Liszt all enjoyed writing music for themselves to perform. The trend also developed to write for well-known virtuoso performers of the day.

The development of the piano

Several developments were made to the piano during the 19th century that gave composers greater opportunities to express Romantic ideas in music. The sound and tone of the instrument, invented during the Classical era, was improved considerably to give the instrument more power over an increased dynamic spectrum, which was vital in expressing the extreme dynamic ranges prevalent in Romantic music. The piano became the supreme solo instrument of the Romantic era. This was achieved through the following developments:

◆ the instrument was reshaped and enlarged to create a greater sound
◆ the number of notes increased in both treble and bass registers to seven octaves, giving a greater pitch range for musical expression
◆ felt replaced leather on the hammers, producing a more rounded and fuller tone
◆ strings were longer, stronger and under increased tensions than previously
◆ the body frame of the piano was constructed of metal (as opposed to wood) to cope with the increased string tensions
◆ the **sustaining** and **soft pedals** were developed.

Glossary

augmented 6th chord chord which contains an augmented 6th interval (e.g. A♭, C, E♭, F♯. A♭ to F♯ = augmented 6th)

diminished 7th a chord made up of superimposed minor third intervals (e.g. B, D, F, A♭)

dominant 13th chord V (dominant) with the added 13th note

neopolitan 6th chord of the flattened supertonic (second degree) in first inversion

virtuoso performer a person – in music or the arts in general – who has mastered the skills and techniques of their art form

Glossary

soft pedal pedal on a piano that, when pressed, softens the tone of the music

sustaining pedal a pedal that, when pressed, sustains all the strings on the piano by removing the dampers from all strings and allowing them to vibrate freely

Chopin's pianistic style

Chopin's piano music is a perfect example of the Romantic ideal for expressing the poetic feelings and emotions through the medium of sound. Chopin was a fitting example of the Romantic artist – he was lonely, aloof and withdrawn – a talented but tragic figure, dying as he did at a relatively young age of 39. He was the founder of the 19th-century school of *cantabile* playing ('in the singing style' – emphasis on held melody lines). Chopin's legacy is found in the development of playing techniques to support the all-important melody line, including such typical features as:

◆ the delicacy of long lyrical melodic lines with graceful ornamentation
◆ spreading **arpeggios**
◆ simple, broken chord accompaniments with subtle pedalling effects
◆ discreet use of romantic *tempo rubato* in the music
◆ passages of rapid articulation and virtuosic display
◆ a range of touch and tone quality and a control of dynamics of volume.

Glossary

arpeggio the notes of a chord played one after the other rather than together, e.g. C–E–G–C etc

cantabile 'in the singing style', meaning that the melody is to be played *legato*

tempo rubato literally means 'robbed' time – this is a technique where the player can pull back (or speed up) the tempo for expressive effect

Background to The Preludes (Op. 28)

The next set work, commonly known as the 'Raindrop', belongs to a body of works by Chopin called The Preludes, which was written between 1835 and 1838 and published in 1839. At the time of publication, the works were criticised for a lack of recognisable structure and for their brevity. The shortest prelude is only 13 bars long, while the longest runs to only 90. The 'Raindrop' Prelude is one of the longest at 89 bars, and in it we can see a clearly worked out ternary ABA structure with a contrasting B section in C♯ minor.

Chopin composed his set of 24 preludes at a time when he was studying *The Well-Tempered Clavier* of J.S. Bach. This is a collection of 48 preludes and **fugues** in every key rising chromatically from C. As there are 24 different keys, Bach wrote two works in the same key. Chopin's arrangement of the 24 preludes is different in that they are arranged in a circle of fifths, i.e. keys a fifth apart.

A prelude is a brief 'opening' piece that sets a particular mood and is linked to a following fugue in the same key. We expect a prelude to be followed by something else! However, the 24 Chopin pieces are all stand-alone preludes, each in a different major and minor key. Each prelude is meant to depict a specific idea or emotion. Although all the preludes, nocturne and etudes had romantic titles in early editions, these were not actually given by the composer.

The 'Raindrop' Prelude was written during Chopin's period of recuperation at the deserted monastery in Valldemossa, Majorca. The piece was written during a storm and the title relates to the dripping of raindrops from the roof of the monastery. In the piece, these are represented by:

◆ the continuously repeating A♭s in section A, which is the dominant note of D♭ major
◆ the continuously repeating G♯s, the dominant note of C♯ minor (enharmonically the same note as A♭) in the middle section B. These repeated pedal notes pervade the work, but do not detract from the beauty of the melodic line.

Glossary

fugue a musical texture involving polyphonic writing for instruments/voices. However, it is also known as a structure in which voice parts enter one after the other in imitation. The fugue has three sections: the exposition – middle entries – final entries

The monastery in Valldemossa, Majorca, where Chopin composed the 'Raindrop' Prelude.

 CD1:3 Close analysis of the 'Raindrop' Prelude (Piano Prelude No. 15 in D flat major, Op. 28) by F. Chopin

Listen to the recording on the audio CD and use your Anthology to study the analysis that follows.

Form and structure

The piece is loosely in ternary form and falls into three quite unbalanced sections.

Section	Key	Length
A (bars 1–27)	D♭ major	27 bars
B (bars 28–75)	C♯ minor (tonic minor)	47 bars
A (bars 75–81)	D♭ major	6 bars
Codetta (bars 81–89)	D♭ major	8 bars

It is interesting to note that over half the piece (section B – 47 bars) is the middle section. The mood of this C♯ minor section is ponderous, dark and stormy, with the melody in the left-hand bass of the piano in thick chordal, almost chorale-like, movement. Yet the piece is remembered and acquired its nickname of the 'Raindrop' from the beautiful elegiac melody of section A!

Keyboard techniques used

The piece is of moderate playing standard and is not virtuosic like many other of Chopin's works. The keyboard range employed is not that great either, keeping mostly to the stave with a few ledger line notes. The top note is only B♭ and the rhythms are quite straightforward. Key playing techniques employed in this piece include:

- *cantabile legato* playing
- careful expressive use of the pedals
- use of *rubato* playing.

Section A (bars 1–27)

The music is marked *sostenuto* (sustained) and the whole section is marked *piano* (soft). The right hand has the melody line throughout in regular four-bar phrases (except bars 16–17 and 18–19, which are two-bar phrases) with a simple left-hand quaver accompaniment incorporating the repeated 'raindrop' A♭s. The musical texture is homophonic (or melody-dominated homophony) throughout the section. Pedal markings are given to help ensure the *legato cantablile* melodic line. Graceful simplicity is the intention with the musical emphasis on the sustained melody. The ingredient not marked, but certainly applied to the whole performance of this piece, is rubato time. Let us now look at this section in further detail.

SECTION A (bars 1–27)	
Bar numbers	**Analysis**
1–4	• Main tune is characterised by the falling motif F–D♭–A♭ – falling raindrops! Traditionally too, as was mentioned in the analysis of the Mozart symphony, a falling motif was common in music from Renaissance times to represent sadness, melancholy and grief. It is a sighing figure. • However, notice how Chopin 'fills in' this initial leap by the stepwise ascent up to a G♭ then stepwise back down again to the D♭ to complete the phrase. • The inner part provides a harmonic support to the melody, doubling in sixths at bars 2–4. The harmony is simple diatonic (in the key) using mainly chords I and V7. • The phrase ends with a perfect cadence at bar 4 (Ic–V7–I) followed by ornamentation over a dominant 7th chord in a septuplet figuration incorporating an **acciaccatura** (a 'crushed' note played as quickly as possible before the main note) followed by a turn.
5–8	• A repeat of bars 1–4.

8 (last beat)–12	• A new, second part of the theme is heard. This undergoes slight variation every four bars. Again this is a simple stepwise melody. • Notice the appearance of the odd chromatic note (C♭ in bars 9 and 11 hinting at A♭ minor) to add colour to the harmony. The G♮ in bar 11 is more important as it modulates the music to A♭ major (the dominant key). • See chords V–I perfect cadence in A♭ at bars 11 (beats 3 and 4)–12 (beat 1). Notice the turn in bar 11 (and 15).

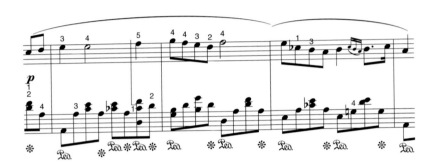

12 (beat 2)–16 (beat 1)	• A variant of the previous four-bar phrase. The A♭ major key is altered by the C♭ at beat 2 of bar 12 as we change to A♭ minor tonality. • The F♮s a bar later take us back to B♭ minor (relative minor to D♭ major). The cadence at bars 15 (beats 3 and 4)–16 (beat 1) is V–I in B♭ minor. • The music through this short section is quite chromatic and modulates (unlike bars 1–8).
16–19	• Two sets of two-bar phrases based on the second part of the theme. These link back to the third statement of the main melody. • Notice how the inner part of the left hand provides chordal support to the melody, effectively filling out the musical texture. • The first two-bar phrase stays in B♭ minor, the second takes us back to the tonic key of D♭ major.
20–23	• A reprise of the opening melody, ending with a chromatic septuplet figure.
24–27	• The chromatic septuplet figure from bar 23 leads to another statement of the opening idea. This is left 'hanging' on a dominant 7th chord at bar 27. • The repeated A♭s are taken over by the right hand. The right hand at this point assumes the role of accompaniment (playing the constantly falling raindrops!) and the left hand now has the melodic interest in the bass. Chopin uses this note again as a pivot note. • The A♭ now changes 'character' and becomes an enharmonic G♯. This is the dominant note of C♯ minor and the music of Section B commences in C♯ minor – the enharmonic tonic minor to D♭ major of Section A.

Section B (bars 28–75)

This is a lengthy and dramatic central section lasting for over half the total length of the piece. For the most part, the melodic interest is in the left hand with relentless G♯s in the right hand. In section A, these were light notes symbolic of gently falling raindrops, but here in the middle section the mood of the storm gives the repeated notes a more insistent quality, rather like a bell tolling! The prominence in the musical texture of these repeated notes is achieved through placing the notes in octaves in the right hand at the top of the musical texture, for example at bars 35–39. However, the right hand assumes the melodic part from bar 60 to the end of the section at bar 75. The musical texture is homophonic throughout but is a much fuller and robust sound with chords in the left hand and at times right hand too. The range of notes is increased with the use of octaves in both hand parts.

If you imagine an orchestration of the delicate music of section A to be suited perhaps to a flute accompanied by pizzicato strings, then the music of section B would require a strong brass and woodwind orchestration of the left-hand chords with strings on top of the texture playing the repeated G♯s!

Although the section starts very quietly *sotto voce* (in an undertone or whisper), the music builds to *ff* and a bright sounding E major at bar 40. This falls away by bar 43 until it builds again at bar 51 to an *ff* E major at bar 56. The rest of the section is more resigned at a lower dynamic level. However, the sense of the romantic passion and storm are to be found within this central section of the work. Let us now look at this section in further detail.

SECTION B (Bars 28–75)	
Bar numbers	**Analysis**
28–35	• Two four-bar phrases with a chorale-like crotchet melody in the left-hand part. Both phrases end on a dominant chord (although in both cases, the third is missing producing a bare fifths chord of G♯ and D♯ – see bars 31 and 35. • Octave G♯s are added in at bar 35.

| 36–39 | • A repetition of bars 28–31, except that the right hand has inner crotchet movement doubling the top notes of the left hand in octaves.
 • This produces a thicker piano texture and reinforces the melody as the music crescendos throughout these bars to *fortissimo (ff)* at bar 40. |

40–43	• The sombre mood is broken by a dramatic chord of E major. These four bars are in G♯ minor (dominant key of C♯ minor) and interestingly the enharmonic of A♭ is the dominant of the key of section A!
	• Chopin has done this by using the tonally ambiguous chord at bar 39 (no third) as a G♯ minor chord. In C♯ minor we would need a B♯ for a dominant chord in C♯ minor. Using this he goes straight into G♯ minor. The E major chords at bars 40 and 41 are chord VI in this key.
	• A perfect cadence in G♯ minor occurs at bars 42–43 (V–I). This is a strong and powerful four bars of music achieved through octaves in the bass and treble. Minim chords appear in the right hand too, providing a strong chordal outline to the tune playing in the bass (left-hand) octaves. This is further emphasised by the accent signs over each note.
	• The texture reduces dramatically to single *piano* quaver G♯s to herald a reprise of this section.

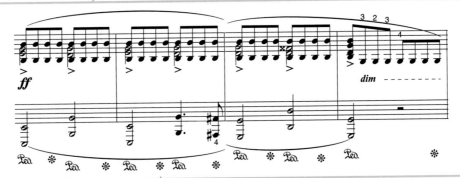

44–59	• A repeat of bars 28–43. The only differences are slight dynamic changes and at bar 59 the repeated G♯s are an octave higher.

60–63	• Back in C♯ minor, the melody moves up to the top part of the texture. This is chorale-like again, moving up and down in step.
	• This melody resembles segments from the first part of section B, e.g. bars 30–31. The first three notes at bars 60–61 are in longer note values, i.e. minims instead of crotchets (this is called augmentation).
	• Note too that the repeated G♯ notes are now in the middle of the texture.

64–67	• Static harmony chords (with quaver G♯s) of the tonic and dominant in C♯ minor forming a series of perfect cadences, e.g. bar 64 (V–I) etc.
	• The repeated minims and crotchets on G♯ form a pedal effect. This is a sustained or repeated note. As it is the dominant note in C♯ minor, it is called a **dominant pedal** and because it is the top part it is in fact an **inverted dominant pedal**. If the pedal was the lowest part, it is just called a pedal, and if it occurs in the middle of the texture, it is an **inner pedal**.

68–70	• A repeat of the music from bars 60–62.
71–74	• A *forte* passage. Two bars take us to F♯ minor (bar 71) then back next bar to C♯ minor (bar 72).
	• Above a dominant/tonic bass there are three repetitions of the notes A♯–A♯–G♯. The note A♯ is a chromatic note in C♯ minor and makes an added sixth chord (C♯–E–G♯–A♯).
	• The feeling in these bars is one of anticipation as we hover on the note G♯, which as the dominant note A♭ of the home key of D♭ prepares for the seamless link back to a reprise of the opening of section A.

75	• This is a link bar into a reprise of the opening melody. The last four quavers in the bass written as G♯–E♯–F♯–D♯ can be read enharmonically as A♭–F–G♭–E♭ in D♭ major.

Reprise of Section A (bars 76–81) and Codetta (bars 81–89)

A short restatement of the opening section of the piece opens the section. On the repeat at bar 80, the music comes to an unexpected halt, as a two-bar monophonic melody phrase leads to a six-bar chordal passage to bring the piece to a very quiet conclusion.

Reprise of Section A (bars 76–81) and Codetta (bars 81–89)	
Bar numbers	**Analysis**
76–79	• A four-bar *piano* statement as at bars 1–4. • The ornament at bar 79 is extended this time into a ten-note figure incorporating an initial turn. • *Smorzando* at bar 79 means 'dying away'.
80–81	• The 'broken off' repeat of the opening figure. The effect is one of a dream-like fading away here into a fantasy 'mini cadenza' at bars 81–83.

81 (last beat)–83	• The listener is made to jolt upright with the *forte* top Bb. This is, incidentally, the highest note in the piece. This two-bar phrase descends in volume and pitch leading to the six-bar phrase that follows.
84–89	• A six-bar phrase based on tonic and dominant chords in Db major. • The repeated Abs are still to be heard in the middle of the texture (left hand). The melodic line is also just above this in the middle of the texture (right hand). The melody resembles that heard in the minor key at bars 60–62. • The piece ends *pianissimo* with a perfect cadence at bars 87–88. A *ritenuto* bar of tonic harmony at bar 88 leads to the final tonic chord at bar 89.

Glossary

acciaccatura literally an ornament – 'a crushed in note' played as quickly as possible before the main note

dominant pedal a sustained (or repeated) note(s) on the dominant note of the key

inner pedal a sustained (or repeated) note(s) in the middle of a musical texture

inverted dominant pedal a sustained (or repeated) note(s) as the highest part in a musical texture

pivot note a note common to both keys and used to pivot between two different keys, i.e. Ab (of Db major) is also G# (in C# minor)

Listening and appraising questions: the 'Raindrop' Prelude

Now that you have listened to Chopin's 'Raindrop' Prelude and studied the analysis on pages 38–44, answer the listening and appraising questions that follow.

1 Why is the piano prelude nicknamed the 'Raindrop'?
2 Name *four* different subjects favoured for musical expression by Romantic composers.
3 What type of piece is a prelude?
4 Describe the basic outline of the structure of this piece.
5 How are contrasted moods achieved in section A and B? Make *two* points.
6 Name *two* keyboard techniques needed for an expressive interpretation of the music.
7 Name the *two* main keys used in this piece.
8 Which note is used throughout the music as a representation of the falling raindrops?
9 Name *two* different ornaments used in the music.
10 What name is given to the prevailing texture found in this music?

Further listening

In addition to this set work, try to listen to other examples of preludes. For example:
- The 24 Preludes by Chopin (of which the 'Raindrop' is no. 17)
- The 48 Preludes and Fugues (*The Well-Tempered Klavier*) by J.S. Bach
- Preludes for piano by Rachmaninov
- Preludes (and Fugues) for piano by Mendelssohn
- Preludes for piano by Debussy
- Preludes for piano by Liszt.

ResultsPlus
Watch out!

Naming musical devices
When asked to name the musical device(s) used in an extract, students often produce vague or incorrect responses. For example:

Question: Name the musical device used in the bass part at the beginning of the extract.

■ Students often have a mental block with the word 'device' and are not clear what is meant by this term. In music, there are a selection of common devices that you need to know to answer this type of question. If you don't have these devices up your sleeve, then watch out: you may come unstuck!

▲ To help avoid this common mistake, here is a basic list of expected musical devices that could apply to this sample question and should be known at GCSE level.

Augmentation – doubling note values
Diminution – halving note values
Sequence – repeating a passage at the same, higher or lower pitch
Ostinato – a repeated chord pattern, melody or rhythm
Pedal – a sustained note in the bass (can be in the middle or top part too)
Retrograde – playing a melody backwards
Inversion – playing a melody upside down
Retrograde inversion – upside down and back to front.
Syncopation – notes accented off the beat

Therefore when you hear the bass part played in longer note values in the sample question, the answer is augmentation. This is far better than just saying 'the melody is slower'.

Composing and performing tasks

The Baroque era (c.1600–1750)

 Vocal composition *Z-Zebediah Zidcup!*

Setting words to music

When studying set work 1, we saw how Handel uses four different short melodies for each line of text and then combines them in different ways.

1 Try setting the following poem by Cara Lockhart Smith in any style you wish (for example, rock, pop, folk, classical) using a different melody for each line as shown.

Z

Zebediah Zidcup	tune 1
Puzzles in his head	tune 2
Round and round and round they go	tune 3
When he lies in bed	tune 4
Zebediah Zidcup	tune 1
Looking at the moon	tune 2
Round and round and round it goes	tune 3
Likewise does the sun	tune 4
Likewise do the elephants	tune 4
Likewise do the sheep	tune 4
Round and round and round they go	tune 3
Till they fall asleep	tune 4

Write for a solo voice, duet, trio or quartet and try to show some of the techniques that Handel uses, namely:

– solo (monophonic) lines

– two-part or three-part imitation combining the same line or different lines of music (polyphonic)

– all parts together (homophonic).

2 Arrange a performance of the finished composition.

Ensemble performance

Use the pentatonic scale notes in C major of C, D, E, G and A in the improvisation performance.

Try the following task in groups of four:

PART 1: Call and response
- Each player needs to make up and learn a melody of eight beats (two bars in 4/4 time).
- The piece starts with player 1 playing their melody as solo (monophonic).
- This is then answered by everyone playing their own melody together (homophony) at the same time.
- Then player 2 plays their melody as a solo followed by everyone again, then player 3 followed by all, then finally player 4 and all together again.

PART 2: Follow me
- Player 1 plays their melody from part 1, and player 2 comes in after one bar, followed by player 3 one bar after player 2, then player 4, one bar after player 3. This should produce some simple imitation.

PART 3: Building up the texture
- Repeat Part 2 above, but this time each player plays his/her own original melody and keeps playing this over and over until the last player has finished playing.

PART 4: The grand finale
- To complete the piece, players 1 and 2 play their tunes together answered two bars later by players 3 and 4.
- This is followed by all four players playing tune 1 together then tunes 2, 3 and 4. Build up the dynamics through this final section, ending *fortissimo*.

The Classical era (c.1750–1830)

Contrasting melodies

In the Mozart symphony you studied sonata form, which is used as a large-scale structure. Despite its size and length, the music features just two contrasting melodies (themes or subjects). In this composing task, you are to compose two contrasting melodies for two contrasting 'characters' or themes.

The two melodies must be different in several ways, for example:
- different keys (major/minor)
- different pitch ranges (treble–bass etc)
- use quite different types of rhythm, articulation etc.

You can also of course think of any other relevant ways to make the melodies different.

You could structure your piece in binary form (AB) or ternary form (ABA) where the contrasting themes appear in section A and B. If you wish to write three different themes, then try a rondo structure (ABACA), with theme A being the dominant character.

Improvisation: *The Angel and the Demon*

To start
With a partner, agree on two contrasting characters for which you will improvise a melody. Experiment with your instrument and start to improvise a melody that you feel represents your character well.

Make decisions about:
- the key
- the number of beats per bar
- the length of the melody
- what scale you might use as the basis of your improvisation.

Now try this!
- With your partner, play your melodies separately one after the other and appraise each other. What was good? What could be improved?
- In the light of this feedback, revise your melody.
- Now try playing the melodies together. What is the effect?
- Now try just playing a fragment (one bar or so) of your melody 'in conversation' with your partner. This is the essence of jazz (see pages 87–101 for more information).
- As you gain in confidence, develop this conversational approach to improvisation. Before long you will have created a short piece.

Play time
Play your finished improvisation to the rest of the class. See if your class can work out your different characters from listening to the music!

The Romantic era (c.1800–1900)

 ## Composing a musical scene

In our study of Romantic music, we have discovered that composers during the 19th century favoured topics such as love, nature, legends and myths for inspiration. Now you can don your wizard's hat to conjure up an imaginary scene to act as a programme to your musical story.

- Write down an outline scene for your musical story in one paragraph – no more!
- Think about how you are going to bring the words to life. For example, is something scary or dramatic going to occur in your scene? Perhaps something tragic or uplifting. If so, you will need to think carefully about how you can use music to represent the scene.

If you can use music technology, this would be an ideal way in which to compose this musical scene.

When it comes to playback time, see if your class can work out what the scene is about from your music! You may be surprised by their responses.

 ## A romantic piece!

Music has often been described as a 'universal language', able to communicate feelings and emotions to all audiences regardless of their nationality.

1 Look through the music you are studying at the moment or a piece that you have played or sung in the past. What emotions do you think the music conveys?

2 In this simple task, you need to put on a short, informal class performance. Do not worry if you can only play half the piece – as it is a 'work in progress', this should suffice for our task!

3 Each member of the class listens to each other performing their chosen piece and then writes down the feelings that the music gives them and the character of the piece. This will be easy of course if you choose to sing a love song!

This task is useful too in getting you to think about what you might like to play for your GCSE solo performance at the end of the course.

Music in the 20th century

The 20th century witnessed more developments in the sheer diversity of musical styles than ever before. Composers reacted to what they saw as the emotionalism or indulgences of the Romantic era in different ways, and this led to the birth of several new styles. The 20th century also saw the birth of popular music in all its different genres and guises, as well as music generated using new forms of music technology, such as electronic and experimental music in addition to a myriad of different forms of dance music that are still evolving today.

Set works

Expressionism and serialism
Set work 4 – 'Peripetie' from Five Orchestral Pieces by A. Schoenberg (1874–1951)

Musical theatre
Set work 5 – 'Something's Coming' from *West Side Story* by L. Bernstein (1918–1990)

Minimalism
Set work 6 – 3rd movement (Fast) from *Electric Counterpoint* by S. Reich (1936–)

A. Schoenberg: 'Peripetie' from Five Orchestral Pieces, Op. 16 (1909)

In the study of this set work you will learn about:

◆ the origins of expressionism

◆ features of expressionism

◆ the life and works of Arnold Schoenberg

◆ how the set work 'Peripetie' is constructed through analysis of the serialism technique.

Before expressionism

Towards the end of the 19th century, composers of the late Romantic era were producing longer and grander pieces of music. Composers such as Bruckner and Brahms produced symphonies vaster than anything ever produced by the previous generation of composers. Composers such as Wagner and Verdi wrote operas that combined the scale of the Romantic era symphonies with theatre, creating works of enormous imagination, pushing the musical language of the day to the very limits. When composers were writing such weighty pieces, they would put a great deal of effort into ensuring that the structure was interesting through the use of different keys, harmonies, themes and textures.

Brahms was interested in writing music in strict forms (mostly borrowed from the Baroque and Classical eras) with Beethoven as his role model, although his music was still very romantic in scale. Wagner made extensive use of **chromaticism** and frequent key changes so that the key of a piece was often unclear. In the Classical era, composers such as Mozart and Haydn used frequent perfect cadences to punctuate their music (much like we use commas and full stops to punctuate sentences) but Wagner used them much less frequently, preferring to keep the tension building in what he called his 'endless melody'.

Glossary

chromaticism music based on the chromatic scale, relating to chords or harmonies based on non-harmonic tones

Expressionism

Most composers of the early 20th century had to react to what Brahms and Wagner had achieved, either by using classical forms and key relationships in their own way or by abandoning them completely. Composers in the **impressionist** style such as Ravel and Debussy wrote music that used recognisable chords and harmonies, but combined them in original ways, using instrumental colour to paint musical pictures. They would use chords out of their normal context to achieve an effect (such as a series of parallel dominant 7th chords) rather than sticking to established harmonic rules (dominant 7th chords should normally resolve to the tonic chord).

Glossary

impressionist a style of music that seeks to describe a feeling or experience rather than achieve accurate depiction

Schoenberg took this idea further, deciding that the combination of instrumental sounds, or 'tone colours' was just as important as melody. He invented the term **klangfarbenmelodie** (tone-colour melody) to describe the concept of how different instrumental colours would contribute to the melody as well as the pitches themselves. As part of this process of experimentation, Schoenberg took Wagner's use of chromaticism to its logical extreme – he abandoned the use of tonality and key relationships entirely, writing **atonal** music.

Expressionist art, music and literature

The expressionist movement (in both art and music) was strongest in Germany during the years immediately after the First World War. At this time there was a strong feeling of disillusionment and discontent concerning living conditions and restrictions imposed on the country by the **Treaty of Versailles**, so the emotions the artists, composers and writers wanted to express were generally related to these feelings. As such, works in the expressionist style tend to make us feel a little uncomfortable at times or at least are a little more difficult to digest than a typical impressionist work of the early 1900s.

Opposite is an example of an expressionist painting from this era, *The Scream* by Edvard Munch. The feelings you get when you look at the painting are likely to be similar to the feelings you get when you listen to the music of an expressionist composer – whether positive or negative, they are likely to be strong feelings! This is what expressionist artists, composers and writers want – for the beholder, listener or reader to experience a strong reaction to their work because they are trying to convey their intense inner emotions to the world.

Glossary

atonal absence of tonality (key)

klangfarbenmelodie literally 'tone colour melody', a word used to describe how timbre contributes to melody in addition to pitch and rhythm

Glossary

Treaty of Versailles the peace settlement signed after World War I had ended in 1918

Features of expressionism

Before we focus on the set work, it is useful to understand some of the hallmarks of the style and the vocabulary used when describing expressionism. The following are features of expressionism in general, most of which are true of the set work and others that are present in other expressionist works:

- expressionist music is atonal – it avoids the normal hierarchy of keys and chords, giving each of the 12 semitones equal importance
- each piece generally confines itself to expressing one intense emotion
- composers make full use of the pitch range of instruments, exploring the difference in instrumental colour that can be heard at the extremes of the instruments' registers
- timbre is felt to be as important as melody – the sound of the instruments is felt to contribute to the melody as much as pitch
- extremes of dynamics are common, from as quiet as possible to as loud as possible. This can be even more dramatic in large ensembles when the music can go from just a few instruments playing very quietly to the full ensemble playing very loudly
- pieces tend to be quite short – it is difficult to write a piece of considerable length without the framework of a key structure and the use of recognisable themes that can be developed in a traditional sense.

It is in this musical style that the next set work – 'Peripetie' by Arnold Schoenberg – was written.

Arnold Schoenberg (1874–1951)

Arnold Schoenberg was born in Vienna, Austria in 1874. He started having violin lessons when he was eight years old. He began composing pieces as a child, mostly teaching himself musical theory through reading books and experimenting – he didn't have any lessons in composition until his late teens. When he started writing music professionally towards the end of the 19th century, he wrote in the style of the late Romantic era, using the large orchestras associated with the period. He supported himself by teaching in Berlin and Vienna (Berg and Webern were two of his pupils). He was Jewish (although he had adopted Protestantism for a number of years), leaving Germany in 1933 to move to Paris and eventually to settle in California after his music was condemned by the Nazis as being 'decadent'.

Schoenberg's move to atonal music in 1908 coincided with a traumatic time in his life – his wife left him for one of his artist friends, who later committed suicide, and he was in severe financial difficulties, so he had a lot of intense emotions to express through his music! Expressionism was the perfect vehicle to do so – the pieces he wrote around this time were generally quite short, expressing extremes of emotion.

Background to Five Orchestral Pieces

Five Orchestral Pieces by Arnold Schoenberg is a set of atonal pieces for full orchestra. They all last between one to five minutes and are not connected to each other by the use of any thematic ideas.

In these works Schoenberg uses pitches and harmonies for effect rather than because of their relationship to each other – he is much more concerned with the combinations of timbres than with melody and harmony as we understand it. In a letter to a colleague he wrote, 'I have high expectations … particularly concerning sound and atmosphere. This is all that is important … a variegated, uninterrupted change of colours, rhythms and moods.'

In 1908 Richard Strauss, an established and popular composer of the time, asked Schoenberg to send him some short pieces to have a look at (with the possibility of getting them some attention from the important musical figures of the day). Schoenberg had not written any pieces for orchestra since 1903 – he had since been experimenting with his ideas of atonality in much smaller-scale works, such as his pieces for solo piano. He responded by writing this set of five pieces for full orchestra. He had had a series of disappointments previously as his works for chamber orchestra were dismissed by one major figure after another, stating that they did not understand his music, so he hoped that his compositions for larger ensembles might be accepted by the conductors of the large orchestras. Unfortunately, the larger-scale works received a similar reception from established composers and conductors – Strauss himself said, 'It would be better for him to shovel snow than to scrawl on music paper!' Schoenberg's reaction was to withdraw further into his small group of like-minded composers and pupils, more determined than ever to succeed in his original ideas.

Schoenberg loved to conceal things within his compositions – he believed that the intelligent and attentive listener would hear the deeper meanings within the music, even if it has not been explained to them previously. He felt that music expresses much more than words possibly can and that a little is taken from the music itself when words are attached to it (for example, giving a title to a piece or describing it in words). As such, titles for each of the Five Orchestral Pieces did not appear on the printed scores until 13 years after they had been composed, and only because one of Schoenberg's colleagues insisted that titles would help audiences respond better to his music.

> **Note**
> Bach used his name as a musical motif – the notes B–A–C–H in German note names translate to B♭–A–C–B♮ in English note names. It is suggested that Schoenberg came up with the idea of a hexachord by finding the musical notes within his name – S C H Ö N B E R G = Es (S), C, H, B, E, G, which translates to E♭, C, B♮, B♭, E♮, G. He rarely used this particular hexachord in his music, but did use other hexachords closely related to his 'signature' hexachord.

One of the main 'codes' concealed within Schoenberg's pre-serialism music is the use of a group of notes called a **hexachord**. As the name suggests, this is a group of six notes that can be played together to form a chord. The group of notes can also be used to form short melodic ideas if they are played one after the other.

A recurring hexachord in 'Peripetie' is played by the horns from the second beat of bar 8. The notes in this chord are C, B♭, E, F, C♯ and A which, arranged in ascending order are A, B♭, C, C♯, E and F. This hexachord can be used as a chord, with the notes arranged in any order and it can be used as a melodic motif with the notes arranged in any order. Either the chord or the melodic motif can be transposed and the notes can be played in any octave. It is used in both forms throughout the piece (see the analysis table for more details).

The **complement** of the hexachord can be constructed by taking the other six available semitones not used in the first hexachord – B, D, E♭, F♯, G, G♯. The complement can be transposed and reordered in the same way as the first hexachord.

In the 1952 revision of the score, edits have been added to show which instrument has the main melodic line at any given time (the **principal voice**) and which instrument has the next most important melodic line (the **secondary voice**) these are represented by the symbols **H** and **N**. Although added after his death, Schoenberg had left instructions as to which instruments were the principal and secondary voices throughout the piece.

H – Hauptstimme – principal voice
N – Nebenstimme – secondary voice

An instrument is no longer considered to have one of the main melodic lines when it is marked with the symbol **⌐**.

'Peripetie' is structured in five sections, broadly in rondo form, but with the returning 'A' sections developed to such an extent that they are hardly recognisable as statements of a theme at all – it is not a rondo in the same way as would have been the case in the Baroque or Classical eras, being more a return of a particular mood or orchestral sound rather than a repeated recognisable theme. See the table on pages 56–58 for a full analysis of the structure of the piece (hexachords have been arranged into ascending order of pitch for clarity).

Glossary

complement the six semitones not used in the first hexachord

hexachord a group of six notes selected from the 12 available pitches that are used as a musical motif or chord

principal voice the main melodic line

secondary voice the next most importance melodic line after the principal voice

CD1:4   Close analysis of 'Peripetie' from Five Orchestral Pieces

Listen to the recording on the audio CD and use your Anthology to study the analysis that follows.

Section	Bar numbers and timing	Description
A	1–18 0:00–0:31	• The piece begins with a bang! The clarinets and flutes state two hexachords (bar 1 = C♯, D, E, F, G♯, A in clarinets and bar 3 = A, A♯, B, C, E, G♯ in flutes) leading to a fanfare-like ***fortissimo*** horn motif which is the first part to be marked as the principal voice **H̄**. • The bassoons in the opening two bars also play the clarinet hexachord from bar 1, which is the same as the horn hexachord from bar 8 (A, B♭, C, C♯, E and F), but transposed up four semitones. • Other variations on the same hexachord can be found throughout the piece (e.g. in bar 6 the loud chord in the strings and trumpets is made up of notes from an inversion of the hexachord – A, G♯, F♯, F, D, D♭). You do not have to be able to find and analyse these complex chords, but should be aware that the piece uses them as the basis for much of the melodic and harmonic content. • In section A most of the ideas that are going to be used in the whole piece are stated one after the other – this was Schoenberg's standard way of working. **Tempo/Rhythm** Tempo marking *sehr rasch* means 'very quick'. The metronome value is approximately 100–108 bpm. The opening contains mostly short triplet and sextuplet (groups of six) bursts, with the fanfare-like horn statement in bars 3–5 played in triplet quavers. After the demisemiquaver hexachord burst the tempo is slightly slower, though the quiet horn passage from bar 6 beat 3 and the expressive, rubato clarinet line from bar 10 beat 2 create the illusion of the tempo slowing more than it actually does. **Instrumentation/Texture** The full orchestra gets a chance to blow out the cobwebs, even if only for one or two notes before they rest for a while. The brass dominate the texture until bar 8, when the woodwind take charge with the low bassoon, bass clarinet ostinato and the silky clarinet line. Instrumental combinations drop in and out in quick succession, with dovetailing, homophonic bursts. The texture thins dramatically after the loud hexachord, gradually dying out to leave the solo clarinet. **Pitch/Melody** There is no sense of key – this is an atonal piece throughout (mostly built on hexachords as mentioned above). After the first six bars we are left in no doubt that we will hear the full pitch range of the orchestral instruments. The clarinet melody from bar 10 beat 2 is expressive and almost gentle, but very angular including dissonant leaps of a minor ninth and major seventh/diminished octave (intervals commonly used to accentuate the dissonance and create tension). **Dynamics** The piece begins loudly, becoming louder with sudden bursts from instrumental groups. By bar 5 beat 3 they reach *fff* before dying away to ***pianissimo***. Note how the trumpets and trombones are playing muted. Normally a mute is used to mellow the tone and allow a player to play quieter, but Schoenberg uses it entirely for the sound quality it produces, and will call for extremes of dynamics for which the mute was not originally designed.

B	18–34	The beginning of the second section is marked by the cello taking over the role of principal voice from the clarinet, handing over the baton to the trumpet after two bars. The intense cello line, played high in its register, immediately gives way to an increasingly frantic section.
	0:31–1:00	

Tempo/Rhythm

The tempo returns to the original marking, with the short durations creating the illusion that the tempo has increased much more than is actually the case.

Instrumentation/Texture

Again, the full orchestra is used, but not all at once except for climactic points like bars 30–34. Even here, not all the instruments are used for the full five bars with most of the string section leaving the wind and percussion to supply the vast majority of the power. Note how, while all the busyness and volume is going on in the wind and percussion, Schoenberg has written a soft line for the first violins and cellos. These parts are all but inaudible, but they do add to the effect and texture, and display Schoenberg's attention to detail. The texture is very polyphonic and complex throughout this section.

Pitch/Melody

The principal voice snakes through much of the orchestra. In bars 24–28 it bounces rapidly from one brass instrument to another, demonstrating the klangfarbenmelodie idea. The secondary voice springs up in this section for its only appearance in the piece (bar 28 beat 2–31 beat 1 in trumpet 1 and bar 29 in the flutes, piccolo and clarinet).

Dynamics

The section begins quite quietly, but there is an immediate crescendo. The dynamics are very varied from instrument to instrument with the principal and secondary voice parts always *f–fff*, but the other parts ranging from quiet to very loud. The dynamics change dramatically and frequently in this section in a very restless fashion.

A'	35–43	The beginning of the third section is marked by the string section rising from the ashes of section B followed by a flourish from the horns and then a return to the *pp* horn hexachord of bar 8. Several other instruments briefly disturb the horn chord, but otherwise this section gives us a brief rest from the turmoil of section B. The mood is more menacing than tranquil, giving the impression that there are more fireworks to come.
	1:00–1:16	

C	44–58	The beginning of the fourth section is marked by the bassoon taking the baton for the principal voice and passing it immediately to a solo cello.
	1:16–1:50	

Tempo/Rhythm

Tempo marking – alternates between *ruhiger* (calmer) and *heftig* (passionate).

Instrumentation/Texture

For the first part of this section the texture is much more sparse, with Schoenberg choosing to focus on overlapping combinations of solo instruments. There is the impression of handling the orchestra like a delicate crystal before hitting it with the full orchestral hammer in bar 53 and standing back to admire the handiwork in bars 56–58.

Dynamics

The dynamics of this section range from *pp* (bars 44/45), with individual instruments rising above the others with individual crescendos, to *fff* (bars 53–55) and back to almost nothing in bar 58.

A″	59–66 1:50–2:09	The beginning of the final section is marked by speeding up to the original tempo and a triplet figure in the clarinets and second violins.

Tempo/Rhythm

Some of the rhythmic motifs from the opening bars return in this section – for example, trumpets bars 61–63 = bars 5 beat 3–6 beat 2 repeated in quick succession, clarinets bars 59–61 = bar 1, flutes bars 62–63 = bar 3.

Instrumentation/Texture

Starting with just the clarinets and strings, the instruments are introduced one by one in quick succession (layering the repeated rhythmic motifs) until the full orchestra comes together for the final climactic chord of bar 64.

Pitch/Melody

The material from the opening is used and developed for this final section. No voice is marked as being more important than any other. The climactic chord of bar 64 is a gigantic hexachord (C, D, E♭, F♯, G, G♯) in most of the orchestra (except the cor anglais and double basses) with the double basses playing an unrelated tremolo chord (very high in their register), which sustains after the rest of the orchestra subside to conclude the piece.

Dynamics

Crescendos quite quickly from *pp* at the beginning of bar 59 to *fff* in bar 64 and immediately dies away to nothing with the tremolo double bass chord (accompanied by *pp* horns).

Serialism

It became clear to Schoenberg that it was very difficult to keep a piece going for any length of time if it did not contain the key relationships and cadences that contribute so much to the structure of music written up to this time. Since a central idea of Schoenberg's work was that there should not be a key, he had to find some other way to organise his ideas.

After some time experimenting he arrived at his 'Twelve-Tone Technique' or, as he called it, 'Method of Composition with Twelve Tones which are Related Only with One Another'.

This technique we now call serialism involves taking the 12 available semitones in the octave and making a 'row' or 'series' by rearranging them in a particular order. Composers who adopted serialism were very careful about the exact nature of their basic series, concentrating on particular types of intervals (such as semitones or perfect fourths) so that these intervals occurred in their series more than any other.

Schoenberg had not invented the twelve-tone technique when he wrote Five Orchestral Pieces, which is part of the reason for their brevity, but an example of its use can be heard in his Fourth String Quartet.

The basic series used to compose Schoenberg's Fourth String Quartet is:

1	2	3	4	5	6	7	8	9	10	11	12
D	C♯	A	B♭	F	E♭	E	C	A♭	G	F♯	B

This is called the **prime row**, shortened to P_0.

Glossary

prime row (P_o) the musical material on which a piece of serial music is based, normally consisting of the 12 notes of the chromatic scale in an order set by the composer

serialism a compositional technique invented by Schoenberg and used by many composers of the 20th century

Note how Schoenberg concentrated here on semitones and major thirds:

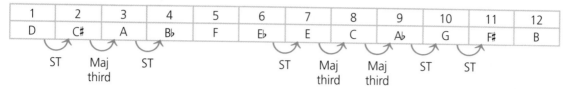

1	2	3	4	5	6	7	8	9	10	11	12
D	C#	A	B♭	F	E♭	E	C	A♭	G	F#	B

ST   Maj third   ST   ST   Maj third   Maj third   ST   ST

(ST = semitone, Maj third = major third)

The prime row can be transformed in three ways – it can be:

1 Turned backwards (**retrograde** – R_0)
2 Have all the intervals inverted (**inversion** – I_0)
3 Turned backwards and have all the intervals inverted (**retrograde inversion** – RI_0).

	1	2	3	4	5	6	7	8	9	10	11	12
P_0	D	C#	A	B♭	F	E♭	E	C	A♭	G	F#	B
R_0	B	F#	G	A♭	C	E	E♭	F	B♭	A	C#	D
I_0	D	E♭	G	F#	B	C#	C	E	A♭	A	B♭	F
RI_0	F	B♭	A	A♭	E	C	C#	B	F#	G	E♭	D

These four versions of the series can each be transposed so that they start on any of the 12 available notes.

For example, the prime row can be transposed up by two semitones. It would then be called P_2. If the starting note of P_0 (D) is transposed up two semitones it would mean that P_2 begins on the note E. The rest of the row is transposed in the same way:

	1	2	3	4	5	6	7	8	9	10	11	12
P_2	E	D#	B	C	G	F	F#	D	B♭	A	A♭	C#

There can therefore be 12 versions of the prime row and each of its transformations – for example, P_0–P_{11}. If the row were transposed up by 12 semitones, it would go back to the original (12 semitones up from D is still D).

When serialism was applied strictly (notably by Schoenberg and Webern), all twelve notes of the row had to be used each time the row appeared. Any note could be repeated and it was possible to use the pitches in any octave, but the entire row had to be used in order.

Chords could be formed by sounding several of the notes (in order) at the same time. In the example above (P_2), a three-note chord of E, D# and B could be formed (notes 1–3 of the row), or a four-note chord consisting of the pitches G, F, F# and D (notes 5–8 of the row). The pitches could be arranged in any order and in any octave within the chord itself. Obviously, most chords formed using this technique are very dissonant, but this is the idea! Some composers constructed rows that deliberately contained major and minor triads (e.g. the notes G, B and D one after the other) so that there were some recognisable chords for audiences to grab hold of while listening. Alban Berg did this in his violin concerto.

Glossary

inversion (I_0) process of turning a part upside down, so that a mirror image is created to the original

retrograde (R_0) a method of developing a series by reversing the order in which the pitches are heard

retrograde inversion (RI_0) a method of developing a series by reversing the order in which the pitches of the inverted series are heard

When composers wrote out their pieces they had to use a lot of accidentals. To avoid confusion they often used **enharmonic** versions of pitches (e.g. E♭ is the same as D♯).

Although the techniques described may not seem terribly creative, the composers were only using them to come up with the basic themes for their pieces. They did not just put the 12 available semitones into a random order and then write them on the page along with a few transformations. Instead, they used the prime row like a classical composer would have used his main theme; the transformations are developments of the theme, but they have to be linked in a musical fashion. Remember that serialism was a natural development from expressionism and existed in order to extend expressionist pieces that rely on texture, combinations of timbres, dynamic contrasts and wide pitch ranges, so it is more of a way to structure the music than being the music in itself. If you write music in a serialist style, it is a good idea to approach it from this point of view rather than treating it like a mathematical exercise.

The Second Viennese School and beyond

Schoenberg's pupils, Anton Webern (1883–1945) and Alban Berg (1885–1935), took up the same style of composition as their teacher and, along with Schoenberg, they came to be known as the 'Second Viennese School'. Other composers also composed in an expressionist style for some of their careers, notably Paul Hindemith (1895–1963).

Many composers other than Schoenberg, Webern and Berg used serial techniques in their compositions, all in different ways to suit their own musical style. Composers made up rows using less than 12 notes, or using odd combinations of tunings. Some composers used a serialist approach, but applied it to tonal music – composing rows that belonged to a key.

Igor Stravinsky (1882–1971) used serialism in many of his pieces after the Second World War. Around this time composers became interested in applying the technique to musical elements other than just pitches. Karlheinz Stockhausen (1928–2007) applied serial techniques to pitch, durations, dynamics and even timbre and attack. Composers who applied these techniques would make rhythmic rows as well as rows controlling the dynamics from *pppp* (as soft as it is possible to play) to *ffff* (as loud as it is possible to play). After the initial rows had been composed, there remained little room for many more compositional decisions, and some criticised the approach as being much too restrictive. Webern said 'only on the basis of these [restrictions] has complete freedom become possible'.

Glossary

enharmonic different ways of 'spelling' the same pitch, for example B♭ and A♯

Listening and appraising questions: 'Peripetie' from Five Orchestral Pieces

Now that you have listened to 'Peripetie' and studied the analysis on pages 54–58, answer the listening and appraising questions that follow.

1 Describe the dynamics of the first section of this piece (up to 0:30).

2 Name the type of ensemble performing 'Peripetie'.

3 Describe the tonality of the piece.

4 'Peripetie' was written in the 20th century. List six musical features you can hear in the piece that are common of music written in the 20th century.

5 What is the name given to the group of notes Schoenberg used as a basis for his melodic and harmonic material in this piece?

6 How might Schoenberg have used this group of notes when he composed 'Peripetie'?

7 The horns play a sustained chord in bar 8. In which section later in the piece can the horns be heard playing the same chord? What is the dynamic marking for this chord?

8 What is the term given to Schoenberg's technique of moving the melodic parts rapidly through the different instruments?

9 What playing technique can be heard in the strings in the last two bars of the piece?

Further listening

In addition to the set work, try to listen to other pieces by Schoenberg.
For example:
- Three Piano Pieces, Op. 11 – 1909
- Five Orchestral Pieces, Op. 16 – 1909
- Variations for Orchestra, Op. 31 – 1928.

ResultsPlus
Build Better Answers

Question: Describe the use of rhythm in this expressionist piece. (3 marks)
If a question has three or four marks, you are expected to make three or four different points.

◼ Basic answers include the basic ideas:
- The rhythms are broken up and do not flow.
- The rhythms are complicated.
- The rhythms are varied and keep on changing.

▲ Excellent answers develop the basic ideas, adding more detail and precise musical vocabulary.
- The rhythms are broken up and do not flow – they are fragmented and erratic with no regular feeling of a beat.
- The rhythms are complicated – complex patterns feature including sextuplets, dotted, reverse dotted and double dotted rhythms, triplets are heard against duplets, constant syncopation etc.
- The rhythms are varied and keep on changing. There is little repetition of rhythmic ideas in the music, creating a sense of unrest, chaos and lack of order.

L. Bernstein: 'Something's Coming' from West Side Story (1958)

In the study of this set work you will learn about:

◆ the origins and development of musical theatre

◆ different types of musicals in the 20th century

◆ some background to the life and works of Leonard Bernstein

◆ the plot of the musical *West Side Story*

◆ Bernstein's compositional style

◆ how the solo song 'Something's Coming' is constructed through a detailed analysis of the music

◆ the key features in the music.

The origins of the musical

The musical as we know it today has a long and colourful history. Music theatre can be traced back to the time of Ancient Greece, where stories and morality plays were acted out for entertainment. Over the last three hundred or so years, the musical has gradually evolved from many different styles of entertainment, both musical and non-musical. Two of the oldest forms are the **vaudeville** and **burlesque**.

Vaudeville and burlesque

The vaudeville was a form of entertainment popular in the 1700s. This work comprised popular songs 'borrowed' from other works but with new, often comical and vulgar words set to the music. The idea was to shock and entertain the audience.

The most famous example of this form is *The Beggar's Opera* by John Gay (1685–1732). The subject matter of this work was a story of thieves and prostitutes! Mozart used to attend vaudeville for entertainment with his wife and son and would hear his own operatic music and plots being made fun of on stage. This was music for the common people, not for kings and queens.

The burlesque was similar in form to the vaudeville but tended to be a little more restrained and classical in style. The subject matter was often a parody of other serious plays.

Two other forms were important in the evolution of the musical, namely the opéra-bouffe and operetta.

Glossary

burlesque a parody or humorous piece

vaudeville a form of entertainment, popular in the 1700s, in which popular songs were performed with alternative words

Rock operas

In addition to the dominance of the Lloyd Webber musicals, there was a whole genre of rock-inspired works. In fact *Jesus Christ Superstar* (1971) was the first in a succession of works. Other important rock musicals include *Tommy* (1969) by The Who, *The Rocky Horror Picture Show* (1973) by Richard O'Brien, *Grease* (1978), *Little Shop of Horrors* (1986) and *Rent* (1996). In more recent times too, there have been musicals that have featured rock songs such as *Mamma Mia* (1999), now made into a film celebrating the music of Abba, and *We Will Rock You* (2002), celebrating the music of Queen.

Styles and forms found in musicals

There are many diverse styles found in musicals, including the popular music of the day, Western classical music, jazz and blues, rock and roll and many more. However, no matter the style of the musical, the forms used by all come directly from the structures and methods employed for three hundred years or so in opera. These include the solo aria (solo song), duets, trios (there is even a quintet in 'Tonight' from *West Side Story*), choruses and dance numbers too.

The next set work from the genre of the musical comes from one of the most famous musicals of all: *West Side Story* by Leonard Bernstein.

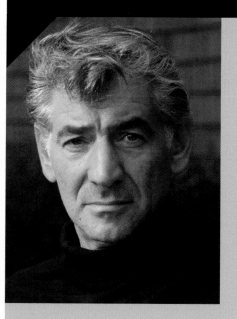

Leonard Bernstein (1918–1990)

Leonard Bernstein was a talented pianist, composer, broadcaster and conductor. He was born in Lawrence, Massachusetts in 1918 and studied composition and conducting at Harvard University. From there Bernstein became assistant conductor of the New York Philharmonic and then the principal conductor from 1958–1969. At the same time, Bernstein developed a career as a composer. He excelled in two principal forms – the ballet and the musical. In 1944 he wrote a ballet *Fancy Free* and his first musical *On the Town*. This was a great success and ran for 463 performances on Broadway. This work was followed by two other musicals, *Wonderful Town* (1952) and *Candide* (1956). He also wrote a film score *On the Waterfront* (1954). However, it was *West Side Story* (1958) that was to make him world famous. Other works include the *Chichester Psalms* (1965), *1600 Pennsylvania Avenue* (1976) and three symphonies.

Background to *West Side Story*

Bernstein's music reflects the styles of his age – bebop jazz and the blues. From bebop, we can see Bernstein's use of dissonances and fast driving rhythms, and from the blues, the use of syncopation and blue notes. *West Side Story* fuses together these elements as well as several Latin American dance rhythms.

The idea for *West Side Story* came from the American choreographer, Jerome Robbins. His idea was to create a musical based on Shakespeare's tragic drama *Romeo and Juliet*. The book of *West Side Story* was written by Arthur Laurents and Stephen Sondheim wrote the lyrics. The romantic world of Renaissance Italy was to be transformed into the run-down, violent world of the West Side of New York. This appealed to Bernstein, who wanted to write hard-hitting, jazz-inspired music about real human conflicts and tensions in a harsh inner-city environment.

The plot of *West Side Story*

West Side Story mirrors much of the Shakespearian play, although now the Capulets and Montagues ('the two households both alike in dignity') are transformed to become two opposing street gangs – the 'Jets' and the 'Sharks'. The basis of the tension is racially motivated. The Jets are white Americans led by Riff and the Sharks are Puerto Ricans led by Bernardo, both protecting their own 'territory'. Romeo becomes Tony and Juliet is Maria, who is Bernardo's sister.

The drama hinges around the love affair of Tony and Maria who meet at a dance at the gymnasium. The love affair creates tension as Tony and Maria are from opposing street gangs. Even the famous balcony scene in Verona is translated into a fire-escape of a run-down apartment block.

The set work – 'Something's Coming' – appears near the beginning of the story, and sees Tony looking expectantly towards a new life away from the gang. He wants to leave the Jets, but as the first song says *once you're a Jet you're a Jet until your last dying day!* He has found a job working at Doc's drug store and the future looks promising. However Riff, the leader of the Jets, is determined to challenge Bernardo to a fight that night at the dance. He calls on Tony just before he sings the song 'Something's Coming' to persuade him to help in the planned 'rumble' (fight). Tony agrees but insists on no future part with the gang. However, the drama is set in motion and from this point onwards the tragedy of the storyline inevitably unfolds.

The music

The music of *West Side Story* was cutting edge when compared to musical theatre pieces up to this time. The new elements in this work were:

- the dark theme rooted in violence and tragedy
- the use of long, extended dance scenes to convey the drama
- the sophisticated synthesis of jazz and classical musical idioms
- the focus on social problems and tensions of contemporary America.

The music used ideas from opera, music hall and Latin American dances. Bernstein's marriage to Chilean Fellicia Monteleagre introduced him to the Latin American dance rhythms that were to be used in much of the music in this work. There is a whole sequence of dances used in the gymnasium scene, including the mambo and cha-cha.

A confrontation between rival gangs the 'Jets' and the 'Sharks' in West Side Story.

The orchestration

Bernstein orchestrated the music himself and called for a larger number of performers, including five woodwind players (all doubling up, i.e. clarinet and saxophone), two horns, three trumpets, two trombones, seven violins, four cellos and two double basses. In addition, he used a drum-kit, two other percussionists, piano and guitar (acoustic and electric). This amounts to some 30 players.

Setting the scene

'Something's Coming' is the third number in the show following the opening prologue and the patriotic war cry of the 'Jet Song'. The scene changes to Tony happily engaged in work at Doc's drug store. He is optimistic about a new and better 'gang-free' future and excited about the dance to be held that night at the gym.

The music of the solo song 'Something's Coming'

In both the instrumental prologue and the 'Jet Song' before 'Something's Coming', Bernstein has already stated the key musical elements that we will highlight in this song and the rest of the work. These are:

◆ jazz-based harmony in which conventional chords have added 'blue' notes and other dissonances

Music extract 1: jazz-based harmony

- syncopated rhythms permeating the music, including the 'push' rhythm anticipating the beat

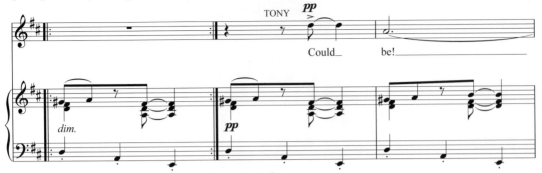

Music extract 2: syncopated rhythms and the push rhythm

- the motif of the interval of the tritone that is used throughout every movement (the notes here are G# to D). The interval is known as the *'diabolus in musica'* (devil in music) and represents evil and sinister moods. In 1949, Bernstein composed the song 'Maria' that appears later in the musical. However, its first three notes use this interval and it became a motif in each piece in *West Side Story*.

Music extract 3: interval of the tritone

- extensive use of short riffs

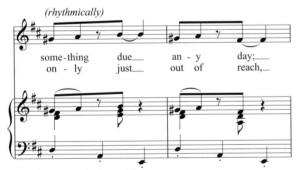

Music extract 4: short riffs

- cross-rhythms

Music extract 5: cross-rhythms

◆ layered textures of independent parts – just listen to the orchestration!

◆ combination of snappy short phrases and long sustained notes.

Music extract 6: short phrases against long sustained notes

 CD1:5 Close analysis of 'Something's Coming' from *West Side Story* by L. Bernstein

Listen to the recording on the audio CD and use your Anthology to study the analysis that follows.

The song does not follow a conventional verse–chorus structure, but has several musical ideas and sections that recur. In broad terms, the structure is shown in the table below.

Part of song	Length
Introduction	Bars 1–3 (bar 3 is repeated *ad lib*)
Section A	Bars 4–39
Section B	Bars 40–105
Section B1	Bars 106–140 (shortened version of B)
Section A1	Bars 141–157 (shortened version of A)
Outro	Bar 158 is a slow fade out

Bar numbers	Analysis

Bars 1–3 INTRODUCTION

1–3	• This sets the breathy and excited mood in the repeated figure (riff) of the accompaniment. This riff pervades the song and the melody is used by the singer (Tony). The key is a bright D major and is in a fast one-in-a-bar tempo (176 crotchets per minute!). • Features of this riff are as follows (look back to page 68 for the relevant musical notation): ○ the tritone used harmonically in the first chord (G♯ to D). This interval appears throughout the work. You could see the G♯ enharmonically as an A♭ which makes it the flat fifth of D major – one of the 'blue' notes in the blues scale in D (see music extract 3 on page 68) ○ the syncopated rhythm of the 'push' on the third beat of the bar (see music extract 2 on page 68) ○ the jazz-inspired harmony. The chords of bars 1 and 2 are as follows: bars 1 and 2, beat 1 is D major with added augmented fourth, bar 1 beat 3 is a B minor chord with added eleventh (B–D–F♯–A–C♯–E) and bar 2 beat 3 is a D major chord with added ninth (D–F♯–A–C♯–E) (see music extract 1 on page 67) ○ three-note ostinato bass up to bar 20. 

Bars 4–39 SECTION A

4–12	• A quiet *piano* section. Tony's sustained opening questions and thoughts '*Could be*' and '*Who knows*?' are two strong statements of tonic (D) to dominant (A) under which the insistent opening riff is played by the orchestra. These driving rhythms create excitement and a sense of urgency to the music. • Notice how Tony comes in with the syncopated 'push' on the third beat. Again Bernstein creates an air of expectancy and tension. • On '*who knows*' at bars 8–9, the interval of the diminished fifth (inverted augmented fourth) is the tritone again. This time it is used melodically.
13–20	• Tony sings a melody closely based on the opening riff. This is constructed of short two-bar phrases – one bar answered by the next (see music extract 4 on page 68). • Look at the triplet on '*soon as it*' at bar 17. This melodically outlines the tritone again G♯ to D. This leads to a long crescendo 'blue' note (flattened seventh in D major) on '*shows*' (and '*trees*' in the repeat).
21–39	• This is a fast, loud, almost declamatory, recitative-like phrase. The orchestra chords just punctuate the music. Again, the chords have added notes to spice up the harmony, such as bar 21 G major seventh chord. • Clear word painting on the fast repeat notes of '*it may come cannon balling down through the sky*'. • Notice too the accents on the weak parts of the beat (syncopated) on '*sky*' and '*eye*' and in the repeat of this on '*due*' and '*true*'. • The riff comes back in the accompaniment at bars 27–30, during which the music diminuendos to link back to the words for the repeat of the section. • After the second time (bar 31), Tony sings a sustained E on '*me*'. This is the highest note in the song so far. At this point too, the music modulates to C major, although Bernstein uses F♯s in the harmony, creating a bitonal effect, that is, the bass is in C major with the other parts in G major. Alternatively, you could regard the F♯s as enharmonic G♭s, and see them as blue notes – that is, flat fifths in C major.

- The accompaniment style changes to an 'um-pah' style bass. The effect is a simple broken chord accompaniment. Importantly too, Bernstein is now using straight on-beat rhythms to contrast with the opening riff. However, the voice part combines both straight and syncopated rhythms (see music extract 4, page 68).
- There is a new layer to the musical texture as a four-note minim riff E–F#–G–F# is heard in the middle part.

Bars 40–105 SECTION B

40–51	<ul><li>This is like the idea first heard at bar 13. However, the phrases are extended and it is down one tone as we are based around the key of C major rather than D major and in 2/4 time. The tritone is now used harmonically from the bass note to the melody note C–F# (see bar 40, beat 1), as well as melodically in the phrases 'something's coming' at bar 44–45, that is, F# to C and then at bar 48 'if I can'.</li><li>The one-beat accompaniment is used and we have the minim four-note riff in the middle of the texture. The B♭ at bar 48 is the flattened seventh – another 'blue note' in the blues scale in C (see music extract 1 on page 67).</li></ul>
52–72	<ul><li>Repeated one tone higher at bars 63–73. A mixture of straight 'something's coming' and syncopated rhythms 'I don't know what it is' are used in this sequence.</li><li>The on-beat crotchets add to the strength and conviction of the belief that something is going to happen at the dance that evening. Notice the 'push' on 'know' (bar 54), 'is' (bar 57) and 'great' (bar 58). The chords used are diatonic to C major but with added notes from jazz-inspired harmony. Just look at bars 52–58. This is all one chord – chord IV (F major) with the added sixth note of D.</li><li>However, the accompaniment reverts to the minim riff as before in G major at bars 59–62 to take the music back for the repeat 'with a click' etc. Much the same happens at the second time onwards from bar 63, except that the music is one tone higher in G major. The music modulates back to D major at bar 70 and proceeds in 2/4 time.</li></ul>
72–105	<ul><li>This is an expansive and lyrical section marked 'warmly, freely' as opposed to the fevered excitement of the snappy one-bar phrases of 'could it be…yes it could' etc. Here we have a sense of line and the whole section comprises four long eight-bar phrases thus:<ul><li>bar 73–80</li><li>bar 81–88</li><li>bar 89–96</li><li>bar 98–105.</li></ul></li><li>The melody employs a higher range up to a top G on 'down' and uses straight rhythms of minims and crotchets. The fluidity of the line is achieved through the use of triplets, making it almost speech like and free of the two-beat harmony of the accompaniment.</li><li>Throughout the section the bass plays on-beat quavers outlining chords of D major, A major and G major (chords I, V and IV respectively). However, the middle parts of the harmony are chromatic throughout the section, often moving in parallel fourths. Just look at bars 77–81 for example. The first two vocal phrases are harmonised in the same way, that is, bars 74–81 and then bars 82–89.</li><li>The effect is one of suspense and mystery, maybe even a foreboding of future events.</li></ul>

- The third vocal phrase starting *'come on deliver'* at bar 89 features a 'blue' note, the flattened seventh on the word *'on'*. Another chromatic chord, the **neopolitan** (chord of the flattened supertonic (second degree) in first inversion) is used at bar 95. As we are in D major, the supertonic note is E, so the flattened supertonic is E♭. The G in the bass is the third of the chord E♭–G–B♭, so the chord is in first inversion. This is a dramatic chord temporarily taking us out of key.

- There is a shift of key to C major with a perfect cadence at bars 97–98. On the long *'me'* at bar 98 above a C major alternating quaver bass, the four-note minim riff returns in the accompaniment in G major creating bitonality of C and G majors. This continues in the return of the shortened B section at bar 106.

Bars 106–140 SECTION B1	
106–140	• This section maps onto the previous section starting at bar 40–105, except that we cut the first time bar at bars 52–62 and its repeat, this time going onto the music heard at the second time bar at bar 63. This is simple, as there is only one set of words this time. • The music repeats the start of the lyrical section of the original bar 72 onwards but this is shortened from three eight-bar phrases to just one and a half phrases.

Bars 141–157 SECTION A1	
141–157	• Bernstein changes back to 3/4 at bar 141, then dovetails in the music from the opening bars 4–20, albeit cutting slightly the held notes on *'coming'* and *'knows'*. This gives a real sense of returning to the beginning and balances the structure effectively. The orchestra plays the one-bar riff. • The hopeful question of *'maybe tonight'* at bar 153 sounds the tritone for the last time G♯ to D as the long-held final vocal 'blue' note of C♮ (the flattened seventh) ends the piece in the air, suspended and unresolved, just like Tony's future! Under the held note the accompanying riff starts to fade *sempre dim.*

Bar 158 OUTRO	
158	• This is a simple 'ad lib fade' bar taking us into the music for a change of scene (instrumental).

Further listening

In addition to this set work, try to listen to other songs from Bernstein's musical *West Side Story*. For example:

- 'Jet Song'
- 'Maria'
- 'America'

- 'Tonight'
- 'One Hand, One Heart'
- 'Somewhere'.

 **CD1:5** Listening and appraising: 'Something's Coming'

1 How does Bernstein create a sense of excitement and expectancy in this song?

2 Mention two techniques or devices that the composer uses in this song and throughout the musical itself.

3 Describe the harmony used in the song.

4 What is a 'push' rhythm? Give an example.

5 What is a 'blue note'? Give an example.

6 Describe the orchestration of the piece.

7 How are the words '*the air is humming*' depicted by the orchestral accompaniment?

8 How does the piece end?

9 This is a solo song or aria. Name two other types of vocal forms used in a musical.

10 What makes the subject matter of *West Side Story* different and new from other Broadway musicals up to this time?

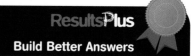

ResultsPlus

Build Better Answers

Identifying instruments.

Question: Name the instrument playing the melody.

This is a common type of question and appears in many guises, such as:

- The theme is shared between two instrumental families. What are they?
- Which other instrument did Reich use in this piece?
- Name the instrument playing the solo.
- Name two folk instruments heard in this extract.
- What instrument is improvising?

■ In past examination papers, the music was unfamiliar and not based on set works, so the instrument could be anything! In these cases, students were reliant on their ability to listen carefully and identify the instruments – something which many students found difficult.

▲ However, with your 12 set works, you should know the instruments. There is no excuse for not knowing that the Chopin 'Raindrop' Prelude is for piano!

The best advice here is to draw up a chart and list all the instruments in each set work. In some cases this is very easy, in others, such as the Mozart symphony, there is more to learn. Also, listen to the main melodies in each work and note down the instrument or instruments playing the melody.

In the examination room, you will be asked several instrument related questions on the paper. If you are unsure, do not just guess the answer. Listen carefully and work out which family they belong to – strings, woodwind, brass or percussion. Then decide whether they are high or low pitched and this should help you get closer to the correct answer. Students tend to struggle to differentiate between the clarinet and oboe, trombone and French horn. Try to listen to recordings of these instruments in preparation for your listening examination.

S. Reich: 3rd movement (Fast) from Electric Counterpoint (1987)

In the study of this set work you will learn about:

◆ the origins of minimalism

◆ the features of minimalism

◆ the life and works of Steve Reich

◆ how the 3rd movement (Fast) from *Electric Counterpoint* is constructed through an analysis of the music.

Before minimalism

Throughout the 20th century, composers sought to push music in new and interesting directions. At the beginning of the century, Schoenberg pushed the boundaries of tonality by abandoning the normal use of keys altogether, developing the style we now know as expressionism. Expressionism led into serialism, which caught the imagination of many composers of the time.

As you have seen in the section on expressionism, serialism is a very tightly controlled way of writing music. Some composers were happy with this approach, so much so that they wanted to control all aspects of music in the same mathematical way. As well as making rows for notes (arranging the 12 semitones in a particular order), they also made rows for dynamics, length of notes and all aspects of the way the note sounded. You can imagine how detailed the music looked when it was written down! Every note would have a different dynamic and articulation marking. This naturally led to some composers (such as Stockhausen) experimenting with electronics so that they could control every aspect of the timbre of the note.

However, some composers felt restricted by serialism, especially this total serialism, so they naturally went in completely the opposite direction, giving the performer back much more control of the composition than they were used to. In fact, the composer handed over many of the composing duties to the performer (this was philosophy, not laziness!) such as letting the performer interpret symbols by choosing any set of notes and durations they felt the symbol suggested. In reaction to the massively detailed scores of serialism, these composers came up with various alternative approaches such as:

◆ scores with little or no detail at all
◆ scores with the staff notation replaced by written directions (text-based scores)
◆ scores with staff notation replaced by symbols and pictures (graphic scores) – the music of Cornelius Cardew is a prime example of this approach.

These composers liked the way instruments used the extremes of their pitch ranges and were being pushed to the maximum by the serialist composers, but thought that the next logical step would be to use instruments in unconventional ways – by hitting the body of the instruments, plucking the strings in the piano, bowing cymbals or immersing them in water and so on. Of course, this can be taken further – why stop at making strange noises with musical instruments when you can make musical noises with everyday objects such as pieces of paper, bottles, doors and cars? This group of composers became known as experimental composers.

La Monte Young and Terry Riley

The composers La Monte Young and Terry Riley belonged to this second group of composers. They were both completely fascinated with drones and repetition, so tended to use these as the basis for their compositions. Young took this to extremes, basing entire pieces on a very long, extended note played very loudly and adding harmonics to it. He would often revisit his pieces, constantly reworking and extending them, so much so that he rarely considers his pieces to be completed. He would also write pieces that were mostly improvised, but based around very carefully controlled rules or themes that might last anywhere from 45 minutes to 6 hours (his piece, *The Well-tuned Piano* (1964–present) is an example of this). Much of his music does not contain many different musical ideas, and this method of making the most of minimal musical resources is where the term 'minimalism' comes from.

Terry Riley was a friend and colleague of Young. He studied with Young and his career as a composer shadowed Young's for a while. In the early 1960s Riley experimented with tape loops of various sounds, combining these with delay and occasional instrumental sounds. He would run the loops through the reel-to-reel tape recorders, out of the open window, around some wine bottles and back in to the tape recorder again. Riley's most important work, which brought minimalism to the notice of the musical mainstream, was *In C* (1965). This piece focuses on repetition of short musical fragments along with a constantly repeating quaver C keeping the pulse. The first performance of this work included Steve Reich in the ensemble.

Hallmarks of minimalism

Before we focus on the set work, it is useful to understand some of the hallmarks of the style and understand the vocabulary used when describing minimalism. The following are features of minimalism in general, some of which are used in the set work and others are present in other minimalist works:

- ◆ drones – a long, continuous note or a constantly repeated note (can be any pitch, but is often a low note)
- ◆ ostinati/loops – repeated musical ideas. The shortest ideas are called **cells**
- ◆ **phasing** – two almost identical parts which go out of sync with each other and gradually, after a number of repetitions, come back into sync again
- ◆ metamorphosis – gradually changing from one musical idea to another, often by changing one note at a time

Glossary

cells short musical ideas

phasing when two or more versions of a sound or musical motif are played simultaneously but slightly out of synchronisation, with the two parts gradually coming back in sync after a number of repetitions

- layering – adding new musical parts, commonly one at a time. The parts will often interact with each other forming a complex texture
- key – in Area of Study 1, it is clear that key has a significant part to play in defining the structure of a piece. In minimalism this is only part of the story – the texture is equally as important as the key in defining the structure of a piece
- **note addition** – starting off with a very simple, sparse ostinato containing many rests, and gradually adding notes over a number of repetitions
- **note subtraction** – starting off with a more complex ostinato and gradually taking notes away, leaving rests in their place
- rhythmic displacement – playing a musical phrase so that the accents fall in different places to what would be expected. For example, playing a three-note quaver pattern in 4/4 time so that the accent falls on the first note, then the second note, then the third note, or playing the same phrase but starting at a different point in the bar (this is what Reich does with 'ostinato 1' as shown later)
- augmentation – extending the durations of a rhythmic pattern. For example, a four-note idea ♩♪♪♩♩ becomes ♩♩♩♩
- diminution – the opposite of augmentation
- static harmony – the piece appears to have one long chord which only changes very gradually, if at all (there is no impression of a chord sequence)
- non-functional harmony – there are chord sequences, but they do not seem to follow the expected hierarchy of tonic, dominant, sub-dominant etc (the chords do not seem to lead from one to the other in the way dictated by classical harmonic rules).

Minimalist art

Parallels can be drawn between minimalism in music and minimalism in art – the use of minimal resources makes us experience the work in a different way, getting drawn into a world of the composer's/artist's creation. People tend to react to this quite strongly, either positively or negatively.

The next set work is in the minimalist style and is by the minimalist composer, Steve Reich.

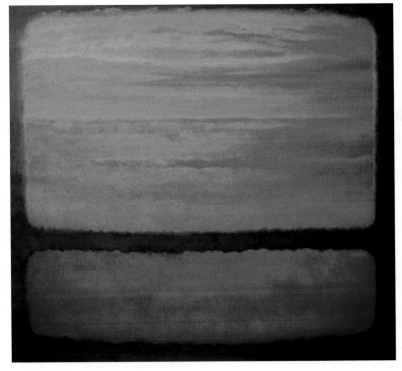

A painting in the minimalist style entitled 'Magenta', by Mark Rothko.

Steve Reich (1936–)

Born in New York in 1936, Steve Reich grew up in New York and California. He studied philosophy at university and afterwards went on to study composition at the Juilliard School of Music and Mills College (where he worked with the famous composers Luciano Berio and Darius Milhaud). He performed in Terry Riley's ensemble for a while and, like Riley, became fascinated with tape loops.

In 1965/66 he composed two pieces called *It's Gonna Rain* and *Come Out*. In each of these pieces he created two identical tape loops of some speech he felt contained musical qualities and played them simultaneously on two different tape recorders. Because the tape recorders ran at slightly different speeds, the loops gradually went out of sync with each other. As the loops become more and more out of sync, the speech becomes less intelligible until it starts to be heard as a rhythm rather than speech. The effect is rather trance-like and is the extreme form of the 'phasing' technique. After a while the loops would come back into sync again. These pieces were a breakthrough in the world of music and would form the basis of Reich's compositional technique.

Reich's music is often rhythmically complex with much repetition. This places very specialised demands on performers, such as the need to concentrate deeply on the exact timing of every note or to count many repeats without cues to tell a performer where they are in the piece. To meet these special requirements, Reich formed his own ensemble in 1966, starting with just three members, but growing to meet the requirements of new pieces he composed.

In 1970, Reich took time out to study African drumming in Ghana. This led to him writing works such as *Drumming* (1970–1971) and *Clapping Music* (1972) that are based around rhythms phasing in the same way as the tape loops did in *It's Gonna Rain* and *Come Out*. He also studied Balinese gamelan music in 1973–1974, but this may not have had such a profound impact on his music other than the extensive use of mallet instruments (such as the marimba) in his ensembles. In 1976–1977, he studied traditional Hebrew chanting which he included in the work *Tehillim* (1981).

He has written major works for various ensembles including *Music for 18 Musicians* (1974–1976), *The Desert Music* (1984) and *Different Trains* (1988). He has been acclaimed as 'our greatest living composer' by *The New York Times*, amongst other accolades, and has won many awards for his compositions.

Background to *Electric Counterpoint*

Electric Counterpoint is the last in a series of three pieces for soloists playing along with pre-recorded multi-track tapes of themselves. The other two pieces in the series are *Vermont Counterpoint* (1982) for flute and *New York Counterpoint* (1985) for clarinet. *Electric Counterpoint* was commissioned for the jazz guitarist Pat Metheny to perform at the Brooklyn Academy of Music's 'Next Wave' Festival. Metheny would record all the instrumental parts himself (12 guitars and two bass guitars) under the watchful eye of Reich, and this would be used as a stereo 'backing track' to which he would perform the live part. The recorded parts are seen by the composer as something more than a 'backing track' – it is a way for the performer to perform in an ensemble with himself, even if it does not allow for live interaction. The act of recording the piece takes an incredible amount of precision, with Metheny himself saying that it was a much more difficult task than he had expected – when you listen to the interweaving parts and the precise timing, you can hear what he means.

This piece takes the act of using tape loops in a different direction – instead of using one, constantly repeating **loop** like that in *It's Gonna Rain* or *Come Out*, the composer uses the tape as a way of capturing the sound of one performer, giving the whole piece a togetherness of sound that would not be possible using different live performers. The piece is like a tape loop that develops – multi-tracking the performer allows note addition and other development techniques that would not be possible with a fixed loop, but the sounds are all coming from an identical sound source – the performer's fingers and guitar.

Glossary

loop a section of a piece of music which is edited so that it can be repeated seamlessly by electronic means

 CD1:6 Close analysis of the 3rd movement (Fast) from *Electric Counterpoint*

Listen to the recording on the audio CD and use your Anthology to study the analysis that follows.

Parts and layers

Like much minimalist music, *Electric Counterpoint* is built up in layers. In the third movement (simply titled 'Fast' by Reich), there are seven pre-recorded electric guitar parts and two bass guitars. The live guitar is then performed along with the recorded parts.

The texture gradually builds up in the first section (section A), with the guitar parts entering in the following order:

1 Guitar 1
2 Live Guitar
3 Guitar 2
4 Guitar 3
5 Guitar 4
6 Bass Guitars 1 and 2
7 Guitar 5
8 Guitar 6
9 Guitar 7

This piece is divided into two main sections with a coda. The main sections are then subdivided into four smaller sections, each of which is defined by changes in key and texture. See the table opposite for a full analysis of the structure of the piece.

Section		Bar numbers and timing	Description
A	1	1–23 0:00–0:42	• The piece begins with guitar 1 repeating a one-bar ostinato. • The live guitar part starts with three notes of ostinato 1, building up to the full ostinato by bar 6 using note addition technique. • Guitar 2 enters in bar 7, playing ostinato 1, but one crotchet later. • Guitar 3 enters in bar 10, building up ostinato 1 using note addition, but by a different route to that used by the live guitar part. The ostinato is displaced by five and a half crotchets. • Guitar 4 enters in bar 16, playing ostinato 1 displaced by two and a half crotchets. • Reich calls this a 'four-part guitar canon' – guitar 4 doubles the live guitar part. • When all the parts have entered, the live guitar starts to play the **resultant melody**. • The piece is in 3/2 time with a clear triple metre. • It is hinting at the key of E minor, but this is not yet completely clear.
	2	24–35 0:43–1:05	• The bass guitar parts are introduced at bar 24, reinforcing the feeling of a triple metre. • A two-bar bass ostinato is introduced gradually, starting with the first bar and then adding the notes until it is played in full by bar 33. It is only at this point that the key of E minor becomes really definite. • Note how the two bass guitars are panned to the left and right speakers – it would normally be considered bad practice to pan a bass guitar to one side, but one instrument on each side balances the sound. • The live guitar continues to play the resultant melody.
	3	36–66 1:05–2:05	• At bar 36 the live guitar introduces a new idea by playing strummed chords. This has a dramatic effect on the texture by introducing a new, rather percussive sound that cuts across the rest of the parts. • Guitar 5 introduces the sequence C, Bm, E⁵ at bar 40. • Guitar 6 introduces the sequence C, D, Em at bar 52. • Guitar 7 introduces the sequence C, D, Bm at bar 64. • Guitars 5–7 play at the same time but, because the chords are played at different times in the bar, there is a new and interesting rhythmic counterpoint introduced and the chords can be heard as distinct chords, even though when the notes overlap they form much more complex chords. • The live guitar continues to play chords through this section, interweaving with the rhythms of guitars 5–7.
	4	67–73 2:06–2:16	• Now that the counterpoint between the strummed guitar parts has been completed, the live guitar returns to playing a resultant melody part (this is not obvious just from listening – you need to tune in to the point where the melody seems to get slightly louder).

B	5	74–81 2:16–2:31	• The first big change of key to C minor at bar 74 is rather startling, signalling the start of section B. • The texture remains the same as for section 4.
	6	82–89 2:32–2:46	• The key shifts back to E minor. Again, there is no preparation for this key shift, it just changes from one bar to the next. • In this section, the metre changes to 12/8 (in all but guitars 1–4) – because the metre does not change in all the instruments, it is not obvious as a change of metre just by listening. • The bass parts play a new ostinato. • At bar 86 the metre shifts back to 3/2 and the bass ostinato changes back to ostinato 2 (bass 1 is inverted and adds one additional note).
	7	90–97 2:47–3:01	• Return to C minor (similar to section 5). • The metre continues to change every four bars.
	8	98–113 3:02–3:32	• Return to E minor at bar 98. • Shifts in key and metre become more frequent, building the tension. • At bar 106 guitars 5–7 and the two bass parts begin to fade out, gradually at first, but quickly at bar 113.
Coda	9	114–140 3:32–4:24	• By bar 114 the texture has returned to the four-part canon of ostinato 1 in guitars 1–4 with the live guitar part playing resultant melodies. • Shifts in key and metre continue until bar 129 when it is finally made clear that the piece will end in the key of E minor. • The piece ends with a crescendo to a final E^5 chord played simultaneously in all five remaining parts at the end of bar 139.

Important points to note

◆ As can be seen in the table, the 3rd movement of *Electric Counterpoint* is basically in E minor, but the composer likes to keep the listener guessing what the key might be right up until the bass guitars finally make it really obvious by bar 33 when they play the tonic note of E at the end of their two-bar ostinato. This is called **tonal ambiguity** – keeping the key uncertain. Reich makes further use of this in section B by the frequent changes between E minor and C minor (a key change that would have felt very odd in the Classical or even the Romantic era). In this piece, the very nature of repeating the key change over and over makes it feel like the most natural thing in the world, even though the two keys are not closely related.

◆ Like much minimalist music, although we can say the piece is in E minor, it is actually **modal** – in the key of E minor we would expect to hear D♯, allowing for the chord of B major (the dominant triad), but because Steve Reich's music does not depend on perfect cadences, he does not need the major chord V (B major). As such, the music is in the aeolian mode transposed to E (E-aeolian).

◆ The texture is built up gradually and it helps to define the structure, particularly the subsections of section A. The texture also thins out towards the end (by guitars 5–7 and the basses fading out), even though the piece finishes quite dramatically with a crescendo and a forceful E5 chord. Once all the parts have been introduced, the texture is quite constant but, with clever use of panning and the interweaving rhythms, the texture always seems to be shifting, a bit like a field of long grass in the wind.

Glossary

modal referring to modes – the precursors of modern scales

resultant melody a new melody produced when a variety of parts each play their melodies at the same time

tonal ambiguity when the key of a piece is uncertain

♦ The piece concentrates on rhythmic development just as much as it does on melodic development – the changes in metre between 3/2 and 12/8 in section B highlight this. Reich feels that the piece ends clearly in 12/8 metre, but you may not feel this. He was very attuned to rhythmic development and the subtleties of metre, but if you are listening to this piece from a more traditional perspective, it feels like it is in triple time all the way through the section with interesting cross-rhythms occurring rather than moving into a different metre. Reich composed his ostinati with little gaps (the quaver rests) so that there would be a rhythmic counterpoint when the two parts were played out of sync with each other. Note that this is not strictly phasing because the parts stay out of sync with each other, separated by the same distance throughout. The interplay of the bass parts is a particularly interesting feature of this piece.

♦ The live guitar part plays a resultant melody – the interweaving of guitar parts 1–4 causes certain notes to leap out at the listener, almost like a melody, but with the notes shared across the instruments. The live guitar part reinforces this by playing these notes in one instrument. Reich uses this technique a lot in his compositions.

Minimalism's influence on other styles

Minimalism has inspired many composers and musicians outside Western classical music. For example, when Steve Reich moved on from his more extreme use of repetition in his works of the 1970s, Brian Eno commented that this was 'rather fortunate because that meant I could carry on with it'. Eno later developed the style into ambient music such as *Music for Airports* (1978). This in turn influenced bands such as The Orb and Orbital to develop their loop-based dance music styles.

Listening and appraising questions: 3rd movement (Fast) from *Electric Counterpoint*

Now that you have listened to the 3rd movement (Fast) from *Electric Counterpoint* and studied the analysis on pages 78–81, answer the listening and appraising questions that follow:

1 Describe the texture of the first section (up to 0:42).

2 What is the term used to describe a repeated motif?

3 What instrument enters at the start of the second section (at 0:42)?

4 What is the tonality of the piece when this instrument enters?

5 There are three strummed guitar parts. What studio effect has been used to help separate out the parts?

6 What other instruments have been separated out using the same effect?

7 The live guitar part plays a melody derived from the notes played in the recorded parts. What is the term used to describe this melody?

8 Why do you think this piece is called *Electric Counterpoint*?

Further listening

In addition to this set work, try to listen to other pieces by Reich. For example:

- *It's Gonna Rain* – 1966
- *Music for 18 Musicians* – 1976
- *The Desert Music* – 1984
- *Different Trains* – 1988.

Composing and performing tasks

Expressionism and serialism

 Composing an atonal piece of music

You have been commissioned to compose a piece of atonal music based on the different stages of life (from birth through childhood, adulthood and old age to death). Your piece should be in five sections to reflect each of these stages of life.

For each section you should compose either one or two hexachords that you will use as the main pitch material for your piece. You can use other notes as required in order to achieve a desired effect, but the vast majority of your pitch material should come from your hexachords or a development of your hexachord (such as transposing or inverting it).

Your piece should be for a small ensemble (you may choose which instruments will be in your ensemble), but should not necessarily be limited to the instruments you have available in your class. You may choose to write your piece for performance on music software, in which case your instruments may include electronic or virtual instruments.

The choice of notes for your hexachord is very important, but you should also develop these ideas in different ways. You should include rhythmic motifs in your piece that can be heard in different guises in each section – for example, in 'Childhood' you may play your motif with short durations at a high tempo, using the same motif with double the durations at a slower tempo for 'Old Age'.

 Group improvisation on a hexachord

This activity is for a group of five performers.

1 In your group, decide on which six notes to include in a hexachord of your own.

2 Practise playing the notes from your hexachord across the full pitch range of your instrument at different dynamics, using different techniques to perform the notes (e.g. tremolo, flutter-tonguing, harmonics etc).

3 Agree on an overall structure for your piece (e.g. ABA where A is fast, mostly loud and with a thick texture while B is slow with gradually changing dynamics and texture). Decide on who will signal when you are to move from section to section and what the cues will be to let you know when to change sections.

4 In your group, improvise on the notes from your hexachord. You must listen carefully to the other performers and decide which of your playing techniques will enhance the sound of the group at any given moment. Remember that you must not play all the time! Concentrate on creating an interesting and varied texture, discovering what unusual combinations you can create within your group.

Musical theatre

 ## Show-stopper songs

West Side Story contains several types of song other than the solo song. If you have opportunity, listen first to some of the following examples from the musical:

- duets – e.g. 'One hand, one heart' and 'A boy like that'
- chorus numbers – e.g. 'Jet Song', 'America' and 'Gee, officer Krupke'
- quintet – e.g. in the song 'Tonight'.

You are going to compose your own song. Choose which type of song you would like to compose and follow these guidelines to help you on your way.

1 PLOT
Create a plot and then focus on a point in the drama, just like the song 'Something's Coming' which concentrates on Tony's excitement and anticipation for his future. Make sure that you understand the character that will feature in your song.

2 LYRICS
You could write the lyrics yourself or adapt lyrics from a novel, a story or a poem that you have enjoyed reading. Try to avoid lyrics from songs you already know as you will subconsciously copy rhythms and melodic ideas from the original.

3 STRUCTURE
Plan the structure of your song. The standard form is an intro-verse-chorus-verse-chorus-middle 8-chorus-chorus-outro pattern. However, you can adapt this as you wish. 'Something's Coming' certainly did not follow this format.

4 CONTRAST
Ensure that you achieve contrast between the verse and chorus sections. It is effective to change key as you go into the final sections. A show stopper has a catchy melody – see what you can do.

5 COMPOSE
You could start by writing out your melodic lines to give you the main ideas for your song. Take care with the word setting to ensure that there is an emphasis on the strong syllables of the words. Your teacher will help you with this. Keep chords and harmony simple. Many popular songs only use three or four chords. It might be a good idea to plan two different chord sequences at the start, one for the verse and one for the chorus.

6 ACCOMPANIMENT
Choose an accompaniment. It is probably best to start with a keyboard or guitar accompaniment, but later you may wish to develop this into an orchestrated version.

When your song is written, arrange a performance and evaluate your work.

Instrumental medley

This is an instrumental composing and performing task based on the dance numbers from *West Side Story*.

'The Dance at the Gym' features several Latin American dances including 'Blues', 'Paso Doble', 'Mambo' and 'Cha Cha'. If you have the CD or DVD of *West Side Story*, you may want to listen to the relevant pieces to get a feeling for the characteristics of each of these quite different dances.

1 Your task is to write an instrumental number or medley of numbers based on one or more of the dances mentioned above using two different riffs (short melodic and/or rhythmic ideas) in your piece.

2 To help you, the table below lists some of the features of each dance. Choose one or more of these dances to base your composition on.

Dance	Features
Blues	Heavy, 4/4 time. Uses blue noted and syncopated rhythms, swing quavers. Use of 12-bar blues chord sequence.
Paso Doble	Stately, 2/2 time. Straight rhythms with some syncopation.
Mambo	Very fast and frenetic. One riff could be the driving rhythm, the other a melodic one.
Cha-cha	Relaxed 4/4 time. Light and staccato melodic part. The bass could be a simple on-beat one-bar riff. Try to use the signature three-quaver cha-cha-cha rhythm.

Minimalism

Composing a piece of minimalist music

Find a picture, image or painting that is either minimalist in style, has a large amount of mechanical parts, repeats in interesting ways or is an optical illusion. You may wish to use the pictures below or find others like them that you feel will give you more inspiration.

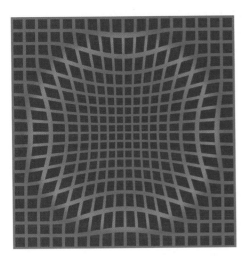

Using your chosen image as a stimulus, write a piece of minimalist music to try and capture the feelings the image conjures up within you.

You may use any of the techniques listed in the 'Hallmarks of minimalism' section on pages 75–76 or you may include some ideas from other genres. It is not necessary to make your piece sound just like a piece by Steve Reich or Philip Glass – the minimalist techniques should just be compositional tools to help you achieve the sound you want. You may even use minimalist techniques in song-writing. Bands such as Snow Patrol and Coldplay use minimalist techniques such as repetition and layering to great effect in their music.

◆ Decide on a structure for your piece. This should be more than just 'build-up, fade out'. You may wish to use a structure you have studied in one of the other set works or a similar structure to *Electric Counterpoint*.

◆ Decide on the instruments you are going to use. Your choice should be guided by the colours of your stimulus image and the sounds you feel would best reflect them.

◆ Are you going to use traditional harmonies and chords or are you going to use drones, made-up modes (making up your own scale by selecting some notes from the 12 available) and static harmonies?

◆ What tempo would best reflect your stimulus image? Should it remain constant or change during the course of the piece?

◆ Should your piece have lots of rhythms set against each other or should it be rhythmically straightforward?

◆ How are you going to develop the texture as the piece progresses?

◆ Only begin composing ideas, motifs, rhythms, ostinati and chord sequences after you have gone through the list above and decided on the general principles of what your piece should sound like – this will guide your musical experiments in the right direction.

Performing a minimalist piece

This activity is for two performers.

1 With a partner, write a short, simple ostinato which is one 4/4 bar in length. It may be easier to perform this task if the ostinato is as simple as four crotchet notes, but you may also make a more rhythmically interesting ostinato with quaver durations and rests.

2 Each performer should sit at a different keyboard or piano. After a count-in, both of you should play the ostinato at exactly the same time, repeating it several times. Ensure your timing is as precisely together as is possible. Repeat this step until you are both very confident of playing the ostinato.

3 Now play the ostinato, but instead of starting at the same time, one of you should start playing one beat after the other so you are deliberately out of time. This is tricky to keep going accurately – it may take several attempts to perfect! Repeat this step with the other partner taking the lead and with different time intervals between entries of the ostinato.

4 Try playing the ostinato at the same time again, but after a few repetitions one of you should speed up very slightly while the other maintains the original tempo – forcing you to go out of phase with each other. This is very difficult, so it may take some time before you are able to do this successfully and keep the ostinato going. Try to block out the other player to a certain extent, concentrating on keeping your own time. If you are able to keep the ostinato going until you have come back into phase with each other, then you are candidates for Steve Reich's group of musicians!

Popular music in context

Record companies are the most powerful entities in the popular music industry, spending many millions of pounds investing in bands and artists that they hope will return a profit on their investment through the sale of their music and concerts. These record companies are always on the look out for upcoming artists who they believe could be the next 'big thing'.

No single element makes a song or piece of music popular. Indeed the term 'popular music' can be somewhat confusing – it is not a genre in itself, rather a term to describe music that a significant amount of people appreciate. Popular music can come from any musical genre, and will usually be popular because of a combination of features which might include:

◆ a good hook line

◆ a strong melody

◆ a strong beat

◆ simply being the right sort of music at the right time that appeals to the right people.

Set works

Jazz
Set work 7 – 'All Blues' from *Kind of Blue* by M. Davis (1926–1991)

Rock
Set work 8 – 'Grace' from *Grace* by J. Buckley (1966–1997)

Club dance
Set work 9 – 'Why Does My Heart Feel So Bad?' from *Play* by Moby (1965–)

Miles Davis: 'All Blues' from the album Kind of Blue

In the study of this set work you will learn about:

◆ the origins and features of jazz

◆ Miles Davis and his influence on jazz music

◆ the 12-bar blues chord sequence

◆ how the set work 'All Blues' is constructed through an analysis of the music

◆ jazz harmony.

The origins of jazz

Jazz began as the coming together of many musical styles and cultures that were stirred together in the mixing bowl of late 19th-century/early 20th-century New Orleans. The music grew organically at the start of the 20th century from mostly African–American musical roots with some important individuals and groups adding their own elements to the mix and bringing the music to the wider public.

Ragtime

At the turn of the century, **ragtime** became a very popular musical style. The piano was becoming increasingly popular in American homes in the early 20th century, so people were hungry for interesting music to play on their new instruments. Ragtime offered an exciting way of making the piano sound like a full ensemble on its own, with the strict, on-the-beat rhythm in the left hand jumping from low bass notes to mid-range chords working alongside the syncopated melody lines played higher up in the register by the right hand. The rhythmically interesting and musically satisfying style caught on very quickly, with the most popular pieces selling hundreds of thousands of copies of sheet music. Scott Joplin (1868–1917) is probably the most famous and popular of all the ragtime composers, his works include *Maple Leaf Rag* (1897) and *The Entertainer* (1902). The popularity of ragtime prepared the ground for the coming of New Orleans Jazz.

New Orleans

New Orleans was a thriving trade centre in the early 1800s when steamboats were the main way to transport goods. This brought many different people from different cultures through the city, some of them deciding to settle there. New Orleans was already culturally mixed, having changed hands from the French to the Spanish back to the French and finally to the US between its founding in the mid-1700s and the early 1800s. The cultural mix continued to grow during the 1800s including people from the Caribbean, slaves brought from Africa and settlers from other European nations.

> ### Glossary
>
> **ragtime** music characterized by a syncopated melodic line and regularly accented accompaniment

Towards the end of the 1800s, the railroad became the most effective method of transporting goods, so New Orleans began to decline, giving the cultural mix time to simmer.

African slaves brought their own style of music with them, including the rhythmic, pentatonic music of their heritage and the work songs they developed while in slavery. During the mid-1800s they often put on performances in Congo Square (a public square in New Orleans) that would not have been out of place in West Africa. When people settle in an area, they take on aspects of their new culture. The African–American people soaked up the music around them, including the hymn songs they were taught. The fusion of the pentatonic scales of Africa and the seven-note Western scales produced a performance technique where the performer would 'bend' a note between the minor and major third, sometimes playing or singing a note that was just in between. These are called **blue notes**. Singers would lament their poor situation in life in the songs they sang, giving the music its title – the blues. The blues would include elements of call and response, improvisation, using whatever musical instruments were easily available or that could be made from objects to hand, had a strong rhythmic content and was part of the social life of the people who performed it. All these elements came directly from the African musical culture.

Bands would form in New Orleans from various combinations of instruments, but the most common melody instruments available tended to be the cornet, clarinet and the trombone (there was a brass band culture in New Orleans in addition to everything else!). Musicians in these bands would all improvise at the same time, bouncing ideas off each other, with the beat kept by an instrument such as the banjo strumming on the beat (playing the role of the left-hand part in ragtime). As this music developed it became known as **New Orleans Jazz**.

It wasn't until the music moved out of New Orleans that it became widely accepted around the US. Around the end of the First World War, musicians started moving north to places that were more tolerant and to better paid gigs. Musicians such as Jelly Roll Morton, Sidney Bechet, King Oliver and Louis Armstrong were not household names until they moved north (often to Chicago and New York).

Glossary

blue note a 'bent' note between the minor and major third

New Orleans Jazz one of the first recognised jazz styles, originating in New Orleans

A traditional New Orleans jazz band.

From Dixieland to Davis

One of the best-known and most loved jazz musicians of all time is Louis Armstrong. He was one of the musicians to move from New Orleans to Chicago, taking his unique, growling vocal style and sophisticated brand of New Orleans jazz cornet/trumpet playing with him. He got together with a variety of musicians, calling his ensembles the 'Hot 5's' or 'Hot 7's' (depending on the number of musicians), and acting as an ambassador for jazz music everywhere he went. At this time, jazz started to focus on a solo artist such as Armstrong who was supported by a band of musicians who, although they got the odd solo, were very much in the background compared to the band leader.

Swing bands

Alongside this focus on the soloist, another style of jazz music was developing in which the ensembles were bigger and so needed more carefully arranged music – the more musicians there are, the more chaos there would be if they all improvised at the same time. This gradually developed into the **big band** phenomenon (in the 1920s) where arrangers would decide who was playing at what time, giving notated parts to the performers. There would still be space for solos, but the emphasis was more on a slick, polished sound. Good quality soloists would always be in demand for the solo spots and some musicians made a name for themselves in these ensembles, such as Bix Beiderbecke and Benny Carter.

After the great Depression, radio became one of the main forms of entertainment and this was the perfect medium to play recordings of big bands. The big bands became bigger and slicker, featuring clever arrangements often based on pop songs and 32-bar song structures rather than 12-bar blues. This was the golden age for jazz. Big band music became known as **swing** and was played at all the dances, becoming the pop music of the 1930s and 1940s. Benny Goodman and Glenn Miller ran two of the more famous bands, gaining widespread acceptance amongst the white community as well as the black community.

The more dance-orientated jazz became, the less room there was for soloists to show off their abilities, so some of the top musicians became a little disenchanted with the popular jazz scene and sought other ways to express themselves. In some Harlem nightclubs, top jazz musicians such as Charlie Parker and Dizzy Gillespie would run late night jam sessions (often going on to 4am) in which they developed a new, technically complex form of jazz called **bebop**. This music was far removed from swing, demanding great technical ability because of the fast tempos and tricky chord changes. The melodies would contain much more dissonance than swing and the ensembles returned to the smaller groups of five or six members. The musicians really wanted to push themselves as hard as they could and would delight in 'cutting sessions', where they would duel with each other in a musical context to see who was the best improviser. By the mid-1940s, people were coming to listen to bebop rather than to dance to it.

Glossary

bebop a jazz style requiring virtuosic technique, including fast tempos and complex harmonies

big band a jazz style popular in the 1920s and 1930s in which the pieces were generally written for a large ensemble to be played in dance halls

swing a development of big band jazz. The term is also used to describe a particular type of rhythmic 'groove' desirable in jazz music

In 1947, Charlie Parker (already a jazz legend because of his prowess on the alto saxophone) formed a band including a young Miles Davis on trumpet. Parker's tone was focused and a little cutting, so he thought that Davis's mellower, more reserved sound would balance this out. Parker had some severe personal problems at this time, including drug and alcohol addiction, making his personality very unstable, so Davis left the band in 1948 to form his own ensembles even though he was a great admirer of Parker.

Miles Davis (1926–1991)

Miles Dewey Davis was born in Illinois in 1926 to a wealthy family. His father was a well-educated dentist who owned a farm, and other members of his family were also well-to-do. His parents were keen for him to follow one of the professions, but it became clear from an early age that he wanted to dedicate his life to music, so he started to have trumpet lessons. He had a number of teachers, but the one he felt he learned the most from was a jazz trumpeter called Elwood Buchanan who introduced him to a variety of jazz music. After high school, he went to the Juilliard School of Music in New York, but spent more time in the local nightclubs trying to find the bebop legends Charlie Parker and Dizzy Gillespie than he did in the classroom. He quit Juilliard after just one year, making his living playing in the jazz circuit.

Parker took him on as a sideman and recorded some songs for the Dial record label. Parker was only a few years older than Davis, but he acted like a father figure or mentor, introducing him to many of the big names of the time and helping him to develop his talents. Davis also played in a number of other bands, touring with them to make his living in music.

In 1948, Davis left Parker's band to form his own ensemble. He began to look for a new way of playing jazz, feeling there was more to be found in the music than the bebop 'quest for speed'. The next year he recorded a number of sessions with his ensemble that formed the album *The Birth of the Cool* – a seminal work introducing a new, more laid back sound to jazz.

Unfortunately, like many musicians of the time, Davis also struggled with addiction, negatively affecting his musical output. He took some time out from New York to deal with this, making a comeback at the Newport Jazz Festival in 1955. In 1955 he put together a new ensemble featuring some of the top musicians of the time (his newfound fame from the Newport Jazz Festival allowed him to pay his musicians better) and this eventually became the ensemble he used for the recording of *Kind of Blue*. It has been widely acknowledged by jazz writers that this ensemble may be the greatest collection of jazz musicians ever assembled.

Background to *Kind of Blue*

Line-up for the album *Kind of Blue*:

Miles Davis: trumpet

Julian 'Cannonball' Adderley: alto sax

John Coltrane: tenor sax

Bill Evans: piano (Wynton Kelly plays on the song 'Freddie Freeloader' instead of Evans)

Paul Chambers: bass

Jimmy Cobb: drums

One of the things that makes this album so special is not just that all the musicians were top jazz musicians of the time playing at the peak of their abilities, but also that they all worked so well together. Adderley and Coltrane pushed each other to new heights in their soloing with Davis's more laid back, 'less is more' approach balancing out their flashy, many-note extravaganzas. Bill Evans' understated piano style was perfectly suited to the sound Davis wanted to achieve in this album, providing the perfect chordal backing to the soloists' explorations.

In this album, Davis wanted to explore the concept of **modal jazz**. He felt that jazz was becoming too dependent on complex chord sequences, with soloists restricted to 'playing over the changes'. He felt that, even in a 32-bar structure, the soloist played over the changes for 32 bars and then had to go back and do it again with variations. If the soloist was freed from the restriction of sticking to the chords by giving them a scale or mode to use, more or less ignoring the changes underneath, he felt this would lead to longer, freer improvisations. The result is that modal jazz songs are significantly longer than the shorter songs of bebop and cool jazz, suiting Coltrane's love of extended soloing.

The album was recorded in three 3-hour sessions in 1959 in New York.

Glossary

changes the chord sequence in a jazz song

head the main melody of a jazz song, generally played at the beginning of the song

modal jazz a jazz style in which the soloists base their solos on modes instead of the chord changes

 CD2:1 Close analysis of 'All Blues'

Listen to the recording on the audio CD and use your Anthology to study the analysis that follows.

12-bar blues sequence

'All Blues' is based around a repeated 12-bar blues sequence with a four-bar linking riff in between each section. The main melody (the **head**) and the solos are all played over the 12-bar sequence (the **changes**). The 12-bar sequence is repeated 19 times in total.

Changes for 'All Blues': Head/Solos			
Bar 1	2	3	4
G7	G7	G7	G7
5	6	7	8
C7	C7	G7	G7
9	10	11	12
D7#9	Eb7#9 D7#9	G7	G7

This chord sequence is slightly different from a standard 12-bar blues sequence. The next table contains what would normally be considered a standard 12-bar blues chord sequence in the key of G. Can you see where the differences are?

12-bar blues chord sequence			
Bar 1	2	3	4
G	C	G	G
5	6	7	8
C	C	G	G
9	10	11	12
D7	C	G	D7

Traditionally, any of the chords in the above sequence could be either the basic triad or a dominant 7th chord (e.g. bar 1 might be G7 instead of G). Adding extra notes to a chord is known as extending the chord. There are lots of extended chords in jazz.

See the table below for a full analysis of the structure of the piece.

Section		Bar numbers and timing	Musical features
Intro		1–8￼0:00–0:21	• The piece begins with the drums (played with brushes), the bass playing riff 1 and the piano playing a **trill** in thirds (A–G and E–F♯). The trill immediately causes a little dissonance. Riff 1 is played by the bass almost throughout the whole piece.￼• The time signature is 6/4 with a tempo of ♩ = 156. Although this may seem rather fast, the bar feels like it is split into two slow beats (two dotted minims), so it feels like a laid back tempo of ♩. = 52.￼• At bar 5 the alto and tenor saxophones join in with a harmonised riff (riff 2).￼• All the parts are played quietly with a rather breathy tone in the saxes.￼
Head	1	9–20￼0:21–0:52	• Davis plays the main melody for the first time.￼• The trumpet is muted and has the distinctive Davis 'vulnerable' tone.￼• The melody is based on a very simple motif – a leap of a major sixth, with the long high note slightly ornamented (adding a **mordent**). The rest of the melody is made up of stepwise movement. It soars effortlessly over the rest of the band.￼• Over the C7 chord the sax parts are more legato than the slightly chopped phrasing over the G7 chord.￼• The altered chords D7♯9 and Eb7♯9 are highlighted by a change in texture and the bell-like piano chords replace the trill for a few seconds.
	Link	21–24￼0:53–1:03	• The link section punctuates the whole piece – it breaks up what would otherwise be 19 straight repetitions of the 12-bar sequence.￼• This section is the same as bars 5–8 of the intro.
	2	25–36￼1:03–1:34	• The same as for the first time the head is played, but the melody is developed slightly.

Solos	Link	37–40 1:35–1:45	• The piano trill drops out with Evans switching to riff 2 – the lack of the trill has quite a dramatic effect on the texture. • Cobb introduces the ride cymbal with a few subtle hits before it plays a major role in the solos to follow.
	Davis	41–88 1:46–3:51	• The first solo focuses on the band leader, Miles Davis, with the other two **frontline** instruments dropping out to emphasise this. He has removed the mute to allow for his tone to come through a bit clearer. • Davis takes four choruses for his solo (he allows himself four repeats of the 12-bar sequence). There is no link between the repeats – the four choruses are played back to back. • The solo is modal – Davis improvises over the changes using the G mixolydian mode over the G7 chords and C mixolydian over the C7 chords. He uses a diminished scale over the altered chords. • Evans (piano) **comps** chords underneath the solo based on riff 2. • Cobb keeps time on the ride cymbal with flourishes and highly syncopated, quite unpredictable snare hits keeping some rhythmic interest throughout.
	Link	89–92 3:51–4:01	• Davis drops out (almost reluctantly), handing the spotlight to Adderley. • The music is the same as the link before, but without the two saxophones. • Each link seems to be anticipating the solo to come, sounding quite eager to hear what the new soloist can do.
	Adderley	93–140 4:01–6:05	• Adderley also takes four choruses for his solo. • His solo is more angular than Davis's solo, including more leaps and shorter phrases. • He includes more **chromatic** notes than Davis. • He has a rhythmic quality to his soloing, placing strong accents on the beats. • He has a thick tone, almost making his alto sax sound more like a tenor sax than Coltrane's tenor! • There are quite a few technically difficult bursts of fast notes thrown in.
	Link	141–144 6:05–6:15	• Similar to previous link. • Adderley drops out, handing the spotlight to Coltrane.
	Coltrane	145–192 6:15–8:17	• Coltrane's tone is very different to Adderley's, with almost no vibrato (or adding it late on in the note) compared to Adderley's wide vibrato. • Coltrane also takes four choruses for his solo. • The first chorus is kept quite simple, with some ideas exploring the mode. • In the second chorus he plays some three- and four-note, short ideas and develops them using sequence and some clever rhythmic development. • The third and fourth choruses successfully combine blindingly fast passages with long, sustained phrases. The phrases are different lengths and come in at different places in the bar, giving the solo the impression of being as natural as speech.
	Link	193–196 8:18–8:27	• Coltrane drops out, leaving the spotlight for Evans.
	Evans	197–220 8:28–9:28	• Evans continues comping in the left hand, but it becomes slightly more intricate. • Evans takes two choruses for his solo. • In the first chorus, his right hand plays a melody line, very much like one of the frontline instruments. • In the second chorus he combines the two hands into a chord-based solo, with some alternate motion in bars 213 and 215 to add some variation. • He uses a fairly limited range of notes around the middle of the piano in typically understated fashion, slipping seamlessly into the link.

	Link	221–224 9:29–9:39	• Evans starts with the chords of riff 2, but drops back into the trill idea after two bars. • The two saxes begin playing their harmonised riff again. • Cobb fades the ride cymbal down considerably.
Head	3	225–236 9:39–10:10	• The same as for head 1, with slight developments of the melody. • The trumpet is played with a mute again.
	Link	237–240 10:11–10:21	• Saxes continue to play through the link, along with the piano trill.
	4	241–252 10:21–10:52	• Further minor developments of the melody.
	Link	253–256 10:52–11:02	• The drums back down quite a lot, contributing to an overall drop in volume.
Outro		257–268/9 11:03–fade	• A final (nineteenth) repeat of the 12-bar pattern with Davis playing a short solo, mostly on the tonic note of G over riff 2 in the saxes and the piano trill. • The song fades out towards the end of the final chorus.

Important points to note

◆ Jazz soloists often think in terms of chords and arpeggios when soloing, so it is almost as if they are spreading a chord out horizontally instead of playing it vertically like a piano or guitar but, in this track, the soloists are using scales or modes a lot more than usual, partly because the chords don't change very quickly.

◆ The solos are much more than simple improvisations using a pentatonic scale over a blues sequence – the soloists combine riffs they have learned previously with arpeggio ideas, the use of scales and modes and some clever rhythmic development to create solos with a sense of direction and development.

◆ The soloists never solo at the same time. When the frontline instruments are playing at the same time, they all have very clearly defined parts to play (saxes play the harmonised riff while the trumpet plays the melody).

◆ The link gives the music space to breathe – the contrast in texture between each section builds up a sense of anticipation for the next section.

◆ The bass part repeats riff 1 constantly throughout the song. This makes it become part of the texture so that it doesn't take away from the soloists' limelight. A bit like wallpaper not taking away from the expensive painting on the wall, but it is necessary to provide a suitable background.

◆ The piano part provides chordal accompaniment throughout the piece, but Evans maintains interest by constantly changing the **voicings** of the chords (see pages 99–100 in this chapter for more detail on chord voicings) and the rhythm of his accompaniment.

◆ The drums provide a constantly shifting backing by Cobb improvising a highly syncopated snare drum part, but he also keeps a steady beat throughout on the ride cymbal, varying how he hits it to create changes in dynamics and texture.

Listening and appraising questions: 'All Blues'

Now that you have listened to 'All Blues' and studied the analysis on pages 91–94, answer the listening and appraising questions that follow.

1 What is the time signature of 'All Blues'?

2 What is the name of the chord sequence on which the changes are based?

3 Name the three 'frontline' instruments.

4 What is the term given to the chordal backing the piano is playing during the solos?

5 What is the tonality of the piece?

6 What is meant by the term 'altered chord'?

7 Give bar numbers where you can hear an altered chord.

8 Describe the dynamics of the first trumpet solo.

9 How do the soloists keep their solos interesting when they are playing over a repeated chord sequence?

Glossary

chromatic music in which notes are used that are not in the key of the piece

comping an abbreviation of 'accompanying'

frontline the solo instruments in a jazz ensemble

mordent ornament in which the written note is played, followed by the note above and the written note again

trill rapidly alternating between two notes

voicings a term used to describe various ways of ordering the notes in a chord from lowest to highest

ResultsPlus

Watch out!

Naming rhythmic devices

When asked to name a 'rhythmic device', students often misunderstand what the examiners are looking for. For example:

Question: Name a rhythmic device that is commonly used in 'All Blues'.

When answering a question like this, avoid the common mistake that many students make by remembering that a rhythmic device is a musical device that specifically focuses on some aspect of **rhythm**. The correct responses to this particular question would be:

• swung rhythm
• syncopation

Other responses that might be acceptable, depending on the context of the question, would be:

• triplet rhythm
• hemiola
• rhythmic displacement
• cross rhythms.

Further listening

• Miles Davis: *Birth of the Cool* – 1950 (Capitol)

• Miles Davis: *Milestones* – 1958 (Sony)

• Miles Davis: *Sketches of Spain* – 1960 (Columbia)

• John Coltraine: *Blue Train* – 1957 (Blue Note)

• John Coltrane: *A Love Supreme* – 1965 (Impulse!)

• Bill Evans: *Blue in Green* – 1974 (Milestone)

Jazz harmony

Jazz harmony can be extremely complicated, but it can also be very logical and is certainly an exciting area to get involved in. If you take some time to study the basics, it can be exceedingly rewarding, no matter what style of music you enjoy personally. Jazz harmony has influenced many styles of music from Gershwin through to modern R'n'B, and even some heavy rock and metal. Artists often take some aspects of the harmony and apply it to their own style, giving their music a harmonic twist that sounds a little more interesting than the norm.

To understand this section, you will need to have a grasp of basic harmony, so refer to pages 181–83.

The 12-bar blues sequence on page 92 is in the key of G. If you want to apply this chord sequence to any key, it is easier to use numbers to describe the chords instead of specific note names – for example, in the key of G:

Chord number	Chord type	Root note	Notes
I	Major	G	G, B, D
II	Minor	A	A, C, E
III	Minor	B	B, D, F♯
IV	Major	C	C, E, G
V	Major	D	D, F♯, A
VI	Minor	E	E, G, B
VII	Diminished	F♯	F♯, A, C

The first two columns in the above table (chord number and type) will remain the same for *all* major keys – the notes in the last two columns will change, depending on what the key is.

The third column will always be the major scale, starting with the tonic note in the first row (G in the example given above). The fourth column can be worked out by starting with the root note (from column 3), miss a note, play a note, miss a note, play a note – for example, for the chord of C, start on the root note C, (miss D), E, (miss F♯), G – so the whole of chord IV is C, E and G.

The following table is for the key of E, so the third column replaces the G major scale from the previous table with the E major scale.

Chord number	Chord type	Root note	Notes
I	Major	E	E, G♯, B
II	Minor	F♯	F♯, A, C♯
III	Minor	G♯	G♯, B, D♯
IV	Major	A	A, C♯, E
V	Major	B	B, D♯, F♯
VI	Minor	C♯	C♯, E, G♯
VII	Diminished	D♯	D♯, F♯, A

Note

In jazz and blues, the roman numerals used to describe chords are always upper case (I, II, III etc), but in classical music upper case is used for major chords and lower case for minor chords (I, ii, iii etc) .

Activity

Copy out the table on the opposite page, completing columns 3 and 4 for the keys of C major.

C major scale: C, D, E, F, G, A, B.

Repeat this process for the key of B♭ major.

B♭ major scale: B♭, C, D, E♭, F, G, A.

In a major key, chord IV is always a major chord. In the key of G, chord IV is C major and in the key of E, chord IV is A major. By using this system of numbers instead of note names, jazz musicians find it easier to transpose songs to different keys – they will memorise the changes in numbers and fill in the notes as appropriate for the key they are playing in.

This is the 12-bar blues given as chord numbers instead of specific note names:

Bar 1	2	3	4
I	IV	I	I
5	6	7	8
IV	IV	I	I
9	10	11	12
V7	IV	I	V7

Activity

Copy and complete the table below for the key of E.

Bar 1	2	3	4
E			
5	6	7	8
9	10	11	12
			B7

Copy out the table above for the keys of C major and B♭ major.

Chord substitution

In jazz music, some of the chords in the traditional 12-bar blues are replaced by other chords – this is called **chord substitution**. As you discovered when analysing 'All Blues', bar 10 consists of the chords of E♭7♯9 and D7♯9, replacing the expected chord IV (C7). The 12-bar jazz blues is a 12-bar blues sequence containing some of the most common chord substitutions (and extensions). The following table is an example of the 12-bar jazz blues in the key of G. Compare this to both the standard 12-bar blues pattern and the 12-bar pattern used in 'All Blues'.

Glossary

chord substitution replacing one chord with another

turnaround a short chord pattern at the end of a sequence signalling the return to the beginning of the sequence

Bar 1	2	3	4
G7	C7	G7	G7
5	6	7	8
C7	C7	G7	E7
9	10	11	12
Am7	D7	G7 E7	Am7 D7

In bars 11 and 12 the chords change twice per bar (like bar 10 of 'All Blues'). The faster chord changes heighten the tension a little and also signpost that this is the end of the sequence. This particular four-chord pattern is called a **turnaround**. Jazz musicians will recognise a turnaround pattern as a sign that they are to repeat the changes again.

Seventh chords

A seventh chord is a triad with one additional note on top, but it is so fundamental to jazz harmony that it is not even thought of as an extended chord – you need to add even more notes before calling it an extended chord. In the 12-bar jazz blues, there are a lot of seventh chords used. In classical music, triads are the basic building blocks of harmony, but in jazz it is seventh chords on which everything else is built. Each of the basic triads can be made into a seventh by continuing the play one–miss one–play one idea. The following table shows how this would work for each of the notes in the G major scale.

Root note	Triad	Notes	Added seventh	New chord type	Chord symbol
G	Major	G, B, D	F♯	Major seventh	maj7
A	Minor	A, C, E	G	Minor seventh	m7
B	Minor	B, D, F♯	A	Minor seventh	m7
C	Major	C, E, G	B	Major seventh	maj7
D	Major	D, F♯, A	C	Dominant seventh	7
E	Minor	E, G, B	D	Minor seventh	m7
F♯	Diminished	F♯, A, C	E	Minor seventh flat 5	m7♭5

We can see then that there are four different types of seventh chord that come out of harmonising the major scale:

1 Major 7th = major triad + major 7th note
2 Minor 7th = minor triad + minor 7th note
3 Dominant 7th = major triad + minor 7th note
4 Minor 7th ♭5 = diminished triad + minor 7th note

This information is important if you wish to compose or perform in a jazz style but, for the study of 'All Blues', you only really need to know about one type of seventh chord – the dominant 7th. Its symbol is the simplest of all – a number 7 is added after the root note (e.g. G7). Every time you see this symbol it means that the notes in the chord form a major triad with a minor seventh note added (e.g. G7 = G, B, D, F).

Extended and altered chords

The rather juicy chords D7♯9 and Eb7♯9 are an important element in making 'All Blues' particularly interesting harmonically, so you should know how to form these strange-looking chords.

It makes sense that, if you could keep the play one–miss one–play one idea going to arrive at seventh chords, you should be able to keep going until there are no more notes left. This is indeed the case with jazz music and is one of the things that gives jazz harmony its distinctive character.

Here is a two-octave G scale with the degrees of the scale written underneath each note. The F♯ has been changed to an F♮ (for reasons that will become clear later).

G	A	B	C	D	E	F	G	A	B	C	D	E	F	G
1	2	3	4	5	6	7	8 (or 1)	9	10	11	12	13	14	1

The root note (G) is the first degree of the scale, no matter where it occurs. It is unlikely that it will be called an eighth. The A in the second octave is called the ninth instead of the second, and the B is the tenth etc until the tonic note occurs again.

If we continue the play one–miss one–play one idea, we would end up with the following chords:

◆ G, B, D, F = dominant 7th (G7)
◆ G, B, D, F, A = 9th chord (G9)
◆ G, B, D, F, A, C = 11th chord (G11)
◆ G, B, D, F, A, C, E = 13th chord (G13)

There are no more notes of the scale left to use!

The 9th, 11th and 13th chords are called **extended chords** – they extend the basic triad and seventh chord, adding some tension and complexity to the harmony.

Extended chords are all well and good, but what does D7♯9 mean?

D7♯9 is an **altered chord** – it started life as D7, was extended to become D9, then the ninth degree of the scale was altered (in this case sharpened) so that it ended up as a D7 chord with a sharpened ninth – D7♯9.

If we use G as the root note, G7♯9 would be worked out as follows:

- ◆ G7 is the symbol for G dominant seventh = G, B, D, F
- ◆ Adding the ninth degree of the scale: G9 = G, B, D, F, A
- ◆ Altering the ninth degree by sharpening it: G7♯9 = G, B, D, F, A♯ (A♯ = B♭)

Transposing this so that D is the root note: D7♯9 = D, F♯, A, C, E♯ (E♯ = F♮).

So, if the chord is spelt out in its simplest form – D, F♯, A, C, F – it can be seen that D7♯9 is actually a D7 chord with a minor third added on top – no wonder it sounds a little crunchy!

Altering and extending the chord works with all four types of seventh chord we found in the harmonised major scale, but the dominant 7th sounds much more acceptable extended and altered than the other chords do – they sound much more dissonant and are only used on occasion, but extended and altered dominant 7th chords are extremely common in jazz. The F♯ of the G major scale was changed to an F♮ because all the extensions were worked out using a dominant 7th chord on the root note of G which requires an F♮, not an F♯.

Chord voicings

When jazz artists play these complicated chords, they take great care as to how the notes are spaced. This is especially important on the piano, on which it is possible to play cluster chords (where all the notes in the chord are bunched together). For example, a G13 chord could be voiced by playing all the white notes in a row from G–F, but it would not sound terribly good. On a guitar it is much easier to voice the chords in a pleasing way because cluster chords cannot be played in the same way as they can on a piano because of the spacing of the strings. In fact, the most pleasing voicing of the 7♯9 chord, and one frequently used by Bill Evans in his piano part, can be heard in 'Purple Haze' by Jimi Hendrix. The 'Hendrix chord' is actually an E7♯9 and is voiced (from lowest to highest note): E–E–G♯–D–G, which transposed to D would be: D–D–F♯–C–F.

Glossary

altered chord a chord in which one of the notes has been sharpened or flattened to become a chromatic note

extended chord a chord in which diatonic notes other than the seventh have been added to the original triad

Note

E♭7♯9 = E♭, G, B♭, A♭, F♯

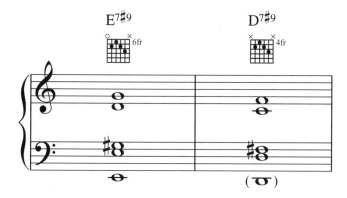

Notice how the A (the fifth degree of the chord) has been left out – this is typical of complex jazz chords – certain notes can be left out to further emphasise the important ones and to thin out the sound a little. The important notes are: root, 3rd, 7th and any altered note or the top note of the extended chord (e.g. the #9th in D7#9 or the 11th in an 11th chord) – all the rest can be omitted.

To prove that the voicing of the chord is important, try switching the F# and F♮ notes around so that the F# is at the top of the chord. Not so nice!

Jeff Buckley: 'Grace' from the album Grace

In the study of this set work you will learn about:

◆ rock and pop music in the early 1990s

◆ the relationship of musicians and songwriters with the music industry

◆ the life and music of Jeff Buckley

◆ songwriting on guitar

◆ alternative song structures

◆ how the set work 'Grace' is constructed through an analysis of the music.

Rock and pop music in the early 1990s

If you listened to guitar-based music in the early 1990s, it would have been very hard to ignore Nirvana's classic album *Nevermind* (1991). It was a refinement of their raw energy into something a little more polished due to the production and mixing of Butch Vig and Andy Wallace. Although it does not sound so ground-breaking now as it did then (it is basically just a well-produced grunge/punk album full of punchy songs and distorted guitar tones), it was to change the face of rock music in America almost overnight and spawn many clone bands. Pearl Jam and Soundgarden were two other bands from the North West of the US who were also having a major impact on the world of rock music, with their own brand of wall-of-sound, powerful guitars, but backed up with more guitar-playing talent.

At this stage in the history of popular music, there were still many of the giants of the music industry releasing albums, for example, U2's *Achtung Baby* (1991), Metallica's self-titled album, *Metallica* (1991), R.E.M's *Automatic For The People* (1992) and Pink Floyd's *Division Bell* (1994), but the industry was crying out for a fresh wave of guitar-oriented music, so the Seattle grunge scene epitomised by Nirvana was aggressively promoted by the record companies and proved enormously popular.

The hip-hop scene was diverging from the more sanitised music of artists such as M.C. Hammer to the heavily censored 'gangsta' rap of Snoop Doggy Dogg. With rap music becoming harder and more political at this time, many albums were censored or issued with stickers warning of explicit content. In the UK, dance music dominated the charts alongside American grunge (see the chapter on Moby for more information on dance music in the 1990s, pages 112–15) and manufactured pop music written specifically for the short-term commercial success of various singers by the 'pop music production line' songwriters.

By 1994 the time was ripe for another change. In the US this came by way of the pop-punk band Green Day releasing *Dookie* (1994) – it's uncompromising energy reminiscent of punk music, but presented in a more polished, radio-friendly package. In the UK, Britpop led the revival of British fortunes in the music industry with the bands Oasis, Blur, Suede and Pulp at the forefront.

Other important guitar-oriented bands of the time include Rage Against the Machine (hip-hop-influenced rock with innovative guitar sounds), the Red Hot Chili Peppers (funk fused with rock) and the UK band Radiohead (fusing hard-edged guitar sounds with progressive rock tendencies).

The artist and the industry

The music industry has an enormous impact on what we hear, determined mainly by what the industry thinks we want to hear, and therefore what they think will sell. This is not a new phenomenon – in the days of Handel and Mozart composers needed to work either to a commission or for a patron who would demand a certain type of musical output. If the composers did not produce music seen as appropriate by the patron, they would not receive payment for their work, so they would have to channel their own creative drive into whatever was required of them at the time. Record companies employ people to find new talent and to gauge what the public wants to hear. They want their artists to fit within a clearly definable category so that people will know what they are getting when they buy the album (e.g. heavy rock, jungle, cool jazz, Texas blues etc) – this means they can market the artist appropriately, targeting the group of people who will most likely buy the music.

The emphasis on marketing has had a significant impact on the way music is written, recorded, packaged, distributed and listened to. In recent times, with the surge in downloadable music, there are new ways to market music (such as social networking sites on the internet) that is then often listened to through a media player on a computer or a portable device such as an iPod. In the early 1990s, it was very important to get your song played on **MTV** in order to generate public interest, encouraging sales of CDs, so record companies would be keen to ensure that albums contained several songs they could release as singles, and each single would have to be accompanied by a video.

Glossary

MTV A TV channel dedicated to playing music videos

Role of a producer

In Areas of Study 1 and 2, the composers for each of the set works will have written and refined every aspect of the music themselves, but this is not the case in the pop music industry. It is possible that the artist will write initial ideas for a song, but may then collaborate with a number of people to write instrumental parts, program drum tracks, alter aspects of harmony, structure and style, and produce, record and mix the track. As such, the artist is only a part of the process that goes into making a song what it is. One of the most important people other than the artist is the producer – they make many of the creative decisions and will work with the artist to come up with a distinctive sound. Producers are generally appointed by the record company, although more established artists may have a say in choosing who produces their work. Modern-day producers make a name for themselves by having a distinctive sound they bring to any recording; for example, a producer may be famous for making rock songs sound particularly cinematic and powerful or another for bringing a sense of intimacy and clarity to recordings.

Jeff Buckley (1966–1997)

Jeff Buckley was born Jeffrey Scott Guibert in 1966 in Anaheim, California. His father (Tim Buckley) was a jazz–folk musician, frequently touring away from home during the pregnancy and eventually deciding to leave Jeff's mother shortly before the baby was born. In 1975 Jeff changed his name to 'Buckley' in honour of his father, who died the same year.

Jeff formed his first covers band in 1982, playing the odd original song written by the band. He had a great appetite for music of any sort, borrowing tapes from friends and family members, no matter what style they happened to be. This openness to a wide variety of styles would contribute to his later music making.

At the age of 19 Jeff started to attend the Musicians Institute (the Guitar Institute of Technology) in Hollywood where he honed his guitar skills. After graduating from the Institute he left to pursue a musical career, playing for any bands he could find that needed a guitarist. This included playing for a reggae outfit, a 1980s 'hair–metal' band and recording backing music for demos for other people to sing over. By 1990 he decided to head for New York, feeling that he needed to break out of a music scene that was stifling him.

In New York, Jeff played in various punk and reggae bands, but was also exposed to a Pakistani devotional music known as 'qawwali' (a type of meditative religious chant), which he loved, adding to his increasingly wide musical tastes. However, things in New York didn't work out initially, so he returned to LA at the invitation of his father's former manager, Herb Cohen, who funded the recording of a demo tape of Jeff's own music.

Jeff's big break occurred in 1991 when he was asked to perform at a tribute to Tim Buckley. Several people who heard him sing his father's songs were so impressed that his name started to create a buzz around the New York music scene. The guitarist (Gary Lucas) who had been brought in to back him up while performing was looking for a singer for his own band, so Jeff was immediately recruited. Lucas wrote music around guitar textures based on **soundscapes** rather than riffs and technical showpieces. Jeff's musical tastes had gradually been growing away from the flash of 1980s guitar rock and the licks of jazz fusion to more experimental music (as well as the music of 'tragic' performers such as Edith Piaf and Billie Holiday), so the two had a great collaborative relationship for a while. Unfortunately, their careers were pulling in opposite directions, so it inevitably ended, but not before they had co-written the songs 'Mojo Pin' and 'Grace'. Although their musical relationship ended just as a recording contract loomed, Lucas was drafted in to add his guitar effects and loops to the album when it was recorded two years later.

At the same time as he was playing in Lucas's band, Jeff was also performing solo sets at a club/coffeehouse in Manhattan called Sin-é. He was given a residency there, gradually attracting more and more people as interest grew in the wide range of musical styles he could perform. By 1992 record companies were taking an interest in Jeff; with the explosion of Seattle grunge music, they were keen to sign someone who could come under their 'alternative' bracket, but Buckley's music was not easy to pigeonhole. Jeff was wary of anything to do with the music business since he regarded it as being responsible for his father's demise but, eventually, he and his manager/lawyer, George Stein, negotiated a deal with Columbia (owned by Sony).

Background to *Grace*

The line-up for the song 'Grace' is:

Matt Johnson: drums
Mick Grondahl: bass
Gary Lucas: guitar
Jeff Buckley: guitar, vocals

Jeff Buckley's music can best be described as 'eclectic' – it covers a wide range of styles, from the classical ballad of 'Corpus Christi Carol' to the metal, noise-making of 'Eternal Life'. The element holding all these styles together is his unique voice, whether he is delivering a tortured howl, or a gentle, lilting melody. A specific sort of producer was required to bring together these elements into one album and make them sound like a unified piece of work, so the record company suggested Andy Wallace (who mixed Nirvana's *Nevermind* and some work by Slayer). Instead of just adding his own style to a recording, Wallace was said to be able to take whatever qualities an artist had and to magnify them, and this was just what Buckley wanted. The basic recording of the main instrumental parts and lead vocals was completed at Bearsville Studios, Woodstock, but Jeff was a perfectionist, wanting to tweak aspects of the recording, adding vocal and guitar **overdubs** in various studios in Manhattan and New Jersey.

Unlike some artists of the past, who would record a whole song in one take, it took Buckley and his band up to 19 takes to get the basic track down! This was exacerbated by his writing methods – he would often be found writing the lyrics for a song on his way into the studio to record them. The band also tended to develop the arrangements of a song while in the studio, taking up some time.

The album was released in August 1994, on the same day as the Oasis album *Definitely Maybe*.

Glossary

soundscapes music concentrating on the manipulation of timbre and texture to create a musical 'landscape' or atmosphere rather than the statement and development of musical themes

Glossary

overdubs the use of a multi-track recording device to layer recorded parts

CD2:2   Close analysis of 'Grace'

Listen to the recording on the audio CD and use your Anthology to study the analysis that follows.

Structure

If you listen to it as a whole, the structure of 'Grace' seems very complicated, but when broken down into its component parts, it is actually just a clever arrangement of several deceptively simple ideas.

Overall 'Grace' is in four large sections, each one subdivided into smaller subsections.

1 Intro – Verse 1 – Pre-chorus – Chorus –

2 Link – Verse 2 – Pre-chorus – Chorus –

3 Middle 8 –

4 Link – Verse 3 – Outro.

The link is the same as the intro and has two distinct parts, labelled part A and part B. The two parts are separated by a sustained chord of E minor. The following are the chord charts for each of the sections:

Link – Part A (three bars)

Bar 1	2	3
Fm	Gm	Em

Link – Part B (four bars)

4		5	
D	A/D	D	A/D
6		7	
D	A/D	D	G5/D

Verse – combination of open fifths (**power chords**) + **drone** strings (6 bars)

Bar 1		2	
Em		Em/F5	Em
3		4	
Em/E♭5		Em/F5	Em
5		6	
Em/E♭5		Em	

Pre-Chorus – repeated six-bar sequence (6 bars)

Bar 1				2		3
Em	F#dim	G6	A6	Bm	A6/9	Em
4				5		6
Em	F#dim	G6	A6	Bm	A6/9	Em

Chorus – 5 bars

Bar 1		2
Em/F5	Em	Em/Eb5
3		4
Em/F5	Em	Em/Eb5
5		
Em		

Chords

The chords for the verse and chorus look very complex (and sound rather crunchy at times) but they are actually very simple on the guitar. They use the old trick of moving the same chord shape up and down the fretboard while keeping one or more open strings as a drone, giving a harmonic richness to the sound without actually having to think about the name of the chords and where to play them etc – the harmonies spring from the ideas played on the guitar, not the other way around. The chord symbols are given as Em over a power chord – this is because the top three open strings on a guitar form the triad of E minor, but Buckley may only have hit one or two of these strings each time.

Below are the chord charts for where you would put your fingers for the chords Em/F5, Em and Em/Eb5. Note how the bottom string on the guitar has been tuned down to D from E (a common trick to make the guitar sound deeper and darker called drop-D tuning) and the chord shape stays the same – it is a 'power chord' shape in drop-D tuning.

$$Em/F^5$$

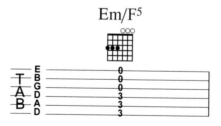

$$Em$$

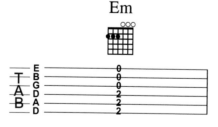

$$Em/E^b5$$

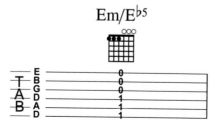

See the table below for a full analysis of the structure and production of the song:

Section		Bar	Description
Intro	A	1–3 0:00–0:11	• The song is in 12/8 time. • The tempo is 64 dotted crotchet bpm (beats per minute). • The key is not clear at the beginning – it is just a series of chords. The combined notes of the first two chords make an ascending F melodic minor scale. • Ripple of notes played on a clean electric guitar sound. • Background guitar 'whisper' made by picking the note with the volume turned down then turning the volume up quickly – lots of reverb and delay on the sound. • Ends with a loud, unison chord of Em, with 'scoops' on the tremolo arm of the guitar adding a little interest and a roll on the crash cymbal.
	B	4–7 0:11–0:26	• Full band play, but no vocals yet. • This section is clearly in D major. • Instruments include drum-kit, bass, two electric guitars and acoustic guitar. A third electric guitar punctuates the texture with a low C♯ note (with wide vibrato) clashing against the pedal D (just added for effect, not for harmonic reasons). • Acoustic guitar and hi-hat work closely together to drive the rhythm. • Bass guitar plays the pedal D, occasionally wandering off for a little ascending riff. • Main feature is the rhythmic, semi-strummed chord pattern played high up on the clean (or very slightly distorted) electric guitar.
Verse 1		8–13 0:26–0:48	• Vocals enter. • High electric guitar riff drops out. • Guitar 'whispers' return, plus occasional additional noises to add interest. • Drum pattern focuses on the toms. • Acoustic guitar seems more prominent, with the sound of the plectrum hitting the strings heard clearly, making it as much a percussion instrument as if it was part of the drum-kit. • Electric guitar plays broken chords. • Bass mainly follows the root note of the power chord. • The harmonies depend on the chord pattern, but overall it is modal, with E as the tonic note.
Pre-Chorus 1		14–19 0:49–1:11	• Guitar 'whispers' drop out. • Electric guitar plays similar rhythm to acoustic guitar with chord shapes moving up the neck. • Other instruments remain as they were for the verse. • The vocal range starts to get higher. • This section is mostly in E minor (with hints of the E-dorian mode).
Chorus		20–24 1:11–1:29	• Backing vocals enter – very subtle, sometimes just doubling the main vocal (double tracking). A whispered voice part can be heard behind the main vocals. • Strings can be heard subtly in the background, more for sound effects than for harmonic reasons. • The harmony is based on the chord pattern, but is again modal, centred on E. • Drum part stops using the toms so extensively – more of a straight rhythm, if a little sparse.

Link	A	25–27 1:30–1:41	• As for section A of the intro, but with a mandolin effect added on the acoustic guitar. • Vocal 'oh' to lead to part B.
	B	28–31 1:41–1:55	• As for part B of intro.
Verse 2		32–37 1:56–2:19	• As for verse 1. • Additional sound effects e.g. descending slide at 2:05 (using **slide** on guitar with lots of **delay**), followed by a slide and trill on the strings imitating the guitar.
Pre-Chorus 2		38–43 2:19 – 2:41	• As for Pre-chorus 1, but strings much more prominent adding considerably to the texture. • *Pizzicato* strings added.
Chorus		44–48 2:41–2:59	• As for previous chorus. • Drum roll leading into middle 8.
Mid 8	A	49–52 3:00–3:14	• Rather intense section with the strings playing long, sustained notes to fill out the chords. • Multi-tracked vocal harmonies in counterpoint with each other (polyphonic texture). • Drum-kit plays a similar rhythm on the snare as to what was played on the toms previously, lending it more intensity – much more cymbal throughout.
	B	53–59 3:15–3:41	• This section is based on the chord sequence for the pre-chorus, but has been produced very differently. • The instrumental backing is similar to pre-chorus 2. • The main vocal line improvises a wordless melody above the backing, then a 'telephone' **EQ** effect is applied to the vocal when the lyrics come back in, giving it a harsh, distant effect. • Beautiful, hummed harmonies follow the chord pattern with the sound opening out to vocal 'aahs' towards the end of the section – an almost angelic quality. This contrasts sharply with the harshness of the vocal part.
Link	A	60–62 3:41–3:52	• As for previous link, part A, but with a rhythmic, percussive sound of hitting the deadened acoustic guitar strings added. • A percussive hit of the acoustic guitar body at the end of the section leads into part B.
	B	63–66 3:52–4:07	• As for previous link part B.
Verse 3		67–71 4:07–4:26	• The backing is similar as for previous verses, but there is much more use of cymbal in the drum-kit. • The vocal part has a much more intense, forceful quality to it, using the higher part of the vocal range. • More and more special effects are added as the section progresses.
Outro		72–end 4:26–5:19	• The strings come to the fore. • Vocal improvisations very high in the vocal range (as high as the top G of a soprano's range!) showing off Buckley's vocal virtuosity. • An electric guitar is added with **flanger** effect (bringing out the open droning, discordant notes), adding even more to the intensity. • The song ends with a short, unaccompanied, modal phrase in the vocal clearly highlighting the influence of qawwali music.

Important points to note

◆ This song is an excellent example of how to arrange a relatively simple idea and make it sound interesting throughout the song. The main chord sequence is just a power chord slid across three frets of the guitar, but it is played in different ways in each section, with different textures making it sound interesting. There is no attempt to do a smooth transition from the modal section into the major section – it always links via a sustained chord. The major section then links to the next section by several of the parts continuing with exactly the same rhythm/strumming pattern as they had before, just with the different chord sequence – this brings a sense of unity to the piece (all the parts feel as if they belong together).

◆ Although the main instruments of bass, electric, acoustic guitars and drum-kit are used most of the way through, the additional instruments are not – the string parts are held back, added either for effects (at the beginning) or to raise the tension by adding to the texture (middle 8). Parts drop out from time to time to let the music breathe (textural contrast). Even the bass, drums and acoustic guitar drop out in the intro and link, section A to give the texture a chance to breathe. The electric guitar 'whispers' are saved for places where they can be heard, adding an eerie effect to the song, emphasising the lyrics.

◆ The lyrics are said to be based on a dream Buckley had about a girl crying on her boyfriend's arm at an airport, not wanting him to leave, but they are also clearly about death. Buckley was fascinated with the subject of mortality, probably because of the early death of his father.

Glossary

delay repetition(s) of a sound after a set time interval, usually at a lower volume and with less high frequency content than the original

EQ abbreviation of equalisation – electronically cutting or boosting specific frequencies in a sound

flanger a studio effect ranging from subtle 'swirling' sounds to 'jet plane' effects

pizzicato playing a string instrument by plucking the strings

slide a playing technique on string instruments by sliding the finger from one note to another or a metal/glass device used to slide from one note to another on guitars

After *Grace*

The record company were always going to struggle to market *Grace* along normal business lines, so they decided to try a different approach, treating Buckley as one of their 'heritage' artists – along similar lines to artists such as Bob Dylan and Bruce Springsteen. This meant that they would not try to get his face on every TV screen and advertising board they could, but would introduce him to the public gradually. Initially this was acceptable – Jeff and his band toured extensively around America, Europe and Australia from 1994 to 1996, but the album did not sell as well as they would have liked. Eventually, against Jeff's wishes, Columbia insisted that he release videos with his new singles from the album. These did help with record sales, but he was still a long way from paying back all he owed to Columbia for the recording and marketing of the album and his tour was just breaking even. The stress of touring and the constant conflict of both loving and hating the life of a famous musician started to take its toll. Jeff became emotionally and physically exhausted, cancelling a section of his tour to recover.

In 1996 Jeff started work on writing the much-anticipated follow up to *Grace*, to be titled *My Sweetheart the Drunk*. He was generally dissatisfied with the results of long jam sessions with his band (which had gone through a line-up change after some tensions on tour) and, after many unsuccessful attempts to come up with something in New York studios and rehearsal rooms, the record company agreed that he should take a break in a different environment, so he relocated to Memphis, Tennessee in 1997 to gather his thoughts.

By all accounts, Jeff's stay in Memphis helped him get back on track. He realised he had manic depressive tendencies, but was seeking help for it. He felt that his songwriting was progressing nicely, putting final touches to many half-formed ideas and writing new material. He was back into a more disciplined lifestyle, focusing on his music and generally getting back into shape after the rigours of the last three years – he seemed to be the happiest that anyone had seen him for some time. On 29 May 1997, just as his band were getting off their flight to join him in the rehearsal room to rehearse the new material, Jeff went off with a friend for a swim in the Wolf river, Memphis. A tugboat passed by, sucking him into an undercurrent of the notoriously dangerous river and he was tragically drowned.

His half-formed ideas for the second album have since been released as *Sketches for My Sweetheart the Drunk*, but nobody knows what alterations he would have made to the material before the perfectionist would have let it be released so, like others before him, we are left wondering what he might have come up with had he survived.

 **CD2:2** Listening and appraising questions: 'Grace'

Now that you have listened to 'Grace' and studied the analysis on pages 106–109, answer the listening and appraising questions that follow.

1 Describe the guitar part in the introduction. You should think about the rhythm and the harmony, and also the mood it creates.

2 What guitar playing technique can be heard frequently in the introduction?

3 What is the tonality of the song in the second half of the introduction?

4 What is the tonality of the song in the verse and pre-chorus?

5 Describe how the drums are played in the verse.

6 How does the instrumentation and texture of verse 2 differ from that of verse 1?

7 How does verse 3 differ from both verse 1 and 2?

8 Describe the vocal parts in the second half of the middle 8.

9 How many different chords are used in the chorus?

10 What effect has been applied to the electric guitar part at the end of the song which cannot be heard previously in the song?

Further listening

- *Sketches for My Sweetheart the Drunk* – 1998 (released posthumously)
- *Mystery White Boy* – 2000 (from a collection of live performances 1995–1996)
- *Live á L'Olympia* – 2001 (live performance – July 1995)

Moby: 'Why Does My Heart Feel So Bad?' from the album Play

In the study of this set work you will learn about:

◆ the origins of club dance music

◆ Moby and his approach to writing music

◆ how the set work 'Why Does My Heart Feel So Bad?' is constructed through an analysis of the music

◆ some of the technology commonly used in club dance music.

Roots of club dance music

For the purposes of GCSE Music, the term 'club' dance music is used to refer to dance music that would normally be played in nightclubs by DJs, as opposed to classical dance styles such as the galliard and the waltz. In normal conversation we would simply refer to it as dance music and understand it to be club dance. For the rest of the chapter, club dance music will be referred to simply as dance music.

Dance music has many different genres and sub-genres, each of which has its own set of influences and developed on its own unique musical path. On the whole, modern dance music can be traced back to the fusion of toasting (where a DJ would talk rhythmically over the music, interacting with the existing song lyrics often in a boastful and rather rude way, so as to hype up the audience) and dub from Jamaica with early hip-hop beats, electro from Europe and disco.

Dub

The art of taking an original song and 'remixing' it can be traced back to the late 1960s when Bob Marley's producer, King Tubby, took some reggae tracks, removed the vocal part and overdubbed some effects (hence 'dub') on the instrumental tracks. The style developed in the early 1970s when King Tubby and Lee Perry (amongst others) turned it into a marketing ploy; they would record the instrumentalists and vocalists in one session and release the song as a single, but on the B-side they would put a dub remix of the track, displaying their own creativity as well as saving money on recording costs.

These dub artists can be considered as the first DJs; they were employed in the mid-1950s (before dub was developed) to use their 'Sound Systems' to play music through. These were basically PA systems through which they were able to amplify their music. They became popular because they were cheaper to hire than a band of musicians. They would often sign artists to record exclusively for them so that they had an edge in the market by playing exclusive tracks on their Sound Systems.

Scratching

In 1975, DJ Grand Wizard Theodore is said to have discovered 'scratching' – a technique where the record is spun by hand, creating a scratching sound. This technique was developed to such an extent that DJs would use the record deck as an instrument, improvising over their beats. The earliest examples of rap music took place in outdoor parties where DJs would play their beats, demonstrating their scratching skills and toasting/MCing over the top. The Sugarhill Gang (named after the label that got them together) released the first recognised rap single called 'Rapper's Delight' in 1979. It was a rather sanitised version of the street music, suitable for public release.

Chicago house

In Chicago, in the mid-1980s, DJs such as Frankie Knuckles and Farley 'Jackmaster' Funk pioneered a sound that was to become known as house (named after the club where it was first played – The Warehouse). The DJs would take existing tracks and remix them, or cut them up, mixing them together with other tracks because they did not have enough new material to play. Frankie Knuckles is sometimes known as 'the godfather of house' because he was the first to bring some of these ideas to the Chicago clubs.

Music played in The Warehouse ranged from disco and soul through to Euro synth-based pop. Sometimes the DJs would bring in a drum machine to exaggerate the **four-to-the-floor** bass drum beat that was characteristic of house music.

Garage

While the popularity of Chicago house music was gradually dying down, another scene was starting in New York. In a club called the Paradise Garage, DJ Larry Levan pioneered a style that was much more melodic than house, taking its influences more from soul and R'n'B. This style again took its name from the club where it was first played, becoming known as garage. In the UK, the Ministry of Sound, based in London, was heavily influenced by the garage sound.

By this stage, Moby was based in New York and was gradually becoming more and more involved in the hip-hop/dance music scene.

Glossary

four-to-the-floor a strong reinforcement of a 4/4 beat by a bass drum

Moby (1965–)

Moby was born Richard Melville Hall in 1965 in New York. His mother was still at university at the time and they moved to Connecticut in 1967 for her to finish her studies. He was brought up in Connecticut, taking classical guitar lessons at school from the age of 9. From 1980 to 1985 he played guitar in a number of punk-style bands including The Vatican Commandoes, Flipper and AWOL. The Vatican Commandoes released an EP in 1983 called 'Hit Squad for God'. Moby attended the University of Connecticut, but dropped out in 1985 to pursue his music career that consisted of DJing at The Beat club in New York and gigging/recording with his band at the time, AWOL.

In 1989, after years of trying, he got his first recording contract (with Instinct Records). By this time he was still DJing around New York clubs, but his living conditions were fairly poor (he lived in a loft with no heat or running water). In 1990 he released his first single called 'Mobility' with limited commercial interest, but his 1991 single 'Go' was the track that gave him his big break, bringing him to worldwide notice. 'Go' makes use of a sample taken from the cult TV series *Twin Peaks*, making it instantly recognisable to millions of listeners. It charted in the top 10 in the UK, giving Moby his first appearance on *Top of the Pops*. This, along with his DJing work, brought him recognition from established acts such as The Prodigy and Orbital, whose work he remixed.

In the early 1990s he released a number of other singles and built up his reputation touring with artists from a range of musical backgrounds including The Prodigy, Orbital and the Red Hot Chili Peppers.

In the sleeve notes for his albums, Moby writes about causes that he feels passionately about. He feels very strongly about human and animal rights, specifically believing that we should do everything we can to alleviate suffering of any kind, whether of humans or of animals. As such, his beliefs have led him to become a vegan, where he avoids the eating, wearing or use of any animal products. He is outspoken about his Christian beliefs, although he is opposed to many of the policies of the Christian right wing in America, holding much more liberal views. He is very happy to write and speak about his beliefs and faith, but does not feel that he should force his opinion on anyone else, believing that each informed adult should make their own choice in everything that they do.

Background to *Play*

In his music, Moby covers a wide range of styles. His first official album release, *Everything is Wrong* (1995), is definitely within the dance genre, but is hard to classify where exactly it fits within this. He immediately followed up this album with a hardcore industrial album called *Animal Rights*, playing as part of a rock band. However, *Animal Rights* did not do terribly well commercially, so he returned to the dance genre with his 1999 album, *Play*.

When Moby works on an album or song, he takes a very long time over it, coming up with the initial idea quite quickly, but spending a long time tweaking and fine-tuning every detail. Because he generally works on his own, he is keen to take time out from his work after he has come up with a mix, revisiting it some time later to make a more objective judgement about the quality of the work. You may want to consider using this process when it comes to your own composition work – if you are not working in collaboration with other people, then it is hard to form an objective opinion of your own work, getting lost in the fine detail of it all, so coming back with a fresh pair of ears is always a good thing. Sometimes Moby says that what initially sounded poor can sound much better, and vice versa, after a break or cooling off period.

Moby spent the majority of 1998 working on the tracks for *Play*, releasing three singles from the album in 1999, which received little public attention in the UK, but his fourth single from the album, 'Why Does My Heart Feel So Bad?', reached number 16 in the UK charts and was received with critical acclaim.

 CD2:3 Close analysis of 'Why Does My Heart Feel So Bad?'

Listen to the recording on the audio CD and use your Anthology to study the analysis that follows.

Sampling vocals

Moby makes extensive use of vocal samples in his songwriting – he says, 'I sample vocals because, try as I might, I cannot sound like a black woman from 1945. I'm a skinny white guy! If I want to have African–American vocals, I either have to bring a woman in to sing them or I need to find vocal samples' (interview in *Sound on Sound*, February 2000).

'Why Does My Heart Feel So Bad?' is built around two vocal samples taken from a recording of a gospel choir made in 1953. Both vocal phrases are in the key of A minor, but Moby has chosen to harmonise one with a sequence that makes it feel minor and the other with a sequence that makes it feel major. How does he do this? Go to pages 181–83 to check how you might harmonise different notes in a scale – you can normally choose between three or more chords in a key to harmonise any given note, with a choice of major or minor chords for any given note. Part of Moby's style is to find new ways of harmonising samples. He may use a similar harmony to that of the original, but he may also find a new and interesting way to harmonise it, entirely depending on what he finds most pleasing to listen to!

Structure

This piece has a very simple structure based around two-chord sequences arranged in eight-bar blocks. Moby develops the texture of the piece around these chord sequences, changing the amount of instruments playing, the rhythms and the effects used.

Chord sequence 1 – Verse: *'Why does my heart feel so bad?'*

Bar 1	2	3	4	5	6	7	8
Am	Am	Em	Em	G	G	D	D

Chord sequence 2a – Chorus (first half): *'These open doors'*

Bar 1	2	3	4	5	6	7	8
C	C	Am	Am	C	C	Am	Am

Chord sequence 2b – Chorus (second half): *'These open doors'*

Bar 1	2	3	4	5	6	7	8
F	F	C	C	F	F	C	C

See the table below for a full analysis of the structure and production of the song.

Section		Bar numbers and timing	Description
Intro		1–8 0:00–0:19	• The time signature is 4/4 and the key is A minor. • The tempo is 98 bpm (beats per minute). • The song begins with chord sequence 1 played on the piano.
Verse 1	1	9–16 0:20–0:39	• Verse 1 consists of four repeats of chord sequence 1. • The first vocal sample is introduced along with the simple piano accompaniment. • The vocal sample is very untidy – echoes, traffic and other noises can be heard in the background.
	2	17–24 0:39–0:58	• The drum/percussion loop is introduced. • A sustained synth pad plays bass notes along with the left hand of the piano. • A similar sustained synth pad (doubled by high piano notes) is the 'response' in a call and response texture with the vocal sample.
	3	25–32 0:59–1:18	• A synth bass part is introduced. • An additional synth string pad fills out the texture with long, sustained chords in the mid–high pitch range.
	4	33–40 1:18–1:38	• Same as part 3, but the main piano part plays a different rhythm, decorating the chord sequence with extra **sus4** and **sus2 chords**.
Chorus	a	41–48 1:38–1:57	• The chord sequence changes for the first time with quite a dramatic lifting effect. Section a of the chorus is chord sequence 2a. • The key is now a little ambiguous – it could be C major or A minor. • The second vocal sample – 'These open doors' is introduced. • The texture is similar to verse 1 part 4, but the answering synth + piano phrases have been replaced by more subtle answering phrases in the right hand of the piano part and the synth string backing is a little more in the background, swelling in towards the end of the phrase.
	b	49–56 1:58–2:17	• Section b of the chorus is chord sequence 2b. • The key is now clearly C major. • The texture is the same as for the first part of the chorus, but this time the sample is retriggered faster than before, so that it answers itself in the call and response pattern.
Verse 2	1	57–64 2:17–2:36	• Similar as for verse 1 part 4. • There is an echo effect on the vocal sample, but the echo has a 'telephone voice' EQ effect applied, making it sound much thinner. The echo itself is also delayed (there are several, quicker repeats of the echo fading into the distance).
	2	65–72 2:37–2:56	• As for verse 2 part 1.

Break		73 2:56–2:58	• A complete breakdown where all the parts drop out for a single bar – all that can be heard are the dying repeats of the delay effect on the EQed vocal echo, a quiet delay repeat of the snare (from the drum loop) and the tailing off of the **reverb** applied to the other parts.
Chorus	a	74–81 2:59–3:18	• Vocal sample 2 is used with lots of reverb and delay making it sound distant and blending it with the lush string pad playing the chords (which is also awash with reverb). • The drums re-enter at bar 81, leading into part b.
	b	82–89 3:18–3:38	• As for part b of the first chorus. • Note how the reverb on the vocal sample has been reduced drastically, making it sound much clearer and to the front of the mix, even though it is no louder than in part a.
	b	90–97 3:38–3:57	• A repeat of part b – this is a little unexpected as we are anticipating an immediate return to the verse. It has the effect of letting us know the song is coming to an end (repeating or elongating the chorus at the end of a song is a common songwriting trick with which we are now familiar at a subconscious level).
Outro		98–105 3:58–4:20	• The texture breaks down to just the first vocal sample accompanied by a soft synth pad playing chord sequence 1.

Important points to note

◆ Moby feels that it is more important for music to trigger an emotional response in the listener than for it to be pristine and clinically well produced. This is why he has left the vocal samples with all the background noise intact. He experimented with removing much of the noise with powerful digital editing tools, but found that this removed some of the emotional content that he particularly liked, so decided to use the unedited version instead. This adds extra texture to the piece – the point where the sample cuts off is very sudden and percussive in its effect, so the background noise acts almost as another percussion instrument.

◆ The use of effects is an important development tool in electronic music, on the same level as traditional development techniques such as melodic and rhythmic development. Listen particularly to the difference in the use of reverb and delay on vocal sample 2 when the section changes at 3:18. Moby uses other subtle effects editing throughout the song.

◆ In addition to the use of reverb and delay, much attention has been given to where the sounds all fit in the stereo field (where they have been placed in the left-hand and right-hand speakers) and the EQ applied to each sound. Listen to the opening eight bars of the piano intro through headphones to hear how Moby has created a sense of movement from side to side. If you can, switch the headphones to mono to hear the difference.

◆ EQ is short for equalisation. It was originally used to even out the problems inherent in early recordings because the media used to record on was far from able to give an accurate reproduction of the original sound – EQ allowed the recording to be more equal to the original sound source. Essentially it is a sophisticated tone control, allowing the relative volume of the treble, middle and bass frequencies to be

Glossary

reverb the reflection of sound off surfaces to give the impression of space – may be natural or electronically applied to a sound

sus2 chord a triad with the major or minor third replaced by the second degree of the scale

sus4 chord a triad with the major or minor third replaced by the fourth degree of the scale

adjusted independently of each other. On modern studio equipment, there is a very high level of control over the frequency of a recorded sound, allowing many EQ settings to be applied at the same time (e.g. the bass could be boosted while there is a slight dip in the low–middle frequencies, but also a slight boost for the very high frequencies). If you listen to the 'telephone voice' effect in verse 2, you can hear that the bass and higher treble frequencies have been almost completely removed, giving an effect similar to that of singing down a telephone.

◆ Harmonies in dance music are generally very simple. Throughout this song, there are only six chords used (see the chord charts for more details). Moby does not have an analytical approach to choosing harmonies – he does not think too much about what chords would be theoretically correct, he just chooses the chords that trigger the appropriate emotional response at any given moment. This means that he probably did not think about the D major chord containing an F♯, which makes the F chord sound so fresh when it occurs in the second half of the chorus, he just harmonised the melody in the second half of the chorus with an F chord, decided that it sounded good, and stuck with it. Strictly speaking, the D major chord makes the verse modal (the A-dorian mode), but to the ear it is simply A minor.

The technology used for 'Why Does My Heart Feel So Bad?'

The following equipment was used on the song:

Equipment	Purpose
Yamaha SPX990 Multi-effects unit	To apply reverb and delay to tracks
Roland TR909 drum machine	Sound source for drum loops
Emu Proformance piano sound module	Piano sound source (there are two piano sounds on the track, one from an old Yamaha synth and another from the Emu)
Roland Juno 106	Synth bass sounds
Yamaha SY22 and SY85 synthesisers	String/synth pad sounds
Akai S3200 sampler	Sampling the vocal sounds off the original record and any subsequent editing

Note that you will not need to learn the model numbers of the equipment for the GCSE listening examination – they have been included here in case you wish to carry out any further research or emulate the sounds of the recording on your school equipment. It is also very interesting to note that Moby did not use the most up-to-date equipment available, even when the track was recorded in 1999.

This song is much simpler than many dance tracks in terms of the technology used. Moby has deliberately made the production simple in keeping with the spirit of the simple, unedited vocal samples. As such, the only effects used are delay and reverb (for our purposes here, echo is the same as delay). The settings change for different sections of the song, but it is still a simple reverb and delay from an aging effects unit.

There is a lot of EQ on the 'telephone voice' effect, but one editing trick has been used in addition to just EQing the sample – Moby re-sampled the original sample at a lower bit rate to give it a grainy, lo-fi sound. If you download an MP3 track from the internet at a very low-quality level, it is likely to exhibit similar effects.

Beyond *Play*

After its release, *Play* initially sold steadily, if modestly, but it gained in popularity until by the end of 2008 it had sold over nine million copies. This established Moby as a major figure, not just in the world of dance music, but also in the music industry as a whole.

The song 'Extreme Ways', from the album *18* was used in the Bourne movies and has since become his most downloaded song.

 **CD2:3** Listening and appraising questions: 'Why Does My Heart Feel So Bad?'

Now that you have listened to 'Why Does My Heart Feel So Bad?' and studied the analysis on pages 115–17, answer the listening and appraising questions that follow.

1 Is the piano in the introduction a live recording of an acoustic piano or a sequenced electronic piano sound? How can you tell?

2 In your opinion, what impact does the use of an 'untidy' vocal sample have on the song? Give musical reasons to justify your response.

3 Why do you think the high string line in the first verse (0:39 onwards) is doubled up by a piano sound?

4 How many chords are used before the first chorus?

5 What effect does the major tonality of the chorus (particularly the first C major chord) have on the mood of the song?

6 Name two studio effects applied to the recorded parts in this song.

7 What studio effect can be heard at the breakdown (2:56–2:58)?

8 Is the drum part a live recording of a drummer? How can you tell?

9 How does the outro differ from the first time the vocal sample is heard (in the first repetition of the first verse)?

Further listening

- *Ambient* – 1993 (Instinct)
- *18* – 2002 (Mute)
- *Hotel* – 2005 (Mute)
- *Last Night* – 2008 (Mute)

Composing and performing tasks

Jazz

 12-bar blues composition

Take another look at how the 12-bar blues sequence has been adapted in 'All Blues'.

Create your own adaptation of the 12-bar blues chord sequence, considering the following points:

- It does not necessarily have to remain 12-bars long – for example, you may find that shortening it to 10 bars has an interesting rhythmic effect or that lengthening it to 16 bars sounds more musically satisfying to you.
- Experiment with a major or minor key (the sequence in the performing activity is in a minor key).
- Experiment with chord substitutions and extensions as described in the section on jazz harmony.
- Try throwing in the odd unusual or unexpected chord, not necessarily for a whole bar, but maybe just in passing.
- Consider the time signature you wish your sequence to be in.

Write a bass riff in your chosen key that lasts for one or two bars. The riff may either repeat throughout the chord sequence or it may change to accommodate the chord changes.

Either record your chord pattern or ask a friend to play it for you while you improvise over it in the same way as for the performing activity. When you find ideas you particularly like, stop and write them down (or at least make sure that you can repeat them and remember them).

Consider how you might extend your piece while keeping it interesting by using the lessons you can learn from the structure of 'All Blues'.

Consider what other instruments you might use in your composition (such as drums, piano, guitar, saxophone, trumpet, flute, voice etc). How might you develop the texture as the piece progresses?

Listen to some tracks from the albums listed under 'Further listening' for more ideas on how to structure your composition.

Improvising over a chord sequence

The following is a very famous chord sequence used in many blues, jazz and rock songs:

Bar 1	2	3	4
Dm7	G7	Cmaj7	Fmaj7
5	6	7	8
Bm7♭5	E7	Am7	Am7

The notes in each of the chords are:

Chord	Full name of chord	Notes
Dm7	D minor 7th	D, F, A, C
G7	G dominant 7th	G, B, D, F
Cmaj7	C major 7th	C, E, G, B
Fmaj7	F major 7th	F, A, C, E
Bm7♭5	B minor 7th flat 5	B, D, F, A
E7	E dominant 7th	E, G#, B, D
Am7	A minor 7th	A, C, E, G

This is an activity for two or more performers.

1 Learn to play the chords on the keyboard, piano or guitar. Don't just play them as block chords – play broken chords (sounding one note at a time) to make it sound more interesting. You could try playing them in different time signatures (4/4, 3/4 or 6/8).

2 Assign one person to play the chord sequence over and over (remembering that there are two bars of Am7 at the end).

3 Player two is to improvise on the chord sequence in the following way:
  a By using only the chord notes – whatever chord is playing at any given time, only notes from that chord can be used for the improvised melody line.
  b By using only the notes of the A minor pentatonic scale (A, C, D, E, G).
  c By combining the two approaches – this will be most useful when playing over the E7 chord where a G♯ sounds particularly effective.

4 Reverse roles so that both players have a chance to improvise. If there are more than two members in your group, you should assign one person to playing the accompaniment part (the broken chords) and take it in turns to improvise.

5 After you get used to the idea of improvising using a combination of the chords and the pentatonic scale, start to think about using short melodic motifs which you develop as you continue your improvisation. Also give thought to structure, the shape of the melody line and try to introduce a sense of direction to your playing so that it sounds as if you are trying to bring the listener on a journey.

Rock

Composing a song

You do not have to be an accomplished guitarist to attempt the following task – ask your teacher to tune the guitar to one of the alternate tunings listed below so that, even when you just strum open strings, you can easily play a consonant chord. Even if you are an accomplished guitarist, it may be interesting to use an unfamiliar tuning to make you listen more instead of resorting to familiar patterns on the fretboard.

1 Tune the guitar strings to one of the following alternate tunings (strings from low to high):

  a DADGAD

  b DGDBGD

  c CGCGCD

  d EBEG♯BE

  e An original alternate tuning of your choice.

2 Experiment with where you need to put your fingers to form pleasing chords. Note that normal chord shapes are unlikely to work (although some of them may make new, interesting chords). Start by just placing one finger on one of the strings and trying out how it sounds on different frets, then try two-finger shapes, sliding up and down the fretboard. Note down any interesting chords you find for later use.

3 Decide on a structure for your song. You may wish to use the structure of 'Grace' as a starting point, or even use one of the structures from the set works in AoS1, but it is always a good idea to adapt existing structures slightly to make them your own.

4 Using the chord shapes from point 2, decide on some chord sequences that will slot into the sections of your structure. Remember to include enough variety between sections so that the song remains interesting. If a chord needs to be changed to fit, even by moving one finger by one fret, do so. Your ears should be the final judge of what works and what doesn't. Remember how simple most of the chords are in 'Grace'!

5 Either choose a poem or write some original lyrics that seem to fit the mood of your song.

6 Say the lyrics over the chord sequences to get a feel for the word-rhythms and decide on the shape of the melody. You may decide to adapt your chord sequence to fit with the lyrical ideas. Gradually your melody will begin to form, but be patient. Be conscious of the leaps and steps in your melody.

7 Decide on any other instruments you would like to include in your song. Take another look at the analysis for 'Grace' and consider the texture of your own song. How can you adapt some of the ideas from 'Grace' to work with your piece?

Performing a cover version

One of Jeff Buckley's most famous songs is actually a cover of the Leonard Cohen classic 'Hallelujah'. Buckley made this song his own by singing it in a particularly emotional way and by adding an interesting introduction and guitar solo.

Choose a song that you would like to perform (either to sing or play on your instrument). How might you adapt this song for your instrument or to suit your own performing skills? In the Romantic era, composers such as Liszt would make transcriptions of operas for piano so they could perform famous operatic numbers in concert, so the idea of cover versions on different instruments is not new.

Consider the following points:

1 Can you perform the piece in its original key or would it be useful to change the key to suit your voice/instrument?

2 Is there a particular aspect of the song you want to draw more attention to than was the case in the original, or is there something in the original you would like to leave out?

3 Would the song work well in a different time signature (e.g., Limp Bizkit's version of 'Mission Impossible')?

4 Are there any interesting ways you can adapt the chord sequence (e.g., The Scissor Sister's version of Pink Floyd's 'Comfortably Numb')?

5 You might want to alter certain aspects of the melody (but remember to keep it recognisable) – for example, there may be some particularly high or low notes you might need to alter.

6 Do you have an idea for completely changing the style of the original – for example, performing a heavy metal version of a Bob Dylan classic or a folk version of a Hendrix song?

Experiment by performing the song (with other performers or on your own), changing your ideas to suit the situation as you go along.

Club dance

Composing a dance music piece

In the analysis of 'Why Does My Heart Feel So Bad?', you can see that the structure is rather simple – there are two basic ideas that are repeated. The most important thing to get right is just how much repetition is enough. Another important aspect of the structure in most club dance music is the breakdown, where the music (and listener) gets a chance to breathe.

With these points in mind, compose a piece of dance music using the following as a guide:

1 You might start by programing a drum loop or importing one from a suitable sample library (bear in mind that, for your GCSE, you can only receive marks for work you have composed yourself, so you will not receive any marks for any sampled drum loops). This will set the mood for the rest of the track. Listen to a number of different loops in different styles to get an idea which style is best for your piece.

2 You will need some sort of hook line – either a simple vocal line and/or a keyboard/ bass riff. Hook lines are always memorable, so keep it simple, short and catchy.

3 Dance music keyboard lines often move in block triads (see page 181 for more information on triads), so you should write a chord sequence that works with your riff or melodic hook and a way to play the triads in a rhythmic fashion (e.g., alternating between the root note and the third+fifth). Listen to the rhythmic piano playing from 1:18 in 'Why Does My Heart Feel So Bad?' for an example.

4 Write a second chord sequence and/or riff. One of the sequences and/or riffs will serve as the verse and the other as the chorus.

5 Look at the way Moby developed the texture in 'Why Does My Heart Feel So Bad?' so as to keep the structure interesting. You do not need to make your song as long as his, but you should use some of the structural ideas, especially the breakdown at just the right moment.

6 Experiment with different reverbs and delays on the keyboard, drums and vocal parts. Sometimes a timed delay effect can be an integral feature of a rhythmic part (e.g., the Edge's guitar work in U2 songs).

Creating a DJ 'megamix'

In this task you are going to create a DJ 'megamix'.

1 Listen to the songs from a recent chart music compilation album. Write down what the approximate tempo for each of the tracks is – count how many beats there are in 15 seconds and then multiply this by four.

2 Decide what the key of each track is by trying to find the tonic note (the note that sounds most like 'home' in the piece) on a keyboard while listening to the track.

3 Select five tracks that have very similar tempi to mix together into your 'megamix'. The songs do not all need to be in the same key, but you may find it easier to make a successful final mix if they are. Import the songs into either an audio sequencing package or a sound-editing package on the computer.

4 Listen to the tracks to see if there are any natural points in the songs which will allow you to fade one track out while fading in the next at the same time. You are not just going to play the full songs one after the other – this is where you use your creativity! Listen particularly for any features such as an interesting build up or fade out, a particular breakdown, an exposed line that might work while playing along with another track or a verse, chorus or middle 8 that might work alongside sections from another song.

5 On your audio editing software, cut the sections of the songs you have decided to use and paste them into a new track. Make sure you leave a little audio before and after the section you want so you can fade the track in and out smoothly.

6 Decide on the order in which your tracks should go. If they are in different keys, then you will need to be particularly careful about the running order. Listen through the raw mix – does it have a sense of direction and does it hold your interest? If the songs do not work in the order you have chosen originally, experiment until you are satisfied.

7 Line up the tracks so that the pulse of the new track falls in the same place as that of the track that is ending. If the tempo of the two tracks is slightly different, you will need to manually alter the tempo of one of the tracks to fit by using the appropriate tool in your software .

8 Decide on whether you are going to fade one track out as the next fades in (cross-fading) or whether it is appropriate for a track to stop suddenly when another begins. Use the appropriate volume editing tools on your software to achieve the desired effect.

9 Listen critically to your final 'megamix'. Do the tracks work together? Is the order appropriate? Is there a sense of direction overall? Is it too long or is there too big a variety of styles? Change the mix and choice of songs as appropriate until you are satisfied with the outcome.

10 Could you add anything else to your mix? For example, MCing, adding samples (individual hits, vocal samples or rhythmic loops). Be creative, but don't overdo things so as to take away from the success of your mix.

Area of Study 4:

World music

This fourth Area of Study looks at aspects of world music. This is a vast subject in itself, comprising numerous cultures and traditions.

Set works

The focus of this area of study will be to look at three aspects from music from around the world, taken from Indian, African and Celtic fusion traditions:

Fusion
Set work 10 – 'Skye Waulking Song' from *Nadurra* by Capercaillie

Indian music
Set work 11 – 'Rag Desh' by three different artists:
- A. Shankar
- C. L. Tanwar
- B. Wertheimer and S. Gorn

African music
Set work 12 – 'Yiri' by Koko

Capercaillie: 'Skye Waulking Song' from the album Nadurra

In the study of this set work you will learn about:

◆ the development of folk music

◆ the music of Capercaillie

◆ how the set work 'Skye Waulking Song' is constructed through an analysis of the music

◆ the key features in the music.

Folk music

Folk music is music of the people – hence the name 'folk' music. It is generally music performed and owned by the lower classes of a society expressing something about their way of life, how they used to live, or about local mythology. It is passed on by the **oral tradition** and is rarely notated.

Folk music is often played at informal occasions, such as jam sessions at pubs or impromptu performances at any social gathering. It is not important to be a trained musician to enjoy folk music – anyone can join in to the best of their ability. Sometimes an individual will display a particular talent for an instrument (such as a child who picks up a tin whistle and begins to copy what their father is playing), in which case they will be encouraged to participate in the instrumental ensemble, but even the most unskilled musicians are encouraged to sing along to the songs. Folk music is about everyone taking part, enjoying the music and passing on the tales of life, legend and heritage.

Folk music around the world

There is folk music in every region of every country, reflecting the traditions, life and myths of that particular corner of the world. In the US, folk music was performed by artists such as Woodie Guthrie, who learned songs from his mother and recorded his own versions of them. He in turn influenced Bob Dylan, who wrote songs in a folk style but whose lyrics were politically charged – he wrote lyrics protesting against the Vietnam War and other things that he felt strongly opposed to. Folk songs with political lyrics such as Dylan's were known as **protest songs**.

Glossary

oral tradition a tradition which is passed on by word of mouth or imitation rather than by written means

protest songs folk songs with political lyrics

Folk instruments

Folk music is traditionally played on acoustic instruments. Some of the most common instruments used in folk music include the following:

◆ accordion
◆ bagpipes
◆ banjo
◆ bodhrán – Irish drum struck with the hand or a double-ended stick called a 'tipper' or 'bones'
◆ bouzouki – a Greek string instrument, generally with four groups of two strings tuned in unison or octaves. It was imported to Ireland and developed into a very similar instrument called the Irish bouzouki
◆ concertina – similar to an accordion, but smaller
◆ double bass
◆ fiddle – the name given for a violin played in a folk music context

◆ guitar
◆ harmonica
◆ hurdy gurdy – a similar shape to a violin, but played by a wheel rotating in contact with the strings. The pitch of the strings is changed by a set of keys rather than direct contact with the fingers
◆ mandolin
◆ piano
◆ tin/penny whistle
◆ uilleann pipes – similar to the bagpipes, but using bellows operated by the elbow rather than blowing. They produce a sweeter and quieter sound than the bagpipes making them more suitable for use in an ensemble of other instruments.

Concertina

Uilleann pipes

Hurdy gurdy

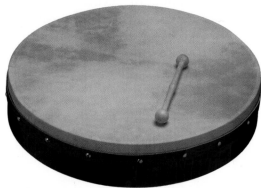

Bodhrán

Electric instruments such as the electric bass, keyboard and electric guitar have been used in folk music almost as long as they have in popular music. However, their introduction into folk ensembles has been met with some resistance from purists who feel that the music should always be played on acoustic instruments – folk music is also called 'traditional music', and electric instruments are not traditional or part of the folk heritage, so some people felt that the use of electric instruments in folk music was something of a betrayal of their values. An example of this was when Bob Dylan introduced the electric guitar to his set in 1965. At the time there was a revival of folk and roots music and his use of electric guitar was seen as a betrayal of tradition. With the introduction of electric instruments into folk music, there is often a cross-over of stylistic influences as well, such as the introduction of elements from pop or rock music (riffs, rock rhythms etc). When another musical style is integrated with folk music, it is called a fusion of musical styles.

Fusion

In a wider musical context, **fusion** is a mingling of more than one musical style or culture – it does not have to include folk music. This could be the fusion of Indian music with Western popular music (Bhangra), jazz with classical music, African music with Celtic music and so on. When talking about fusion, it is important to know what musical styles are fusing together in order to understand the term. Capercaillie are an example of a band that fuse Celtic folk music with the instruments and production values of Western popular music.

Glossary

fusion a mingling, or blending together, of more than one musical style or culture to create a new 'fused' sound

Waulking songs

Waulking is an ancient process used for making tweed fabric more flexible and windproof. A waulking song refers to a song used to make this process into a more sociable occasion. To keep everyone in time, the work was accompanied by song – waulking song. There would be one person leading with lyrics based on a well-known story, some aspect of village life or general gossip, and the others would join in after each line with some nonsense syllables (serving the same purpose as 'la-la-la' might do in a modern song). It was considered unlucky to repeat a whole verse, so the songs often had many verses with each line repeated once to form a verse, perhaps giving the lead singer time to think of the next line. Although machines are used now to produce Harris tweed commercially, the process of waulking by hand or feet still continues in some parts of Scotland as a means of preserving the tradition and as a social occasion for the women of the region. Waulking songs are still sung by these societies and collections of waulking songs have been produced in notation and recordings.

Capercaillie

Capercaillie were formed in Oban High School, in the West Highlands of Scotland, in the early 1980s by Donald Shaw (accordion and keyboards) and several of his friends on other instruments. The name is taken from a Scottish grouse (a native bird) that was at one point nearing extinction, but has since undergone a successful preservation campaign. There are hints of something similar in the way the band preserve Scottish folk music, often singing in the Scots Gaelic dialect. They were first spotted as a potential recording act while performing in the Mull Music Festival in Tobermory in 1983. Singer Karen Matheson (winner of a national Gaelic singing competition) joined them in 1984 when they recorded their debut album, *Cascade*. Fiddle player Charlie McKerron joined the band in 1985 and Manus Lunny (guitar and Irish bouzouki) in 1988. In 1988 the band wrote and recorded the music for a Channel 4 series on the history of the Scottish Gaels called *The Blood is Strong*. With this, they continued to cement their roots in the folk music scene and as champions of their national heritage.

Manus Lunny's brother, Donal, was already very well known in the traditional Irish music scene, but he also had links in the mainstream music industry. He brought some production skills to the band when he produced their 1989 album *Sidewaulk* – their first album to contain songs with English lyrics (all their previous songs had been in Gaelic). The decision to record songs in English brought the band to a wider audience and they started to gain recognition outside of the folk music scene. In 1991 they recorded the album *Delerium* with a new record label (Survival). This album contained an arrangement of a folk song 'Coisich a Ruin' – a 400-year-old work song that they brought new life to with their fusion sound of electric instruments and interesting rhythms. This became the first Scots Gaelic song to reach the top 40 in the UK charts. Even with this commercial success, Capercaillie have always resisted the record company's desire to push them in more commercial directions, always sticking closely to their folk music roots, even if they have experimented with modern treatments of the songs. As the 1990s progressed, they released the self-titled album *Capercaillie*, which did very well commercially, but was slated by the folk community as a 'disco' record because of the dance music-influenced percussion parts in the album. Unperturbed, Capercaillie have continued recording their own brand of folk music fused with the rhythms and production values of popular music, releasing albums regularly throughout the past two decades without compromising their own musical principles.

Background to *Nadurra*

Nadurra was released in September 2000 featuring Capercaillie's highly acclaimed touring line-up as follows:

◆ Donald Shaw: accordion, piano, synth
◆ Michael McGoldrick: flutes, whistle, uilleann pipes
◆ Karen Matheson: vocals
◆ Ewen Vernal: acoustic and electric bass
◆ Charlie McKerron: fiddle
◆ Manus Lunny: bouzouki, guitar, bodhrán, vocals
◆ James MacKintosh: drums, percussion

This line-up was acclaimed as 'the marriage made in heaven' because of their individual virtuosity on their own instruments, and also because of the way they gelled together so well as an ensemble, seeming to create a sound greater than the sum of the parts. The line-up for the band has gone through many incarnations over time, but this particular line-up stayed together for several years in a row, allowing them to build up a real musical partnership. If you listen to the opening of 'Skye Waulking Song', the sound of the band is almost that of one instrument, the musicians understand each other so well.

 CD2:4 Close analysis of 'Skye Waulking Song'

Listen to the recording on the audio CD and use your Anthology to study the analysis that follows.

Story and lyrics

'Skye Waulking Song' is a waulking song telling the tale of Seathan, son of the king of Ireland, from a collection of Gaelic folk songs by Alexander Carmichael. The original song was nearly 200 lines long and would have taken over an hour to perform, but the Capercaillie version uses just an extract from the Alexander Carmichael collection. The original song was a lament sung by Seathan's wife, telling of his deeds, his character, her recollections of times spent with him and his demise. The long lament is a way of grieving, of sharing her feelings and as a sort of therapeutic way of dealing with her loss. The full title for the song, as recorded by Capercaillie, is 'Chuir M'Athair Mise Dhan Taigh Charraideach' (My father sent me to a house of sorrow).

The full lyrics are as follows (nonsense syllables are shown in italics):

Hi ri huraibhi o ho
Chuir m'athair mise dha'n taigh charraideach
O hi a bho ro hu o ho
Hi ro ho
Chuir m'athair mise dha'n taigh charraideach

Hi ri huraibhi o ho
'N oidhche sin a rinn e bhanais dhomh
O hi a bho ro hu o ho
'N oidhche sin a rinn e bhanais dhomh

Hi ri huraibhi o ho
Gur truagh a Righ nach b'e m'fhalairidh
O hi a bho ro hu o ho
Gur truagh a Righ nach b'e m'fhalairidh

Hi ri huraibhi o ho
M'an do bhrist mo lamh an t-aran dhomh
O hi a bho ro hu o ho
M'an do bhrist mo lamh an t-aran dhomh

Hi ri huraibhi o ho
M'an d'rinn mo sgian biadh a ghearradh dhomh
O hi a bho ro hu o ho
M'an d'rinn mo sgian biadh a ghearradh dhomh

Hi ri huraibhi o ho
Sheathain chridhe nan sul socair
O hi a bho ro hu o ho Hi ro ho
Tha do bhata nochd 's na portaibh

Hi ri huraibhi o ho
Och, ma tha, chaneil i sociar
O hi a bho ro hu o ho
Och, ma tha, chaneil i sociar

Hi ri huraibhi o ho
O nach roch thu, ghaoil, na toiseach
O hi a bho ro hu o ho Hi ro ho

Hi ri huraibhi o ho Hi ro ho

See the table below for a full analysis of the structure and production of the song.

Section	Bar numbers and timing	Description
Intro	1–8 0:00–0:33	• Begins with a sustained keyboard chord hinting at the key of E minor. • The fiddle joins in, more for effect than anything else, with a tremolo note (rapid repetition of a note to create a 'trembling' effect). • After a few bars the drum part comes in along with a second keyboard sound (electric piano with a tremolo effect) working in counterpoint with the bouzouki to give a sense of movement. • The bass plays staccato, almost imperceptible notes working almost as one instrument with the bass drum. • By the end of this section, the chord sequence has been established as Em–G. • The time signature is ambiguous – it feels like it might be 6/8 or 12/8, but the shaker and hi-hat are playing every two beats, giving more of a triple time feel.

Verse 1	9–11 0:33–0:51	• The instruments continue in the same way as for the introduction, but the voice enters to sing the first line of the verse ('*My father sent me to a house of sorrow*'). • The voice sings the characteristic lilting rhythm, but this is working against what the other instruments are playing, so the time signature is still a little ambiguous.
Break	12–15 0:51–1:03	• The backing instruments continue with their atmospheric background sound, while the fiddle becomes a little more prominent, but still concentrates more on effects than on melody as such.
Verse 2	16–20 1:03–1:24	• The voice begins to establish itself as the main rhythmic feature, setting the 12/8 time signature.
Verse 3	21–24 1:24–1:41	• Continues seamlessly from verse 2. • The last line is sung unaccompanied, serving as a link between the opening section and the next section.
Verse 4	25–28 1:41–1:58	• The accordion joins in along with a strummed accompaniment on acoustic guitar/bouzouki. • Backing vocals join in for the nonsense syllables, leaving the main lyrics for the lead vocal. • The drum part is now clearly setting the 12/8 feel along with the rest of the band. • The bass part has much more substance than previous sections. • The chord sequence changes here to C–G–Em–G, adding some harmonic interest.
Verse 5	29–32 1:58–2:14	• The same for verse 5. • The accordion provides countermelodies to the vocal.
Verse 6	33–36 2:14–2:31	• The same for verse 6.
Instrumental	37–43 2:31–3:01	• The uilleann pipes solo along with the fiddle in a **heterophonic texture** while the accordion provides accompaniment and occasional melodic doubling. • The instruments (particularly the accordion) emphasise the second and fifth beats, adding some extra rhythmic interest.
Verse 7	44–48 3:01–3:21	• The chord sequence changes to Am7–Em–Em–G for one verse only. • The dynamics drop considerably, with all the instruments leaving room for the intimate vocal sound (with backing vocals on nonsense syllables). • All instruments drop out for the last line, adding to the contrast as the drums build up to the last verse.
Verse 8	49–52 3:21–3:38	• Chord sequence returns to C–G–Em–G. • Full band plays.
Outro	53–end 3:38–4:38	• Vocals improvise to the nonsense syllables as the instruments weave a counterpoint with each other. • The chord sequence alternates between C and G for the remainder of the song. • A long fade out brings the song to an end.

Important points to note

◆ Harmony in this style of music is less important than melody and rhythm. The harmony is very simple throughout the song (there are only four chords in the whole song), but the changes in chord sequence, while infrequent, are very noticeable when they happen, highlighting a change of section and mood.

◆ The melodic lines are played in the folk style – the instruments improvise around the melody simultaneously, sometimes playing a very similar melody in slightly different ways (creating a heterophonic texture) and sometimes weaving a complex, improvised counterpoint around the melody and scale (G major).

◆ The vocal part is sung using the scale of E minor pentatonic (or G major pentatonic) throughout.

The traditions of waulking song can be heard in the use of the nonsense syllables between each sung line and the repetition of each line of the verse. Also, the backing vocals join in for the vocalising of the nonsense syllables in between each line of lyrics.

CD2:4 Listening and appraising questions: 'Skye Waulking Song'

Now that you have listened to 'Skye Waulking Song' and studied the analysis on pages 131–34, answer the listening and appraising questions that follow.

1 What playing technique is used in the fiddle part at the very beginning of the song? Describe the sound in as much detail as you can.

2 In what language is the vocalist singing?

3 Describe the texture of the opening (up to 1:41).

4 Name two instruments that join in at 1:41.

5 Repeated nonsense syllables are sung frequently in this song. What was the original purpose of these in waulking songs?

6 Name the traditional pipes played in this song.

7 Describe the tonality of the song.

8 Why is this song considered a piece of fusion?

Further listening

- *Sidewaulk* – 1989 (Green Linnet)
- *Delirium* – 1991 (Survival)
- *Beautiful Wasteland* – 1997 (Survival)
- *Roses And Tears* – 2008 (Vertical)

Rag Desh

In the study of the set work you will learn about:

◆ the importance of improvising music as part of the oral tradition

◆ the rag as a form of Indian melody

◆ the tala as the basic cyclic rhythm pattern

◆ the musical characteristics of the different sections of a raga performance

◆ common Indian instruments and playing techniques

◆ an analysis of Rag Desh.

Indian music

Indian music has a long history, going back more that 2000 years. It is closely linked to Hinduism and religious philosophy. The many Hindu gods are often worshiped through performances of **raga**, both vocal and instrumental. In particular, the god Shiva is associated with music and dance in Hindu philosophy and there are many pieces in praise and honour of this particular deity.

The music of India can be divided into two great musical traditions:

◆ the music of Northern India (the Hindustani tradition)
◆ the music of the South (the Carnatic tradition).

The set work is taken from the Indian classical tradition of Northern India.

The oral tradition

Unlike Western classical music, Indian music is not written down as conventional musical notation. Instead, it is taught through listening and by word of mouth – called the oral tradition.

Indian families have a system of master–pupil teaching known as a **gharana**. A father might teach his son how to play through an intensive course involving listening and memorising. The son would then pass on his skills to the next generation and so on. However, playing styles will inevitably change as new techniques are added by subsequent generations and so the process is a duel one of consolidation and evolution of playing skills.

The Hindu god Shiva.

Glossary

gharana Indian system of master–pupil teaching

raga improvised music in several contrasting sections, based on a series of notes from a particular rag

Elements of a raga

The three most common elements or strands in Indian classical raga music are:

◆ the melody – made up (improvised) from notes of a particular rag. Sung by a voice or played by an instrument such as the sitar or sarod
◆ the drone – a supporting 'drone' of usually one or two notes provided by the tambura
◆ the rhythm – a repetitive, cyclic rhythm pattern played by the tabla drums.

Melody – the rag

The rag is the set melody on which the music is improvised. This is a cross between a collection of pitches and a scale. Like a scale, a rag ascends and descends, but the pitches often differ in each direction. Unlike the pattern of scales in Western classical music with the same number of notes, the number of notes in a rag will vary considerably. Some rags have just five notes, rather like the **pentatonic scale**.

Other rags commonly have seven or eight notes. Here are two examples: one an early morning rag called *Vibhas* and the other a night-time rag called *Kalyan*

There are over 200 different rags in existence in Indian classical music, and each has a particular mood (called a **rasa**) associated with it. Not only are there morning and night rags, but also celebration rags, seasonal rags and even some associated with certain feelings and emotions. Others are even deemed to be male and female! There is virtually a rag for every occasion. The chosen rag will be used as the musical material in a full raga performance, and the music is then made up by the performers. This technique of making up music without notation is called improvisation.

Drone accompaniment – the tambura

There is no sense of harmony in Indian raga music – the emphasis is placed purely on the melody and is therefore linear in concept. However, from the very first notes of a piece, you will hear a supportive drone played by the tambura. This usually sounds the tonic and dominant notes of the chosen rag. Its function is to keep a sense of tuning or intonation as a reference point for the melodic part, such as the sitar. Its ever-present sound adds texture to the music as a whole.

Glossary

pentatonic scale a scale built on five notes (penta=5) of the scale on the first, second, third, fifth and sixth degrees of the scale. In C major, these are C, D, E, G and A

rasa mood created by the sounds of the pitches in a particular rag

Rhythm – the tala

The rhythm provided by the small tabla drums is organised into repeating rhythmic cycles called tala. The most common tala is the **teental (or tintal)**, which is a 16-beat pattern (with each beat called a **matras**) organised in four bars as 4+4+4+4. There are many other talas with different numbers of beats per cycle, including 6, 7, 8, 10, 12, 14 and 16.

The complex rhythms sound exciting when played against this steady beat by both the tabla player as well as the instrumentalist (or singer). These rhythm patterns, called **bols**, are independent of the beat and can be inventive, displacing accents off the beat to create **syncopations**.

However, these rhythms must start and end together precisely on the first beat of the cycle, called **sam**. In a raga performance, this can lead to exciting competitions between instrumentalist and drummer as they attempt to copy and out do each other's clever and novel rhythmic ideas whilst still keeping within the cycle of beats – a sort of musical duel!

The structure of a raga performance

A raga performance usually has a structure based on defined sections called the **alap**, **jhor**, **jhalla** and **gat** (this is called a **bandish** if the piece is vocal).

However:

◆ some sections can be omitted, for example a raga might just have an alap and a gat.

◆ raga performances can vary vastly in time – up to five or more hours in some cases! Some performances can last all night!

The table below shows the main characteristics of each section of a raga.

Section	Tempo	Metre/rhythm	Musical features
Alap	Slow and meditative	No sense of metre (free time)	• Soloist 'explores' the notes of the rag, setting the mood, accompanied by the tambura drone. • Music is improvised.
Jhor	Steady/ medium	A real sense of a regular pulse is established	• Improvised music becomes more rhythmic. • Music becomes more elaborate and the tempo increases.
Jhalla	Fast/lively	Fast pulse with exciting and complex rhythms	• High point in piece. • Virtuoso display using advanced playing techniques.
Gat/ bandish	Moderate to fast	Tabla drums introduce the rhythmic cycle 'tala'	• The 'fixed' composition is introduced. In the case of a vocal piece, a song, in an instrumental piece, a prepared solo. • Musical dialogue takes place between the instrumentalist and drummer, as well as improvised flourishes on the prepared melodic line.

Glossary

bols in a tala, these are the independent rhythm parts that go against the main beat of the cycle creating exciting syncopations

matras individual beats in a rhythmic cycle

sam the first beat of the rhythmic cycle

syncopations notes accented off the beat. The weak part of the beat is often emphasised

teental (or tintal) common 16-beat (4+4+4+4) rhythmic cycle

Glossary

alap the opening unmetred and improvised section of a raga

bandish the last section of a vocal raga – a 'fixed composition' in the form of a song

gat the final section of an instrumental raga – a 'fixed composition' with some improvised embellishments

jhalla the third section of a raga – a lively tempo and virtuoso display of improvisatory skills. The climax of the whole piece

jhor the second section of a raga – a medium tempo with improvisation

Indian instruments used in raga performance

The voice

There are many different Indian instruments but the most highly regarded is the human voice, as in Indian philosophy it is thought that by singing it is possible to talk directly to the gods. All other instruments are ranked according to how close their sound or **timbre** resembles the sound of the voice.

The sitar

This is the most well-known plucked string instrument. It has seven principal metal strings of which two are used as drone notes. Below these are usually up to a dozen loose-fretted strings called 'sympathetic', as they vibrate when the top strings are plucked. This gives the traditional 'twangy' sound that makes the instrument instantly recognisable. The main strings are played by plucking with a wire plectrum. Two common playing techniques are:

◆ sliding between notes (called **meend** or **mind**) in intervals of quarter tones or less
◆ playing rapid scale-like flourishes called **tan**. These virtuoso passages of improvisation feature in later sections of a typical raga performance, i.e. the jhalla and gat.

Glossary

meend/mind the sliding effects between notes

tan the rapid scalic flourishes on the sitar/sarod or sarangai

timbre particular tone colour of an instrument or voice

The sarangi

This is smaller than the sitar and differs in that it is fretless and uses a bow rather than plucking the strings. A bit like a violin, the instrument has a gentle tone and is ideally used to accompany singers.

The sarod

The sarod is also smaller than the sitar but like a sitar it has two sets of strings to create the distorted effect common to the sitar. It is fretless and has a metal fingerboard so that the player can slide up and down the strings to obtain different notes. The instrument has a lower range and heavier tone than the sitar.

The tambura

A simple instrument with only four strings and a resonator. It is used to provide the drone notes to accompany the singer or instrumentalist.

Tabla

This is a small set of two drums of different sizes – the smaller one made of wood is called the *tabla* and the larger one made of metal is the *baya*. Both drum heads are of skin and the black centre circle is made of a paste of iron filings and flour. The drums play the chosen rhythm cycle, known as the *tala*, as well as improvisatory rhythms.

Other instruments

Many other instruments are used, the most common being two woodwind types of flute and oboe. The flute (**bansuri**) and oboe (**shehnai**) do not have keys like modern Western equivalents but a series of holes. The players skilfully managed to produce a wide range of pitches by half covering the holes and varying the blowing. Sliding effects, as on string instruments, are possible too.

Glossary

bansuri Indian flute without keys

shehnai a double reed Indian instrument, similar to the Western oboe

A bansuri, the Indian equivalent of a flute.

Close analysis of Rag Desh

Listen to the recording on the audio CD and use your Anthology to study the analysis that follows.

This rag is traditionally played at night. Rag Desh (which translates as 'country') is also known as a rainy season or monsoon raga. The primary moods (*rasa*) expressed are devotion, romance and longing, with origins in courtly love songs called *thumri*. The notes used in Rag Desh are based on the Indian system known as *sargam* in which the notes are named Sa, Re, Ga, Ma, Pa, Dha, Ni, Sa. The tonic note is C (Sa) and this forms the principal drone note.

The notes in Rag Desh are:

| Sa | Re | Ma | Pa | Ni | Sa | Ni | Dha | Pa | Ma | Ga | Re | Sa |

There are three versions of the Rag Desh for you to study and compare and contrast with each other.

Version 1: Anoushka Shankar (sitar)

Instruments: sitar and tabla

Structure: three movements – Alap, Gat 1 and Gat 2

0.00–0.55 Alap This is slow and unmetered. The sitar is unaccompanied and explores notes of the rag. Rhythms are fluid and free and sound improvisatory due to a lack of regular pulse. There is some decoration to the notes of the melody line.

0.55–9.27 Gat 1 The sitar plays the fixed composition (i.e. it has been previously worked on and thought out rather than spontaneously improvised). Decoration is added to this composition. The tempo is medium speed (called *madhyalaya*). The tabla enters at 0.58 seconds and plays the 10-beat *jhaptal* tala.

Jhaptal (10 beats): (2+3+2+3)

1	2	3	4	5	6	7	8	9	10
clap		clap			wave		clap		

The tabla player adds decoration to this basic pattern. There are also flourishes and ornaments in the sitar part. This comprises complex patterns of scalic passages including dialoguing with the tabla in short melodic and rhythmic improvisations. A *tihai* is heard to indicate the end of these improvisations. This is a short phrase played three times, across the beat, before finishing on the first beat of the cycle (sam). Examples of these section endings can be heard in many places, for example at 3.40-3.50.

3.55 The sitar starts to improvise in triplets (called *chand*).

5.02 Improvisations with four notes per beat. There are passages for sitar followed by tabla in alternation. The *tihai* is used to mark out the end of solo sections.

9.27 Gat 2 This is faster than the first gat and uses the common *teental (tintal)* 16-beat tala. This is grouped in four, four-beat units (4+4+4+4).

10.10 In this final part of the rag, drone strings are used on the sitar in strumming fashion providing a striking rhythmic effect called *jhalla*. The piece concludes with a *tihai*.

Version 2: 'Mhara janam maran' performed by Chiranji Lal Tanwar (voice)

Instruments: voice, sarangi, sarod, pakhawaj, cymbals and tabla

The pakhawaj is a large double-headed drum. Descriptions of the other instruments can be found in previous pages in this chapter.

This song is a Hindu devotional song from Rajasthan and is known as a *bhajan*. The song tells of tender waiting in longing anticipation of the arrival of Lord Krishna in the morning.

The words in translation from the Hindu are:

You are my companion through life and death and I cannot forget you night and day.
My heart pines for you and I feel totally restless when I am not able to see you.

Structure: two movements – Alap, Bhajan (song)
The tal used in this piece is the eight-beat Keherwa Tal (2+2+2+2).

Keherwa Tal (eight beats): (2+2+2+2)

1	2	3	4	5	6	7	8
clap		clap		wave		clap	

0.00–0.50 Alap Short introduction as the sarod player, then the singer, vocalises a melody in free time based on notes of the rag. This is a version of the chorus from the song.

0.50–end Bhajan This is the 'fixed composition', in this case a song in verse form. The tabla joins in at 0.50. There is a short sarod solo at 1.10 and then the sarangai at 1.22. The dynamics and tempo increase and the music becomes fast and exciting. The pattern established is a verse (heard at 1.32/3.04/and 4.50) followed by the first line used as a refrain (chorus), followed by more solos for sarod and sarangai.

Version 3: Benjy Wertheimer (esraj and tabla) and Steve Gorn (bansuri)

Instruments: bansuri, esraj, tambura and tabla

The esraj is a bowed fretted string instrument played sitting on the floor rather like the sarangi. Like the sitar, the instrument has a number of sympathetic and drone strings.

Descriptions of the other instruments can be found in previous pages in this chapter.

Structure: three movements – Alap, Gat 1 (slow) and Gat 2 (fast)

0.00–8.35 (Part 1) Alap This is a slow and unmeasured section. The drone is established from the outset by the tambura which plays the notes Sa (C) and Pa (G) (tonic and dominant). The bansuri (flute) then comes in, taking up notes from the rag itself. This develops from trying out the various pitches in short fragments to a more developed melodic part.

0.00–4.41 (Part 2) Gat 1 This is at a slow tempo. There is a lyrical unaccompanied melody for the bansuri and the tabla comes in at 0.31 playing the seven-beat rupak tala.

Rupak tal (7 beats): 3+2+2

1	2	3	4	5	6	7
wave			clap		clap	

The fixed composition then starts at 0.43. Following this, the music becomes more agitated and dramatic as improvisation takes over around the gat, while the tabla player also embellishes upon the original tala pattern. The bansuri then plays the gat repeatedly whilst the tabla player improvises around the tala cycle. At 3.32 the two instruments swap function, so that the bansuri improvises while the tabla accompanies. Several *tihais* are heard to mark out section ends. The last of these leads into the second gat at 4.41.

4.41–end (Part 3) Gat 2 A fast tempo (*drut*) in ektal tala.

Ektal tal (12 beats): 2+2+2+2+2+2

1	2	3	4	5	6	7	8	9	10	11	12
clap		clap		wave		clap		wave		clap	

This is a 12-beat ektal tala The tabla sets a fast tempo and the bansuri plays an elaborate gat containing wide ranges of pitch, scalic runs and slides. These fast scale passages are called *tans*. Several *tihais* are heard as the music draws to a close.

(CD2:5,6,7,8 & 9) Listening and appraising questions: Rag Desh

Now that you have listened to Rag Desh and studied the analysis on pages 140–41, answer the listening and appraising questions that follow.

1 All three pieces start with an alap section. Name three characteristics of this opening section of a raga.

2 Name two common playing techniques employed by the sitar player in the music.

3 What is the 'fixed composition' and where is it to be found in the raga?

4 Describe the role played by the tabla player.

5 Which musical skill is featured in the performance of Indian raga?

6 Indian raga music is described as linear in concept. What does this mean?

7 What is the role and function of the tambura in the music?

8 Each rag has its own particular *rasa* associated with it. What does this mean?

9 Name two other sections of a full raga performance.

10 Describe two features of the rhythm in all three versions.

11 How is Indian raga learnt and then performed?

ResultsPlus
Build Better Answers

Question: State **three** differences between the two extracts (an alap and a gat).

This comparison question is quite common and requires the use of topic specific vocabulary. The more detail you can include in your answer, the higher your mark will be!

■ A basic answer might be:
- The second extract has drums in it. No drums in the first extract.
- The second extract is faster than the first.
- The first extract has only a few notes in it compared to the second extract.

▲ An excellent answer might be:
- There is a rhythmic tala (teental) played by the tabla in the second extract. This rhythmic element is absent in the alap section.
- There is a regular pulse and metre in the second extract. The tempo is quite fast compared to the slow, unmetered alap section in free time.
- The sitar player tries out, improvises and experiments on notes of the rag in the alap. This is quite fragmentary melodically compared to the rhythmically complex lines in the gat section.

Koko: 'Yiri'

In the study of this set work you will learn about:

◆ the rich and diverse musical cultures of sub-Saharan Africa

◆ the social importance of African music

◆ how music is learnt and passed on through the oral tradition

◆ the key common techniques employed in African music

◆ rhythmic and melodic patterns and procedures in African drumming, balophon music and choral singing

◆ how the set work 'Yiri' is constructed through an analysis of the music.

African music in society

The music of sub-Saharan Africa is extremely rich, colourful and diverse. This covers a region of fifty different nations, each with its own musical traditions and languages. The music plays an important role in African society and is used to communicate many different feelings and emotions. Music is nearly always part of any social gathering, be it to celebrate the harvest, a birthday, wedding, funeral or even a gathering of chiefs. On all these occasions, the music is often combined with speech and dance as well as vibrant costumes to produce exciting and dramatic performances.

In the set work you will study, there is a strong emphasis on dance. The music is frequently linked to movement, which is regarded as an important mode of communication – as important as the music itself. The dancers dress in vividly coloured costumes replete with body painting and elaborate masks. Stories may also be related through body actions and mime. African music falls broadly into three strands:

1 drumming
2 choral song (tribal music)
3 instrumental music.

A traditional African drumming scene.

Common features of African music

Several common elements can be identified in the different types of African music, ranging from the drumming to the singing and the instrumental pieces. These are terms that you should have met before in some of the other GCSE topics, that is:

◆ *Repetition*. The restatement of a section of music. This might be just a few notes or a whole section of music.
◆ *Improvisation*. The process in which music is made up spontaneously, without the use of written musical notation.
◆ *Polyphony*. A texture featuring two or more parts, each having a melody or rhythm line and sounding together. This creates a multi-layered texture.
◆ *Call and response*. Simple form involving a solo (call) followed by a group answering phrase (response).

African drumming

In African music, the drum is considered to be the most important of all the instruments. It has been a means of communication, with certain rhythm patterns meaning different things. For example, a slow beat could signal a sad occasion, such as a funeral. The drum also has religious significance and is used in all forms of ceremonies, including weddings, funerals and the celebrations of the annual harvest.

There are hundreds of drums in African music and their names vary from region to region, and even from one tribe to the next. The most common drum is called the **djembe**. This is a single-head instrument shaped like a goblet and is made in a range of sizes to produce different pitches. The drums can be played on their own, but will frequently be heard in ensembles where there is usually a solo drum played by the master drummer and a set of accompanying drums. The most famous of these groups is called The Royal Burundi Drummers.

As well as the single-headed drums, there are double-headed drums that can be played using sticks. The drums heads have different sizes and will produce two different pitches – for example, the **dundun**. One of the other famous types of drum of West Africa – the **donno** – is known as the talking drum. This is held under the arm and played with the hand.

Glossary

djembe goblet-shaped drum from West Africa

donno hourglass-shaped 'talking drum' held under the arm and played with the hand

dundun double-headed drum (in several different sizes) played with sticks

Different sounds can be made on these drums using different playing techniques. For example:

◆ playing hands on the skin of the drum – different sounds are made when the fingers are open or closed
◆ playing hands on the wooden edge of the drum
◆ using sticks to create a sharp staccato sound
◆ stretching the drum membrane to produce a range of pitches, particularly on the donno.

A typical performance

African music is founded on the **oral tradition** and therefore has no musical notation. The master drummer stands in the centre of the ensemble and is responsible for directing the whole performance. He will be surrounded by other drummers and percussion instruments. The master drummer will signal to the other players when he is ready to start, often with a vocal cry followed by a short rhythmic solo to set the mood and tempo of the music. This is called a cue and the other players will then come in together to play the response. The response could be an exact copy or even a different rhythm entirely. This call and response technique is a main feature of tribal music. Cueing will happen throughout the music, creating a structure of contrasted sections. The music is essentially a series of variations on rhythmic patterns.

During the course of the piece, the master drummer will signal to the other individual players to perform a solo. This again will be a variation or development of the original rhythm pattern and will lead to further rhythmic development by the players. A steady continuous beat, called the timeline, is often played by the master drummer and there may also be a percussion rattle or bells, the most common being the agogo bells.

The complex rhythms played by the drummers create polyrhythms often with stresses that conflict with each other and with the steady constant beat of the timeline – creating **cross-rhythms**. The result is a **polyrhythmic texture**.

The music will usually increase in tension as the piece progresses, and sections and the tempo and dynamics will vary from section to section to provide interest and variety in the music. It is the responsibility of the master drummer to control the changes and to make sure that the music never becomes monotonous.

Some of these performances can take up to five hours or even longer. As well as solo drumming spots, which give the individual players a chance to show off their skills of improvisation, there is often movement and dance.

Glossary

cross-rhythms rhythms that literally cross the usual pattern of accented and unaccented beats creating irregular accents and syncopated effects

oral tradition music that is learnt by listening and repeating, and passed on orally from generation to generation (without being written down in traditional notation)

polyrhythmic texture a texture made up of many different rhythms

African choral singing

Sub-Saharan musical traditions are centred around singing. Many Africans believe that music serves as a link to the spirit world. Singing is a vital part of everyday life and is heard at religious ceremonies, rituals and celebrations. Singing unites whole tribal communities and everyone takes a part, regardless of ability.

The songs provide a means of communication. African languages are **tone languages** – that is, the pitch level (high or low) determines the actual meaning of the words. Therefore, the melodies and rhythms can be made to fit in pitch outlines to match the meanings and speech rhythms of the words of the song.

Common features of African songs

The common features of African songs are as follows:

- the basic form of the songs is *call and response* where one singer sings a line and the whole group then makes a vocal reply
- melodies are usually short and simple and repeated over and over, and usually in a scale of only four, five, six or seven different tones
- these melodies can be changed at will by other singers, so that what we end up with is a theme and then variations on that theme
- performers often improvise new melodies while the other singers continue the original melody, and it is common to have different melodies sounding simultaneously resulting in polyphonic textures
- the music can often be sung in rounds – for example, in Zulu choral music, individual voices enter at different points in a continuous cycle, overlapping in a complex and ever-changing musical texture
- harmony, which will vary from tribe to tribe. In some communities, the voices sing only in unison or parallel octaves, with the odd fourth or fifth. However, other groups will freely harmonise in thirds or fourths and can even sing in two or three different parts.

African instrumental music

There are many different instruments in African music and they vary from region to region. The many different types of drum are called **membranophones** (because they have a skin). The other main types of instruments can be categorised as shown in the table below.

Idiophones (resonant/solid)	Aerophones (wind)	Chordophones (strings)
Rattles (shakers)	Flutes (bamboo, horn)	Zithers
Bells	Ocarinas	Lutes (kora)
Mbira (thumb piano)	Panpipes	Lyres
Xylophones (balaphones)	Horns (from animal tusks)	Musical bows
Clap sticks	Trumpets (wood, metal)	
Slit gongs	Pipes (single and double reeds)	
Stamping tubes	Whistle	

Body percussion is also used, which includes hand clapping and foot stamping, as well as vocal effects such as shouting and other **vocables**.

The instruments are selected for performance according to the nature and mood of the instrumental music or song. These instruments have more complex tuning systems than used in vocal music and are capable of playing quite demanding rhythms and melodies. As in the drumming music, the melody often consists of several different parts which interlock and overlap to form polyrhythmic structures.

Xylophones (balaphones)

Xylophones, or balaphones, are one of the most common African instruments. These African instruments are made in several different sizes, providing a wide range of pitches from the deep resonant bass notes up to the high pitches of the smaller xylophones. The wooden bars are set on a framework, and to allow the bars to vibrate and resound, a membrane is needed between the bars and the frame. On your school instruments, this is most likely to be rubber, but the African instruments use naturally occurring materials such as orange peel.

Common features of African instrumental music

The five common features of African instrumental music are:

1 repetition (including ostinato)
2 improvisation
3 cyclic structures
4 polyphonic textures
5 intertwining melodies.

We shall identify all these features again as we look in detail at the set work.

Glossary

membranophones category of instruments that have a drum skin (membrane)

vocables effects made by the voice, using vowel sounds such as 'eh', 'ah', 'oh'

Background to the set work 'Yiri'

The musicians in the group Koko are:

◆ Madou Kone: vocals, balaphone, flute
◆ Sydou Traore: vocals, balaphone
◆ Jacouba Kone: djembe
◆ Francois Naba: vocals, tam-tam, dundun, maracas
◆ Keresse Sanou: talking drum
◆ Tidiane Hema: vocals, maracas

This set work comes from Burkino Faso, which is a landlocked nation situated in West Africa. It is surrounded on all sides by other countries: Mali, Niger, Benin, Togo, Ghana and Cote d'Ivoire. Renamed by President Thomas Sankara in 1984, Burkino translates as 'men of integrity' and Faso means 'father's house' and its inhabitants are called Burkinabe.

The themes in music from the region of Burkino Faso conjure up some of mankind's greatest battles in life, including the fight for survival and looking after the environment. In addition, the music focuses on creation, community celebrations and friendships.

In the set work there are three clear strands:

1 The balaphone ostinati – in combination, these produce a complex polyphonic texture.
2 The drum ostinati – in this work they play a relentless one-bar pattern (albeit with a little variation at the beginning of the bar of two semiquavers–quaver–two semiquavers–quaver).
3 The vocal line – this is a simple pentatonic call and response structure.

 CD2:10   Close analysis of 'Yiri'

Listen to the recording on the audio CD and use your Anthology to study the analysis that follows.

Timing	Analysis
0.00–0.18	Introduction The piece starts in free tempo with a high balaphone improvised solo played at a soft dynamic level, setting the scene in a **monophonic** texture. The solo comprises a melody in G♭ major with fast high and low rolls on every note. This is a simple and repetitive idea.
0.18–0.34	A moderato tempo is established by the first balaphone as a second (lower pitched) balaphone joins in at the end of bar 9 playing mainly in octaves. There is a strong sense of major tonality as the opening two notes of the melody are dominant (D♭) to tonic (G♭). The melody has a strong rhythmic basis too and is built on two-bar phrases. The second balaphone plays the same melody but with a few different pitches (see bars 11–12) in a **heterophonic** texture as the contours of the melody are roughly the same. The rhythms are mainly semiquavers and quavers with some tied notes.
0.34–1.09	Large talking drum, small talking drum and djembe come in playing an insistent half-bar ostinato of quaver–two semiquavers–quaver–two semiquavers. Balaphones continue to play a melody which is a variation on the first melody. The lower balaphone plays an ostinato figure in bars 17–20. There are occasional djembe fills in this section of music too. The melody includes syncopated rhythms and lots of octave repetitions on the tonic note of G♭ and the dominant note of D♭. From bar 21 the simple melodic phrases are repeated with slight variation in short two-bar phrases.

1.09–1.25	Chorus A1 Voices in unison. Melody is short, simple and repetitive. The semiquaver–quaver–semiquaver rhythm is a feature of the vocal writing. No harmony.
1.25–1.44	Short instrumental for balaphone (solo break) and drums play continuous ostinati as before.
1.44–2.01	Chorus A2 Voices in for second verse (music much the same as before).
2.01–2.10	Voices out, then solo instrumental break on lower pitched balaphone. Some variation in balaphone melody (continuous semiquavers on Gb).
2.10–2.45	Solo with choral responses A solo voice (call). A dramatic and new melody features long held notes and short punctuated notes on 'Yiri'. The drum ostinato continues. Vocal melody now incorporates triplet figures. This again is a variation on the original melody. The lower pitched balaphone plays the same ostinato figure we heard at bars 17–20. Voices (choral response) in unison to call at bar 63. New melodic riffs in balaphones based on original.
2.45–3.14	Solo voice (call) again featuring long held notes. Drums continue as before. Balaphone now plays a rhythmic three-note semiquaver melodic figure creating cross-rhythms. Bar 71 features the solo voice again singing yet another variant of the melody. The triplet idea, syncopated rhythms and semiquaver–quaver rhythms heard before in the music all feature here too.
3.15–3.19	Vocal response from the choir in unison.
3.20–3.28	Solo voice (call) with some varied balaphone rhythms in a solo break.
3.28–3.59	Instrumental solos carry on. New melodies on the balaphones. Short three-beat (one-bar) rest before we have the next chorus.
4.00–4.31	Chorus B1 Full choir in unison singing 'Yiri' with some short instrumental interjections to break up vocal lines.
4.31–4.45	Dialogue effects between voices and instruments.
4.45–5.20	Instrumental as a balaphone break. Riffs with variations. This is quite extended and is based still on the original melody with variations. This is more virtuosic with rapid figuration featuring octave leaps and semiquaver and demisemiquaver patterns.
5.20–5.36	Chorus A3 Full choir again in unison with instrumental interjections.
5.36–6.24	Instrumental ending played as a balaphone break. This is very syncopated and the drums re-enter at bar 153, one bar before the coda.
6.24 to end	Coda Five two-bar phrases mostly in octaves end with dramatic rests observed by all instruments. This has the sense of a strong riff. There are some differences in notes on occasions (see bars 154–end) creating an heterophonic texture. Drums provide the familiar ostinato from bar 153. The piece finally concludes with a single 'ting' on the bell.

In addition to the above analysis, there are also some constant features of the music that you should be aware of:

- the tempo is unvaried
- the beat is regular and unvarying
- the drum ostinato persists throughout the music
- the pattern of voices followed by instrumental breaks
- the dynamics are largely unvaried.

Glossary

heterophonic a musical texture in which several parts play the same melodic part but with slight differences in pitch

monophonic a musical texture of a single melodic line with no accompaniment

CD2:10 Listening and appraising questions: 'Yiri'

Now that you have listened to 'Yiri' and studied the analysis on pages 147–48, answer the listening and appraising questions that follow.

1 How does the piece start and what is the texture of the music at the opening?

2 Mention two techniques or devices that are used in the music.

3 How many different groups of instruments/voices feature in the music?

4 How is variety achieved in the music as a whole?

5 What is the mood of the piece, and how is this achieved?

6 Describe the structure of the piece as a whole.

7 How would you describe the texture when all parts are playing/singing?

8 How does the piece end?

Results**Plus**

Watch out!

Question (based on an extract from 'Yiri'): Describe the music played by the **three** different instrumental parts in the extract.

BALOPHONES...

DRUMS...

VOICES..

The key thing here is to make sure you describe the music as accurately and precisely as possible. You will have studied this work in detail and therefore you will already know these key elements of the musical texture.

■ A basic answer might be:

• The balophones play simple melody patterns.
• The drums play repeated rhythms.
• The voices sing a simple song that repeats.

● A better answer might be:

• The balophones play repeated patterns at various different pitches according to the size of the instrument.
• The drums play a simple ostinato for much of the piece. Occasionally they drop out of the instrumental texture for variety.
• The voices sing a simple call and response style song.

▲ An excellent answer might be:

• The balophones play ostinato figures based on the major scale of Gb. They also have short improvised instrumental breaks in free time between sections of the music. These solos also features fast tremolos (rolls) etc.
• The drums play a simple ostinato figure of two semiquavers followed by a quaver for much of the music. This provides a good, strong rhythmic backing to the piece, especially if it is to accompany dance. On occasions, the drums stop playing for short sections for textural variety.
• The voices sing in typically African call and response style. This involves a solo call which is then answered by the chorus in the response. The same music is used again for each verse, with slight pitch and rhythm differences to accommodate the word setting.

Composing and performing tasks

Fusion

 Composing a song with world music influences

A lot of modern pop music makes use of world music instruments to make the texture a little more interesting or exotic. Some pop music styles are fusions of a world music style with Western popular music (such as Bhangra and Celtic rock).

Try introducing some elements of world music into a song you have already written or write a new song which making use of folk or world music influences alongside your own favourite style of Western popular music.

Below are some possible examples:

1 Writing in a singer–songwriter style, replace the acoustic guitar with a mandolin, bouzouki or banjo and add a bodhran part and tin whistle counter-melody.

2 In a dance music style, replace the standard drum loop with some African drumming, ensuring that the drum part includes African rhythms (not just standard dance rhythms played on different drums).

3 'Dream Brother' by Jeff Buckley includes tabla as additional percussion to add a mystical air to the song. What world music instruments would add mystique to your compositions?

4 Adding an Irish reel as an instrumental middle section to one of your songs, but played on electric guitars to maintain the rock feel.

 Fair Haired Mary

Below is an Irish reel called 'Fair Haired Mary' along with some suggested chords. Practise playing the melody until you are able to play it quite quickly. If you play a chord instrument, practise the chord changes, especially the faster changes.

Fair Haired Mary

The melody is modal – it is in the dorian mode (it sounds like D minor, but without the B flats and C sharps).

When several members of the class are able to play the tune accurately, try playing it in unison. One or more of you may make a mistake here and there, but that doesn't matter, in fact, it's more in keeping with the style! When folk musicians play tunes, they may play the same melody all at the same time, but they each introduce their own subtle changes to the melody, so that it is not just one tune played in unison – this is known as a heterophonic texture.

What little changes can you introduce? Try some of the following:

1 Add a grace note here and there.

2 Where the tune is just a broken chord (for example, the first half of bar 2 is just a C triad), try breaking up the chord in a different order (for example, C–E–G–E instead of E–C–G–C).

3 Hold the root note of the marked chord instead of playing the written melody.

4 Try improvising around the dorian mode (all the white notes) for a few bars before returning to the written melody.

This sort of music works best with an ensemble of at least four or five people and is very rhythmic, so you may include a hand drum, a bodhran or just stamp your feet loudly to keep the beat. You will also need a guitar (or bouzouki!) to help maintain a driving rhythm.

Indian music

Interpreting *Rag Desh*

You have already listened to three versions based on the notes of *Rag Desh*. Now it is your turn to create your own interpretation.

1 Use the notes of this rag as a basis for a short musical improvisation on your own instrument. You will need to rehearse the music but you will not need to write anything down.

2 You should create two contrasting sections – an alap followed by either a jhor, jhalla or gat to demonstrate progression of the notes from the opening alap section.

3 Once you have finished your work and are happy with your improvisation, work with a partner to incorporate drone notes (played on a keyboard or cello for example). If possible, use a rhythmic tala (played on a drum) in the gat section.

Vocal rag

The task is to write a vocal rag incorporating an alap using improvised vowel sounds (vocalise), followed by a setting of the words below as a song (bandish).

1   Start by exploring the notes of *Rag Desh* to create short melodic phrases using only vocal vowel sounds (as in one of the GCSE recorded versions of this raga) This is exactly the same approach as composing an instrumental alap.

2   Set the following words about Kanhaiya (Krishna) to music to produce a song designed to be played as the final section as the 'fixed composition'.

Come clever beautiful one
Oh my darling Kanhaiya
We are meeting after many days
Well, now take what is yours, you clever beautiful one

3   You may like to do this task using Sibelius or another software program.

African music

 Improvisation

This is a group activity featuring improvising on the spot. For this task you are to create a tribal dance celebrating a gathering of chiefs and elders. There are to be the following four strands:

a) a drum-based one bar ostinato in 4/4 time
b) a pentatonic xylophone (or glockenspiel) part lasting for eight beats (two bars) using the notes C, D, E, G and A.
c) a percussion part featuring several different rhythmic ostinati (each lasting for two bars)
d) a vocal 'call and response' – based on the major pentatonic again.

Try to write your own words for the call and response, such as:

1st Call: Come on join in and celebrate!
Response: We all celebrate our new great chief
2nd Call: Today is our festive day!
Reponse: We all celebrate our new great chief
3rd Call: Clap hands, dance and sing!
Response: Long live our great new chief

Try to create an imaginative structure, perhaps based on 'Yiri'.
Below is a possible plan for your piece:

Introduction – drums set up ostinato
Section 1: Xylophone ostinati come in one at a time (and percussion)
Section 2: 1st vocal call and response
Section 3: Instrumental section (solo xylophone melody?)
Section 4: 2nd vocal call and response
Section 5: Instrumental section (drums only – perhaps a drum solo?)
Section 6: 3rd vocal call and response
Section 7: Instrumental section (solo xylophone melody?)
Section 8: All instruments

African moods

This task involves writing an African instrumental rondo (ABACA structure) for drums and xylophones in which rhythmic contrasts provide contrasting moods in the B and C sections.

This piece can easily be done on Sibelius or other software notation packages.

Section A must:
- be in 6/8 compound time
- be fast and lively featuring dotted rhythms and groups of three quavers
- include loud dynamics.

Section B must:
- be in 3/4 simple time
- be slow and feature only straight crotchets and quavers
- include soft dynamics.

Section C must:
- be in 4/4 time
- have a moderate tempo featuring off beat (syncopated) rhythms/swing quavers etc
- include moderately loud dynamics.

Once you have composed your piece, perform it to the class.

Preparing your coursework

In this section we will look at:

◆ the requirements of the specification
◆ the pitfalls to avoid in choosing performance pieces
◆ what examiners look for in a good performance/composition.

Paper 1 – Performing Music

For this paper, Edexcel requires you to submit the following pieces:

Requirement	% of overall GCSE mark	What can be submitted
One solo performance	15%	• Traditional solo performance • Solo improvisation • Sequenced performance • Realisation
One ensemble performance	15%	• Traditional ensemble performance • Improvising as part of an ensemble • Multi-track recording • Directing an ensemble

Traditional solo performance

This refers to the submission of a solo in any style that is seen as a 'standard' solo – it does not mean that you have to perform in a traditional style or in a classical style.

The solo performer must play a 'significant role' in the performance. Obviously a solo study or the flute part in a flute sonata qualifies as a solo performance, but so do the following:

1   If the part to be assessed has a particularly important solo – for example, the lead guitar part in a rock band where the guitar has a clearly defined solo.

2   Where the instrument does not have much in the way of solo repertoire – for example, the bass guitar or rock drums – but the part to be assessed is particularly to the fore of the ensemble and has obvious flourishes or fills to satisfy the 'significant role' criteria.

The situation as set out in point 2 makes it much more difficult to state categorically whether the piece qualifies as a solo or not, so it is best to ask your teacher to contact Edexcel if in any doubt.

It is possible to download MIDI files from the internet (there are many free collections available in addition to the commercial ones), mute the track you are going to play and record it as a backing track. This option would be much better than point 2 above as it leaves no room for doubt and means that even the simplest bass line can count as a solo without sounding incredibly exposed by playing it without accompaniment.

In fact, the Teacher's Guide states that if a solo piece has an accompaniment part, then it should be present on the recording submitted to the examiners. This is particularly important in situations where a violinist might perform a movement from a violin concerto, but waits for the eight bars rest, imagining the piano accompaniment and counting audibly.

If backing tracks are to be used, they **must not** contain the part to be assessed. This is most common in the case of vocalists performing their favourite songs – it is not acceptable to sing along with the original CD. It is perfectly acceptable to sing along to a professional backing track with the original vocal removed, or to use a MIDI file as the backing track (with the guide vocal track muted).

Your choice of piece for the solo performance plays an extremely important part in the process, as we shall see later in the chapter.

Solo improvisation

It is acceptable to submit an improvisation as a solo performance. This can be in any style, but must always be well thought through. Try to ensure that your improvisation:

For rock instruments such as electric guitar, bass guitar, keyboards and drums, Rockschool provides grade exams in the same way as the Associated Board and Trinity Guildhall do for classical instruments. At each grade level they provide backing tracks with the solo instrument removed, so are a good resource for performance pieces, even if you do not intend taking the grade exam itself.

- has a clear structure
- shows use and development of the stimulus material
- has very little waffle or padding
- demonstrates what you are capable of without going beyond your abilities
- is of a suitable length (does not go on forever or last for just two repeats of the stimulus)
- sounds as if it has been rehearsed – there must be no hesitations.

Your choice of stimulus is important. If it presents lots of possibilities for further exploration, then it is a good choice. If it locks you into one idea or tempts you just to repeat it over and over with little alteration, then it is a bad choice.

You need to practise the art of improvisation over the whole two years of the course if you want to attempt it as a solo performance option. For a traditional performance you have to practise the piece, but for improvisation you have to practise improvising.

A good idea would be to ask your teacher to provide you with an improvising stimulus at the beginning of a lesson, work at it during the lesson and play the piece to your teacher near the end of the lesson, inviting comments about how well you did. This way you will build up your improvising skills and confidence.

Sequenced performance

This is the music technology option for the solo performance. The following information refers to sequencing music that has been composed by someone other than you. If you are intending to sequence your own composition, then you should look at the section on realisation instead, applying the general sequencing principles described in this section.

Sequencing involves using a MIDI keyboard and a sequencing package to input and edit a piece of music. It is not necessary to be able to play the keyboard because you can actually input the notes using the mouse in one of the edit screens of your software. Pieces input in this way will require more editing afterwards to make them sound musical (rather than wooden and electronic), while pieces input using a MIDI keyboard will probably be more musical from the outset but require more editing for accuracy afterwards. You may use any software package as long as it allows you to do the following after you have finished inputting the sequence:

◆ edit the pitch of any note
◆ edit the start time of any note
◆ edit the duration of any note
◆ alter the dynamics – both the loudness (or velocity) of notes and the volume of the note as it is playing
◆ change the sound (timbre) of any part
◆ pan parts to different positions in the left and right speakers
◆ adjust the tempo of the song, both globally and as the song progresses.

The specification requires you to submit a piece of suitable length containing at least three different parts. Drum-kits count as one part only, but the piano would be considered to be two parts if the two hands are independent of each other.

As with any performance, your choice of piece is very important. Before you choose a piece to sequence, you should spend some time experimenting with the school equipment to see what instrumental sounds sound best. Make a list of all the sounds that impress you, and also make a list of the sounds that are particularly poor. When you choose a piece to sequence, it should contain instruments from the 'impressive' list and avoid those from the 'poor' list.

You do not have to choose sounds from just one sound source – it is acceptable to use various plug-ins and multiple sound modules at the same time if your setup allows this.

Avoid choosing a song to sequence where the vocal part depends more on the delivery and style of the vocal than the melody itself (e.g. where the singer has a semi-talking quality to their voice or often bends up to or away from the notes). It is extremely difficult to make a good job of imitating vocal parts like this on a computer.

After you are satisfied with the accuracy of the piece, you need to think about making it sound as musical as possible. Try to ensure that you include the following:

◆ dynamics as marked in the original score
◆ appropriate timbres

- use of controller 7 (main volume) to achieve crescendos and diminuendos over the duration of some long notes (only as appropriate to the piece)
- use of controller 10 (pan) to place the different timbres to the left and right. Keep bass instruments and lead instruments central unless there is clear reason to do otherwise (e.g. double basses in an orchestral setup)
- reverb (controller 91), but be careful not to overdo it
- varied articulation of individual notes – you should have accented the notes that need accents and observed staccato and slur markings etc
- appropriate phrasing – perhaps getting softer at the end of a phrase, applying a little *rit.* if required etc.

Note that Edexcel will not accept the following as sequenced performances:

- a piece containing parts sequenced by anyone except yourself (e.g. drum loops programmed by someone else or parts input by your teacher)
- a piece using the automatic backing feature available on most keyboards – a performance of this nature would be better submitted as a straightforward solo performance.

If you intend to submit a piece containing audio loops, it must be submitted as a realisation.

It is not advisable to use this option if you only have a keyboard sequencer available that does not allow editing of individual notes (i.e. you have to play in each line in one go and can't access individual notes to change errors).

Realisation

Sometimes it is inappropriate or just impossible to get a score for a performance. For example, if you sequence your own composition it would not be appropriate to submit it as a standard sequenced performance as well, because the notated score would always be 100% accurate (all you would have done was to just print it off!). Examiners recognise that there are some circumstances in which a performance itself is completely valid as a GCSE submission, but it is necessary to submit it without a normal score. For these circumstances there is another performance option called 'realisation'.

The following is a list of performances that will be accepted as realisations:

- Sequenced compositions
- Performances of compositions where it has been inappropriate or impossible to submit a score
- DJ performances (possibly including MCing)
- Music from the oral tradition (such as learning a tabla piece directly from a teacher rather than from written notation)
- Electro-acoustic sound diffusions (using a mixing desk to move recorded sound around different speakers that have been carefully positioned in a performance space)

For all realisations it is vital that you submit a written account of what the piece demands of you as a performer. You need to let the moderator know why they should be giving you marks for this performance. You can prepare the written commentary on your realisation in conjunction with your teacher to ensure that you write everything necessary to access the full range of marks.

Do not begin work on a realisation without first consulting with your teacher to ensure that it is a suitable performance option for you.

Traditional ensemble performance

An ensemble is where more than one human performer is playing at the same time. The following are good examples of an ensemble performance:

◆ a small chamber group (e.g. string quartet, brass quintet)
◆ the piano accompaniment for any solo instrument
◆ a vocal duet/trio/quartet etc with or without backing track
◆ a rock band
◆ a large ensemble where the part to be assessed is clear on the recording and is not doubled up by other instruments (e.g. first trumpet in a concert band)

The following are to be avoided as examples of ensemble performance:

◆ large ensembles where the part to be assessed is not clearly heard or is doubled up by many others on the same part (e.g. the soprano part in a large choir)
◆ a solo piece with a minimal accompaniment added (e.g. a solo song with a bongo part added for good measure).

The following are not examples of ensemble performance:

◆ the solo part in solo + accompaniment (this is essentially the same as a solo)
◆ one soloist + backing track
◆ two vocalists + backing track where both sing the same part or very slightly altered versions of the same line in different places.

The choice of piece for an ensemble is just as important a factor as it is in any performance, as is adequate rehearsal of your chosen piece.

Improvising as part of an ensemble

This option is intended for musicians who are used to playing in styles that usually require an element of improvisation – for example, jazz saxophonists who usually take a solo spot or lead guitarists who usually improvise a solo as part of their band's performances. It is not a good option to attempt unless this is the case.

The requirements are essentially the same as for solo improvising except that the actual improvising element does not have to be so long in duration – it is acceptable to present a performance for this option if the improvising element is a 16-bar solo in the middle of an otherwise fully notated piece.

You are marked according to your ability to improvise and to fit within the ensemble. As with solo improvising, you are strongly advised to actually practise improvising over the duration of the course, rather than just attempting it once at the end for your recorded submission.

Multi-track recording

This is the music technology option for the ensemble performance. To fulfil the requirements for this option, you must record at least three different parts onto a multi-track recorder (again, drums count as one part no matter how many microphones are used to record them).

Most schools use computer software packages such as Logic, Cubase and Sonar for this option at GCSE level, but others use stand-alone hard disk recorders and all-in-one devices which feature a small mixing desk, hard disk recorder, effects unit and CD burner in one package. The equipment you use is not nearly as important as the care you put into the capture of the sound sources, the editing process and the mixdown. It is possible to gain full marks in this option using almost any modern recording equipment if you pay attention to every detail of the process.

To obtain the best results, it is advisable to record each part with a separate microphone, either all at once (careful placement of the microphones will be required to avoid microphones picking up sounds you don't want them to) or one at a time.

It is perfectly acceptable for you not to play any of the instruments you are recording – you will be assessed on the quality of the recording and on your skills as a producer/director – you should not accept poor quality or out of time performances from the live musicians (be polite and diplomatic when you inform them that they need to do another take!). Similarly, it is acceptable for you to be the only performer on the recording, overdubbing all the individual parts.

It is also possible for you to sequence some tracks (for example, a rhythm track with some keyboard parts) and record some additional parts – this is counted as a multi-track recording rather than a sequence.

When recording, pay careful attention to the following:

- ensure the original sound recorded is as clear as possible, with no external noise getting onto the recording (place the microphones carefully)
- the wanted sound should be as loud as possible without distorting – if it is too quiet, then there will be too much noise in the final mix
- balance all the tracks carefully so that no instrument is too loud or too quiet, according to how important it is
- if you have a favourite instrument, be careful you don't make this too loud in the mix – guitarists often mix the guitars too loud and the drums too quiet
- apply effects carefully – don't overdo them or the recording will sound amateurish, and try to avoid 'novelty' effects
- use some panning to place instruments in the stereo field
- listen critically to your final recording a few days after you have mixed it. Is there anything you could have done better? If so, mix it again.

Do not try to be too ambitious with your recording – a simple ensemble of between three and six instruments/voices is sufficient. If you try to record too many parts, the mix may become muddy.

Directing an ensemble

This is another option in which you display your musicality in a way other than actually playing the instruments. You are marked on the final performance, so you are expected to have rehearsed the ensemble to the highest standard they are capable of. Do not take this option if you intend to show up before the recording and hope that all will be well – you are expected to have led several rehearsals of the group you are directing so that you can build up a rapport with them.

Take notes on what your music teacher does when they direct the school ensembles. What do they ask of the performers? How do they approach a new piece with the ensemble? How do they actually rehearse the piece to make it sound good? How do they communicate with members of the ensemble?

You should take the following into account:
◆ treat members of the ensemble with respect
◆ always expect the best from them
◆ insist on everyone observing all markings in the score (dynamics, articulation, tempo markings etc)
◆ listen to as many recordings of the piece you are directing as possible. Which did you like best, and why? How could you get the same results from your ensemble?
◆ make all your directions clear, both when you are conducting and when you are speaking to the ensemble
◆ remember that you are in charge!

General points about performance

Your choice of piece is probably the most important part of the whole performance.

Do choose a piece that:
◆ shows off your abilities
◆ is within your capabilities of playing well
◆ allows you to put appropriate expression into the performance
◆ is a suitable length for your standard of performance
◆ you enjoy playing (and practising) – it must motivate you to work hard at it.

Do not choose a piece that:
◆ is too easy
◆ is pushing your abilities to the very limit or makes you concentrate so hard on getting the notes right that you can't think about expression
◆ is too long (see opposite)
◆ is too short (see opposite)
◆ you dislike (you will not be motivated to practise)
◆ you can only play a part of (rather than the whole piece or whole movement).

Length of pieces

The maximum length of piece for a GCSE performance is **5 minutes**. Do not go beyond this time limit if you can possibly avoid it. Similarly, if a piece is too short, then you will be unable to put enough expression into it.

Difficulty level

Edexcel applies three different levels of difficulty to all pieces presented for coursework – standard level, easier level and more difficult level.

These levels do not correspond to particular grades – it is not accurate to say that grade 3 is always standard level. There are grids given in the specification for the different difficulty levels for most of the commonly played instruments. Choose your piece carefully, asking your teacher to guide you in terms of level of difficulty.

Grade 4 and 5 pieces will normally be more difficult, but so will some grade 3 pieces (although not all!). If you have reached grade 5 or 6, you might want to consider performing a piece that is a little easier than this (if it is still at 'more difficult' level), paying particular attention to interpretation. Once the more difficult level is reached, there is nothing else above it, so it is better to choose something you feel you can play particularly well rather than the most difficult piece in your repertoire. Similarly, many grade 2 pieces will be of standard difficulty, but some might fall into the easier level, so make sure you choose your piece carefully with the aid of your teacher.

Make sure that you have a good quality 'insurance piece' recorded as soon as you can in the course. Your teacher will probably insist on you recording approximately one performance a term so as to give you a choice of pieces for your final submission. There is a maximum of four additional marks for your performance if you opt for a higher level of difficulty, so do weigh up the benefits against the disadvantages of choosing pieces that are of a higher level.

Paper 2 – Composing

For this paper, Edexcel requires you to submit the following pieces:

% of overall GCSE mark	Requirement	
15%	Composition 1	• A composition or arrangement based on one of the Areas of Study (AoS)
15%	Composition 2	• A composition or arrangement based on a different AoS from Composition 1

What does 'based on' mean?

Each piece must show influences from one of the Areas of Study. It is not necessary to base your composition on one of the set works – it is the *titles* of the Areas of Study that your piece must refer to. For example, you could write a piece linked to Area of Study 3 (Popular music in context). This could be a piece of dance music or a jazz-blues song, but it does not have to be. It could be anything that has used 'Popular music in context' as an influence. So, you could write a rock song with some blues influences, or you could write a pop ballad because it clearly falls under the Area of Study title.

It is sometimes a good idea to write music that draws its influences from the set works, because you have been taught the composition techniques associated with them. For example, you will know how a minimalist piece is put together after you study *Electric Counterpoint*, and will probably have completed several short composition tasks based on it, so it makes sense to build on this knowledge and develop the short tasks into a complete piece.

However, you should not feel constrained by the set works. An exciting option would be to see how you could combine influences from two contrasting set works, or even from two separate Areas of Study. You could use material you had already written as compositional tasks for one set work and combine elements of these themes with the structural ideas of another piece – for example, Moby's *Play* album features blues vocal recordings applied to a dance music structure, or you could write a piece using modern instruments and harmonies in sonata form.

The composing brief

A brief is a set of criteria or instructions you must meet within your composition. It is not set in stone, so you may find that the brief develops along with the composition, but it is a useful guideline and a way to focus your creative ideas. The specification does not require you to have a brief for your compositions, but it is a good idea to start with one anyway.

The criteria set out by the brief should be within your ability to fulfil, preferably playing to your strengths. The brief should contain some statement about the Area of Study you are basing your composition on (for example, Area of Study 1 – sonata form), the instruments you are going to write for (e.g. a string quartet), possibly something about structure if it is not already obvious from the title, and anything else that you feel would be a good boundary to set (e.g. key, context, mood, texture etc).

By setting boundaries for yourself (or getting your teacher to set boundaries for you), it gives you a framework within which your creative imagination can run riot. Having a blank piece of paper can be very daunting, but if you create a framework by starting with a brief, then you can start to fill in the blanks, even if you decide to change everything later.

What makes a good composition?

The answer to this question changes depending on the style, but there are some general points that examiners look for in all pieces:
- development of ideas (melodies, riffs, themes, rhythms)
- how well the resources (instruments, vocals, sound sources) have been used
- a clear and well-balanced structure, appropriate to the style.

Development of ideas

There are many ways to develop your ideas, depending on the style of your piece, but some styles lend themselves more to this than others. You can develop a motif by splitting it up, expanding or contracting the intervals, keeping the rhythm but altering the melody (or vice versa), inverting it, playing it backwards etc. Even rock guitar-style riffs, which lend themselves to development much less than classical style themes, can be developed in many ways (e.g. playing in a different register, playing power chords instead of single notes, altering the way a chord pattern is plucked, changing the chords slightly, adding extra notes or techniques etc).

Developing pre-recorded samples can be more challenging because of the lack of control you have over the individual notes. As technology progresses, there is an increasing range of tools available for manipulation of samples, so there is no longer a restriction on the use of samples in your compositions. The main thing to bear in mind is that you can only get marks for any work that you have done yourself – you cannot get a mark for rhythm just by inserting a pre-programmed drum loop because someone else came up with the rhythm, not you. If you significantly develop the rhythm by chopping up the sample and using individual sections of it to create a new loop, then you can gain credit for the work you have done. In all cases where you have used samples, you should submit additional information with your composition outlining what you have done with the original material.

Use of resources

When you write for an instrument, you should use more than just one octave of its range. If you are writing for your own instrument, look at what other composers have done in pieces you have played. How did they use the full potential of the instrument?

Do not feel limited by what you can play yourself when composing – none of the great composers could play all the instruments they ever wrote for; they just understood the capabilities of the instruments (through research and asking musicians who were particularly good at the instrument) and had some idea of what they would sound like.

When composing instrumental parts, you should be aware of the following:

◆ Any techniques specific to the instrument (e.g. pizz/arco in string parts).
◆ Is the part possible to play on the instrument – are all the notes within range and have you avoided overlapping notes in instruments that can only play one note at a time?
◆ Is the part too difficult for the performers you have in mind? If so, is there a way around this without compromising your composition?
◆ Do the instruments work well together or do some of them overpower the others? This could be solved by doubling up the quieter parts – an orchestra has lots of violins playing the same part, but maybe only one trumpet per part.
◆ Have you made good use of the instrument's range? You do not have to use the full range of any instrument, but you do need to consider that when instruments are playing notes low in their range, they sound different to when they are playing notes at the top of their range.

Structure

Your piece should have a clear and well-balanced structure, appropriate to the style. This may be something less obvious than ternary form if you are writing a minimalist piece. A structure appropriate to minimalism may consist of a gradual build-up with a sudden change to a different combination of rhythmic motifs, which build-up in turn. Similarly, dance music may have a structure based on repetition and the gradual build-up of texture within a verse–chorus structure. Most styles will have a preferred set of forms that are used commonly by the main composers in the style.

Music is unsuccessful if it does not have a sense of direction. Most music has a series of highs and lows, with clearly defined sections.

Melody, harmony, accompaniment, texture, tempo, rhythm, dynamics

These are the optional criteria listed in the specification. It is a good idea to think about which criteria will be most appropriate to your composition from the very beginning of the process, perhaps working them into your composition brief. Look at the mark scheme for each of the criteria and consider how you may achieve the full five marks. The style you are writing in will have a major impact on which of the criteria will be chosen for marking the composition. For example, it is unlikely that an expressionist or serialist piece will be marked on harmony or a traditional piece for string quartet will be marked on the use of technology, but it is highly likely that a minimalist piece will include texture or a ballad will include melody in the optional criteria. This does not mean that you should explore one or two elements to the exclusion of all else – you should consider all the musical elements in your composition, but you should ensure that the three optional criteria meet the requirements of the mark scheme.

Time management

All coursework must now be completed under 'controlled conditions'. This means you must be supervised when you write out the score for your composition and when you record your performances and compositions.

Each performance and composition has a time limit of 10 hours and you must ensure that you complete the work within the time limit. This does not include time you spend preparing the coursework. You are allowed to practise for your performance unsupervised and there is no time limit on this, but when it comes to the actual recording of your final performance you have a maximum of 10 hours in which to complete the recording procedure.

Similarly, you are allowed to make drafts of your composition work, figuring out melodic ideas and possible developments of your motifs, but any work that goes into creating the final recording of the composition and final score must be done under supervision and within the limit of 10 hours.

You should discuss with your teacher any questions you have regarding specific circumstances as they will have more information on the exact terms of controlled assessment. Controlled assessment is not the same as examination conditions – you are still allowed to discuss things with your teacher and to ask questions while you are completing your composition work. It is important to ensure that you use your free preparation time to prepare enough material to make the most of your supervised time.

Welcome to examzone

In this section of the book, we'll take you through the best way of preparing and revising for the listening exam to ensure you get the best results possible.

Zone In!

Revising for the Listening Paper can be a daunting prospect: you may have studied some of these topics and set works some 18 months ago, so you are entitled to be a little rusty! Now is the time to get in the right frame of mind for revision. The fact that your course is conveniently divided up into 12 pieces in four Areas of Study lends itself well to a bite-sized approach topic by topic.

Here is Lucy's story on how she prepared to 'zone in' to the business of revision.

First, I made a timetable to help plan my revision. The structure of the timetable helped me to ensure a good work-rest balance!

I began by writing notes on each of the four Areas of Study of the specification. For this I used different techniques such as mind maps for key themes, and bullet points for summarising my knowledge. I left my notes then returned to them a couple of days later making sure I understood and recalled everything correctly. I summarised those notes further so that only a small number of key words and ideas remained. Finally, I summarised those notes again, so that I could keep all the information on a few cards.

Check out our top tips for avoiding common problems and to build your confidence prior to the exam.

UNDERSTAND IT
Understand the exam process and what revision you need to do. This will give you confidence but also help you to put things into proportion. These pages are a good place to find some starting pointers for performing well in exams.

FRIENDS AND FAMILY

You should let your family and friends in on your planning strategies too, as you will need them to cooperate to allow you time and space for revision. If they know what you are up to, they will support you and not see you as an anti-social recluse!

BUILDING CONFIDENCE
This whole process will help you to build confidence as you go along. The more you do, the more you will learn, and the more confident you will become. Work in small chunks and set yourself small, achievable goals.

DEAL WITH DISTRACTIONS

Distractions come in all shapes and forms. This might simply include your home environment and demands made on you by brothers, sisters, parents and relatives! If you have a study area at home, perhaps in your bedroom or a study, then use it! Find a quiet place – the local library if need be. Silence can be guaranteed and the actual process of *going* to a place for this purpose will help you. If a library is not local to you, your school library will suffice.

COMPARTMENTALISE

Having to juggle many issues including work, family and other commitments is not easy. You can help to sort things out by mentally putting all of these things into an imagined box at the start of the revision process and mentally locking it, then opening it again at the end of your revision session.

Planning Zone

Preparation is vital. Success in anything in life is often related to planning and preparing in advance. If you are well-prepared, then you should enjoy a stress-free experience. Here are some tips for creating a great personal revision plan.

In the first place, you should be aware of the parts of the subject you have found easy as well as difficult. Write down your strengths and weaknesses. Go through each of the 12 prescribed set works and decide which you feel fall into the 'strong' and 'weak' camps. Gather other evidence to help you decide on this from mock examination results, tests, etc taken from over the two years of the GCSE Music course.

You should build in more time to deal with your 'weaker' areas. Perhaps when you create the plan you could ensure that you put down both a strong topic with a weaker one so that you are not overwhelmed with a heavy demand from the outset!

Next, create your plan!

Here are some useful pointers to help you structure the plan. Please feel free to edit to your own needs!

MAY 2011

SUNDAY	MONDAY	TUES

1 Draw up a calendar of all the dates and times from when you will start and finish your revision.

2 Find out the examination date and write this in as the focal end point of your revision plan.

3

8 Plan enough revision slots to cover all the set works and the background information. It is best to use short 30-minute slots with breaks. Long revision periods are less effective, as concentration levels begin to fall.

9 Break your revision down into smaller 'bite-size' chunks and sections. For example, in the first set work, you need to look at the features of Baroque style, what an oratorio is, the life of Handel, background to *Messiah*, the analysis of the set chorus, features of the choral style in the music, different musical textures and so on.

The final essay question of the Listening Paper needs separate revision notes based on the musical elements of melody, harmony, tonality, texture, rhythm and structure. Why not create an A3-sized table with these headings and complete as you revise each set work!

Finally follow your plan! The plan will only be successful if you stick to it. Once you get behind or miss a few sessions, it will become an uphill struggle. Keep ahead of the game and enjoy a stress-free revision!

24 EXAM DAY!

3

and spend long sessions trying to cram information into their heads. However, if you have stuck to your plan, this should not be a concern for you. Here are some last minute learning tips from Lucy again.

So, if you follow Lucy's advice it should help you to control your nerves and stay in charge! In summary then, the final revision should be focused on:

- revision 'short cut' cards covering the key facts and musical vocabulary associated with the 12 set works

- running though your mind mapping plans as a secondary back up

- looking over your chart of the key musical elements in each work for the final essay question.

To have the cards with you just before the exam is very reassuring because you can scan down your key words and feel confident before you enter the exam room. I actually found that discussing with friends was also very helpful because they are bound to have had a slightly different slant on their revision strategies. However, just keeping calm about the exams is the most important thing! Getting worked up won't help – there is more to life than taking exams!

Exam Zone

What to expect in the exam paper

The exam paper is divided into two sections.

- Section A contains eight short questions requiring you to identify musical features from the chosen extracts.

- In Section B, you will answer one set work question (from a choice of two) in more depth. This is an extended writing question.

Section A: Questions 1-8 (68 marks in total)

The main types of questions in this section can be summarised as:

- multiple choice

- single-word answers

- short responses (one sentence)

- responses involving notation

- free response questions

- tables for completion

- multi-section questions.

Each question will be made up of a combination of these types of question in varying proportions year on year.

Questions that ask students to identify key musical features

These questions assess your ability to listen to an extract from a set work and comment on the musical features you can hear. Question types include one-word or two-word answers, multiple choice, and comparisons of extracts. Answers are short and generally 'right or wrong'. These questions will be based around the following aspects of the set works:

- the musical elements (pitch, duration, dynamics, tempo, timbre, texture, structure)
- identifying instruments and groups (families) of instruments
- identifying musical and melodic features (ornaments, ostinati, riffs, imitation, pedals and sequences)
- rhythm features (syncopation, swung rhythms, dotted rhythms)
- keys (major, minor, modal, pentatonic, chromatic and atonal).

Hint: make a list of these features in each of the 12 set works as a revision exercise.

Here are some examples of these types of questions.

Is the music in this extract in a major or minor key?

How many beats are there in each bar?

What scale is the vocal melody based on?

| Minor | Major | Modal | Pentatonic |

Apart from the instruments playing, state *two* other differences between the two extracts.

Questions that ask students to place music in a wider context

These questions require you to place the music in a social and historical context. You need to know about the work as a whole, its historical background, the composer and so on. For example, related to the set work on Mozart's Symphony No. 40 first movement, you need to know about the features of the Classical style, the symphony, the structure of sonata form, the classical orchestra etc.

Answering these questions requires knowledge beyond that which is on the CD. The answers are short or multiple-choice types.

Here are some examples of questions.

The first main section in a sonata form movement is called the **exposition**. Name the other two sections?

This piano prelude was composed in the Romantic period. State **four** key features associated with Romantic music.

In which decade was this music composed?

This piece is based on traditional folk song. **Who** would have originally performed the folk song and **what** would they have been doing?

Questions that ask students to express and justify opinions

In these questions, you will have to give reasons and justify opinions on music. These responses will require longer answers of two or three sentences.

Here are some examples of questions.

> Give **two musical** reasons why you like or dislike this piece of music?

> How does the composer create a mood of excitement and anticipation in the music?

Hint: when you are asked the 'like' or 'dislike' question, you must make sure that your answer has *musical* reasons attached to it. A poor answer would be '*I dislike it because it is boring*'. An improved answer would be '*I dislike the music because the rhythms are too repetitive*'.

Musical dictation questions

The exam will always contain at least one exercise in dictation. This will either take the form of the completion of a few notes of melody and/or a short rhythm. The other type of exercise would be the completion of a chord pattern or sequence. These questions will always be based on the featured extract from the set work concerned.

Hint: make sure that you write out and learn all the main themes from the set works, as they could well feature in dictation exercises.

Section B: Questions 9-10

This type of question can be summarised as extended writing. You will have to answer **either** question 9 **or** question 10. The quality of written communication (QWC) will be assessed, so ensure that you check your spelling, grammar and punctuation! To achieve a top mark you need to use accurate and extensive music vocabulary.

Questions in section B are divided into three sub-sections: (a), (b) and (c). Questions (a) and (b) are two short response questions in which you are required to place the work in a wider context. For example:

> 'Why Does My Heart Feel So Bad?' by Moby
>
> (a) In which year was this track released?
>
> (b) What style is this piece written in?

Part (c) is the long answer question, testing your ability to answer questions relating to:

● how the musical elements are used by the composer (pitch, duration, dynamics, tempo, timbre, texture, structure)

● how the instruments are used

● other musical features particular to the style/genre of the set work.

Hint: write out bullet points for each of the 12 pieces under headings such as structure, harmony, texture, instruments, melody, technology and samples (if relevant), dynamics and tempo.

Meet the exam paper

The illustration shows the front cover of the exam paper. These instructions, information and advice will always appear on the front of the paper. It is worth reading it carefully now. Check you understand it. Now is a good opportunity to ask your teacher about anything you are not sure of here.

Print your surname here, and your other names afterwards.

Fill in your school centre name and number here.

The exam will last for 1 hour 30 minutes. All announcements willl be made on the CD and you will be guided through the examination by the announcer on the CD. You will also be given 10 minutes reading time before the examination begins to read through the paper.

Note that the quality of your written communication will also be marked. Take particular care to present your thoughts and work at the highest standard you can for maximum marks.

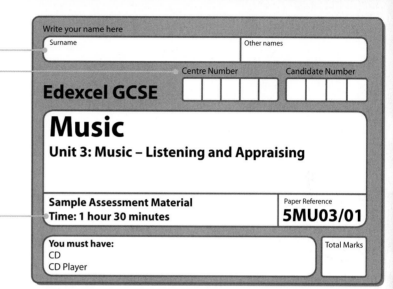

Write your name here

Surname

Other names

Centre Number

Candidate Number

Edexcel GCSE

Music

Unit 3: Music – Listening and Appraising

Sample Assessment Material
Time: 1 hour 30 minutes

Paper Reference
5MU03/01

You must have:
CD
CD Player

Total Marks

Instructions

- Use **black** ink or ball-point pen.
- **Fill in the boxes** at the top of this page with your name, centre number and candidate number.
- Answer **all** the questions in Section A and **one** question from Section B
- Answer the questions in the spaces provided
  – *there may be more space than you need.*

Information

- The total mark for this paper is 80.
- The marks for **each** question are shown in brackets
  – *use this as a guide as to how much time to spend on each question.*
- Questions labelled with an **asterisk** (*) are ones where the quality of your written communication will be assessed
  – *you should take particular care with your spelling, punctuation and grammar, as well as the clarity of expression, on these questions.*

Advice

- Read each question carefully before you start to answer it.
- Keep an eye on the time.
- Check your answers if you have time at the end.

Turn over ▶

N35690A
©2008 Edexcel Limited.
3/3/

N 3 5 6 9 0 A 0 1 1 6

edexcel ::::
advancing learning, changing lives

Edexcel GCSE in Music   Sample Assessment Materials   © Edexcel Limited 2008   3

Zone Out

This section provides answers to the most common questions students have about what happens after they complete their exams. For much more information, visit www.examzone.co.uk

About your grades

Whether you have done better than, worse than, or just as you expected, your grades are the final measure of your performance on your course and in the exams. On this page we explain some of the information that appears on your results slip and tell you what to do if you think something is wrong. We answer the most popular questions about grades and look at some of the options that face you in August.

When will my results be published?

Results are published on the third Thursday in August each year.

Can I get my results online?

Visit www.resultsplusdirect.co.uk where you will find detailed student results information including the 'Edexcel Gradeometer' which demonstrates how close you were to the nearest grade boundary.

I haven't done as well as I expected. What can I do now?

First of all, talk to your teacher who will have the breakdown of marks for each of the three components of the GCSE. Your teacher is the person who best knows what grade you are capable of achieving. If you feel that there is something wrong with your grade, the school or college can apply for a re-mark immediately. These are known as EARS – Enquiries about Results. However, a word of caution – marks can go up as well as down in a re-mark and your overall grade can be affected!

How do my grades compare with those of everybody else who sat this exam?

You can compare your results with those of others in the UK who have completed the same examination using the information on our website at:

www.edexcel.org.uk/sfc/feschools/stats/

What happens if I was ill over the period of my examinations?

If you become ill before or during the examination period, you are eligible for special consideration. This also applies if you have been affected by an accident, bereavement or serious disturbance during an examination.

If my school has requested special consideration for me, is this shown on my Statement of Results?

No, special consideration is not shown on the results slip, but will be shown on a subject mark report that is sent to your school or college. If you want to know whether special consideration was requested for you, you should ask your examinations officer.

Can I have a re-mark of my examination paper?

Yes, this is possible, but remember that only your school or college can apply for a re-mark. You should remember that very few re-marks result in a change to a grade. Check, too, the closing date for application for a re-mark.

When I asked for a re-mark of my paper, my subject grade went down. What can I do?

Grades can go up as well as down, so be prepared for this. Once a re-mark has been done, the only way to improve your grade is to take the examination again. In the case of music, this can only be done in the May (Summer) session.

For much more information, visit www.examzone.co.uk.

Understanding music

In this topic you will learn about:

◆ clefs, note names, tones and semitones, flats and sharps, note values, dotted notes and rests
◆ time signatures and key signatures
◆ scales – modes, major, minor, pentatonic, chromatic and whole-tone scales
◆ degrees of the scale and intervals
◆ simple harmony – triads and inversions, the primary triads, the secondary triads and cadences
◆ musical devices and the elements of music.

This chapter is intended for reference, for you to dip into during your GCSE course.

Staff and clefs

The two most common **clefs** that you will come across are:

◆ the **treble (or G) clef**
◆ the **bass (or F) clef**.

Two other clefs that you may come across are:

◆ the **alto C clef**
◆ the **tenor C clef**.

The clefs are written on a five-line **stave** (or **staff**), as shown below.

G
Treble clef

F
Bass clef

C
Alto clef

C
Tenor clef

The instruments that use these different clefs depend on their pitch range.

◆ Treble clef instruments include the piccolo, flute, clarinet, oboe, trumpet (cornet), French horn, saxophone, violin, recorder, soprano and alto voices.
◆ Bass clef instruments include the bassoon, tuba, cello, double bass and bass voice.

Glossary

alto C clef clef used mainly by the viola

bass (or F clef) clef that fixes the note F on the fourth line of the stave

clef French for key, clefs fix a particular note on the stave

staff/stave the five parallel lines upon which music notation is written

tenor C clef used in conjunction with the bass clef for high notes on the bassoon, trombone, cello and double bass

treble (or G clef) clef that fixes the note G on the second line of the stave. The treble clef is used for high-pitched instruments and voices

◆ The alto C clef is mainly used for the viola.
◆ The tenor C clef is used in conjunction with the bass clef for the high notes on the bassoon, trombone, cello and double bass.

Note names

The musical language uses the letter names **A**, **B**, **C**, **D**, **E**, **F** and **G**, and then starts with A again. The distance between one A and the next A is eight notes. This is called an **octave** (oct = 8). The following extract shows the notes on the lines and spaces of the treble and bass clefs.

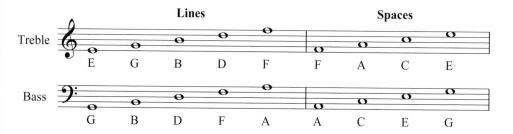

Tones and semitones, flats and sharps

The distance between two notes is called a **tone**. The two exceptions to this are between the notes E to F and B to C. In these cases, the distance between the notes is only a **semitone**. You can see this in the picture of a keyboard below.

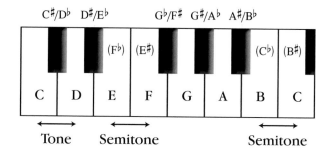

If we raise a note by a semitone, we sharpen the note. If we lower a note by a semitone, we flatten it.

As the distance between the notes E to F and B to C is a semitone already, if we sharpen the note E, it becomes E♯, which is also the note F. In the same way, F♭ is also E, B♯ is C, and C♭ is B.

Glossary

octave the interval of eight notes – for example, C to C eight notes higher

semitone half a tone – the distance between a white note and an adjacent black note

tone interval of two semitones – for example, F to G is made up of F to F♯ (a semitone) and F♯ to G (a semitone)

Note values

The different note values all stem from the longest note, called the **breve**, lasting for eight beats. The diagram below shows how the division of the breve includes the **semibreve**, minim, crotchet, quaver and semiquaver.

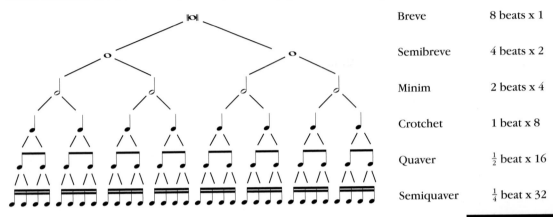

Breve	8 beats x 1
Semibreve	4 beats x 2
Minim	2 beats x 4
Crotchet	1 beat x 8
Quaver	$\frac{1}{2}$ beat x 16
Semiquaver	$\frac{1}{4}$ beat x 32

Dotted notes

The effect of placing a dot after a note increases the length of the original note by half as much again (that is, an extra 50 per cent).

Therefore:

◆ a dotted crotchet = a crotchet (one beat) plus half the value of the original note (half a beat) equals one-and-a-half beats

◆ a dotted minim = a minim (two beats) plus half the value of the original note (one beat) equals three beats

◆ a dotted quaver = a quaver (half a beat) plus half the value of the original note (quarter of a beat) equals three-quarters of a beat.

Glossary

breve literally 'a breath' – a long note of eight crotchet beats duration

semibreve long note lasting for four crotchet beats

Rests

Rests that provide silence in music are just as important as sound created by notes.

The common rests are:

| BREVE | SEMIBREVE | MINIM | CROTCHET | QUAVER | SEMIQUAVER | DEMISEMIQUAVER |

A dotted rest has the same effect as a dotted note – for example, a dotted crotchet rest = a crotchet (one beat) plus half again, that is, a quaver (half a beat) = one-and-a-half beats.

Time signatures

The two figures at the start of a piece of music are called the **time signature**. The top figure is the number of beats in each bar. Two beats in the bar is called duple, three is triple and four is quadruple.

Glossary

time signature the two numbers at the beginning of a piece of music. The top number refers to the number of beats per bar and the bottom figure indicates the type of beat

The bottom figure is like a code to represent the type of beat – for example, a 4 represents the crotchet. Therefore 4/4 means there are four crotchet beats in each bar, that is:

4 = number of beats
4 = type of beat

The important thing is to know what the bottom figure represents. The common ones are:

2 = minim   4 = crotchet   8 = quaver   16 = semiquaver.

Simple and compound time signatures

Time signatures where the beat can be divided into two are **simple time signatures**. Time signatures where the beat can be divided into three are **compound time signatures**.

The beat is divided into two, so it is simple time. As there are two beats in each bar, it is simple duple time. So 3/4 = simple triple and 4/4 = simple quadruple.

The beat is divided into three, so it is compound time. As there are two beats in each bar, it is compound duple. So 9/8 = compound triple and 12/8 = compound quadruple.

Key signatures

Music can be written in a variety of different keys, both **major** and **minor**. Each major key has its own related minor key with the same key signature – for example C major has A minor as its relative minor.

The diagram opposite shows all the major and minor keys. Each key is five notes apart, and this is called the circle of fifths, as eventually you arrive back at the start. The order of sharps proceeds in a clockwise direction (C, G, D and so on) and the flats in an anti-clockwise direction from C (C, F, B and so on). The diagram below will provide a useful reference chart for you.

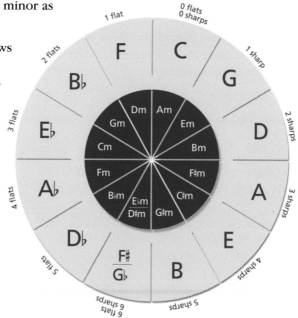

> ## Glossary
>
> **compound time signature** a time signature where the beat is dotted and subdivides into groups of three, as in 6/8 which has two dotted crotchet beats, each of which comprises three quavers
>
> **major** Western tonal music in bright sounding keys. A major key has four semitones between the first and third notes (C–E)
>
> **minor** Western tonal music in solemn sounding keys. A minor key has three semitones between the first and third notes (C–Eb)
>
> **simple time signature** a time signature where the beat can be divided into two, such as 2/4 which has two crotchet beats, each made up of two quavers

Order of sharps and flats

Scales

There are many types of scale and you should have an understanding of:

◆ modes
◆ major
◆ minor
◆ pentatonic
◆ chromatic
◆ whole-tone scales.

Modes

Modes came into use a long time before the major/minor scales. These modes are easy to understand at the piano or keyboard. They are basically constructed of eight consecutive notes but only using the white keys, for example take the notes D to D, that is, D, E, F, G, A, B, C and D. This is a mode called the dorian mode and each of these modes has a different name, as can be seen below.

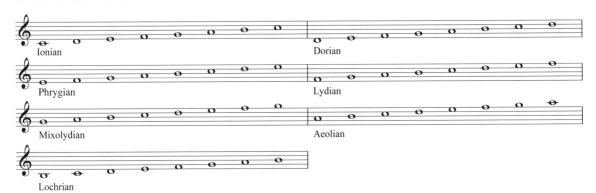

The modes differ in terms of their sound when played and the arrangement of tones and semitones in the pattern. Look at the difference between the mode on A (aeolian) and the mode on G (mixolydian):

Aeolian	Mixolydian
A – B – C – D – E – F – G – A	G – A – B – C – D – E – F – G
t s t t s t t	t t s t t s

Modes are still commonly used today in popular music, as well as in British folk music. One example is 'Scarborough Fair' written in the dorian mode.

Major scales

The major scales are constructed of eight notes that all follow the same pattern of tones and semitones, in the set sequence:

tone, tone, semitone, tone, tone, tone, semitone.

The following music shows how this works with C major.

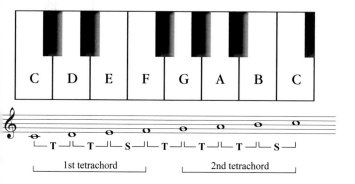

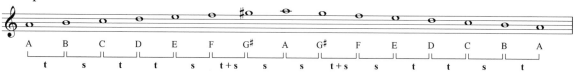

Minor scales

There are two forms of minor scales: **harmonic** and **melodic**.

The harmonic minor scale is the same ascending and descending and has a semitone between the seventh and eight notes, which gives the interval of a tone-and-a-half between notes 6 and 7. This gives these forms of minor keys their characteristic 'Turkish' sound. Look at A minor (harmonic) as an example:

The melodic minor scales are a little more complex in that they have different versions ascending and descending. In simple terms, the sixth and seventh degrees are raised by a semitone on the way up and then flattened on the way down.

Using the previous example of A minor, here are the basic notes:

Now we add the sharpened sixth and seventh, and then flatten these two notes on the way down. A sharp flattened by a semitone becomes a natural. Likewise, a flat sharpened becomes a natural.

Pentatonic scales

'Penta' means 'five', as in pentagon, a five-sided shape. Pentatonic scales are built up using the first, second, third, fifth and sixth notes of the scale. They are commonly used in folk tunes and other melodies such as the hymn tune 'Amazing Grace'.

In C major, these notes would be:

Another easy way to compose using just pentatonic notes is to use only the black keys on the keyboard: G♭, A♭, B♭, D♭ and E♭.

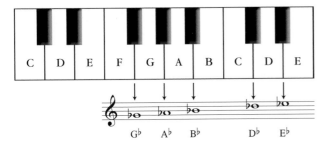

G♭ A♭ B♭ D♭ E♭

Chromatic scales

The word 'chromatic' means 'colour' and is a scale that comprises the 12
semitones within an octave, that is:

C C♯ D D♯ E F F♯ G G♯ A A♯ B C

Whole-tone scales

These scales were popular with the 20th-century impressionist composers
such as Debussy (1862–1918) and Ravel (1875–1937) and, as the name
suggests, they are made up of a sequence of tones:

C D E F♯ G♯ A♯ (C)

Degrees of the scale

The eight notes in a scale have specific technical names assigned to them.
The three most important are those based on the first, fourth and fifth
degrees. Roman numerals are used to describe the degrees of the scale:

◆ I = tonic
◆ IV = subdominant
◆ V = dominant.

However, it is useful to know all eight, as printed below.

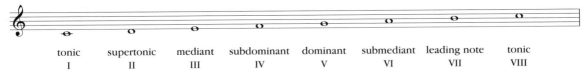

| tonic | supertonic | mediant | subdominant | dominant | submediant | leading note | tonic |
| I | II | III | IV | V | VI | VII | VIII |

Intervals

The distance between any two notes is called an **interval**. To work out the
number of the interval, simply count up from the lowest note (count this
note as 1) up to the next note, counting lines and spaces. See the extract
below:

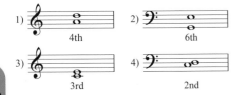

1) 4th 2) 6th

3) 3rd 4) 2nd

An interval greater than an octave is often called a **compound interval**. Therefore a ninth can also be called a compound second.

This gives you the basic numeric description of the interval, but you also need to know what is called the quality of the interval, that is, major, minor, **perfect**, **augmented** or **diminished**.

If you imagine the bottom note to be the key note of the scale (in this case, the note is C, so we are in C major), then you can work out the following intervals.

Maj 2nd	Maj 3rd	Perf. 4th	Perf. 5th	Maj 6th	Maj 7th	Maj (or perfect octave) 8th

Simple harmony

Triads

A **chord** is made up of at least two notes sounded simultaneously. There is no maximum number of notes in a chord! A **triad** is a three-note chord, the prefix 'tri' meaning 'three'.

The basic triad uses a root note plus a third above this and a note a fifth above the root note, as shown in the C major triad below. There are triads on each degree of the scale, too.

C major

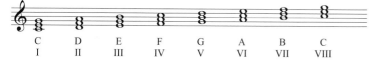

C	D	E	F	G	A	B	C
I	II	III	IV	V	VI	VII	VIII

Triads can also be built on notes from minor scales.

A minor

I	II	III	IV	V	VI	VII	VIII

Inversions

Look at the C major triad above. This is in **root position** because the root of the chord (C) is in the bass.

To 'invert' the chord, we can do two things:

◆ have the third in the bass – this is called **first inversion**
◆ have the fifth in the bass – this is called **second inversion**.

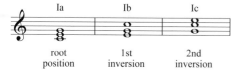

Ia	Ib	Ic
root position	1st inversion	2nd inversion

To tell the chords apart, root position chord I = Ia, first inversion is Ib and second inversion is Ic.

The primary triads

Primary triads form the basis of all harmony and are therefore of primary importance. They comprise the three chords of I, IV and V in every key.

These primary triads provide the basic 'colour' of the harmony. By using just these three chords, we can harmonise every note in the key of C major. The 12-bar blues and reggae songs were often based solely on these three chords, and many popular songs also only use a limited number of chords.

The primary triads in C major and C minor are shown below.

The secondary triads

The secondary triads are chords II and VI, and in a major key these are both minor chords. In C major, for example, this would be a chord of D minor (II) and A minor (VI). In a minor key, chord II is diminished and chord VI is major. The secondary triads in C major and C minor are shown below.

Cadences

Cadences are a type of musical punctuation. There are four common types of cadences that you need to know. Each cadence consists of two chords only.

◆ The **perfect cadence** (or full close) = chords V–I. This is like a full stop as it is conclusive and is often used to end a passage or section of music.
◆ The **imperfect cadence** (or half close) = chords I–V, or II–V, or IV–V (in fact, anything–V). The imperfect cadence is the comma. As it ends on the dominant chord, we are aware that the musical sentence is not complete and that there will be more to come.
◆ The **plagal cadence** (sometimes called the 'amen cadence') = chords IV–I. The plagal cadence is a gentler version of a perfect cadence. Chord IV is literally softer than the strong dominant chord and this cadence has associations with sacred music of the church and sounds like an 'amen'.
◆ The **interrupted cadence** = chords V–VI. The interrupted cadence literally 'interrupts' a perfect cadence. The listener is expecting chord I after chord V, but this is followed by chord VI, effectively like a semicolon, the music has more to add before concluding its musical sentence.

The four cadences written out in the key of C major and C minor in four-part harmony set for a four-part SATB choir (soprano, alto, tenor and bass) is shown as follows:

Glossary

imperfect cadence a cadence ending on chord V which sounds incomplete. Usually preceded by chord I, II or IV

interrupted cadence most commonly comprises chord V followed by chord VI. So called because the expected perfect cadence V–I has been interrupted by the unexpected chord VI

perfect cadence chord V followed by chord I

plagal cadence chord IV followed by chord I – the 'Amen cadence' or English cadence

a) **Perfect cadence**

V   I

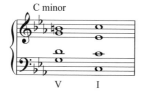

V   I

c) **Imperfect cadence**

I   V

I   V

b) **Plagal cadence**

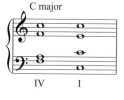

IV   I

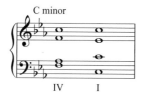

IV   I

d) **Interrupted cadence**

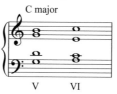

V   VI

V   VI

Musical devices

There are many devices used in music. The following are some of the most common that you will come across.

Drone

This usually features the sustained tonic and dominant notes together, although the two notes can alternate. It is commonly a feature of the harmony and will be used to support a melody. Bagpipes use this principle of a drone bass with a melody played on the chanter.

Pedal

A sustained note, usually dominant or tonic, hence called a tonic pedal or a dominant pedal. If the sustained note is the lowest part in the musical texture, it is called the **pedal**. If the sustained note is in the middle of a texture, it is called an **inner pedal**, and if it appears as the highest part, it is called an **inverted pedal**.

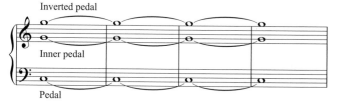

Glossary

inner pedal a sustained note in the middle of the musical texture

inverted pedal a sustained note at the top of the musical texture

pedal a sustained note usually in the lowest bass part

Alberti bass

This is a common type of figuration used as an accompaniment. It was invented by Alberti during the Classical era and has been extensively used since.

Arpeggio/broken chords

Two useful types of accompaniment (or figuration) that can easily be
adapted to fit a particular passage of music.

Ostinato/riff

An ostinato (or 'riff', as it is called in popular and jazz music) is simply a
short repeated phrase. An ostinato can be a repeated rhythm, melody or
chord sequence.

Quite often, the ostinato will be a combination of these features – for
example a rhythmic melodic idea. This well-known football chant is an
example of a rhythmic ostinato.

repeat

The elements of music

This final section looks at the key elements of music that you will be
expected to understand and recognise by the end of your GCSE course.
They are also tested in Questions 9 and 10 of the listening paper. These are
the key elements of:

- pitch
- duration
- dynamics
- tempo
- timbre
- texture
- structure.

Pitch

Pitch refers to how high or low the music sounds at a particular point. Pitch
can include reference to both melody and harmony, and involves all types
of notation, including conventional staff notation, non-standard and graphic
score notations.

The musical vocabulary that you need to be familiar is summarised in the
following table.

Pitch	Melody	Harmony and tonality	Notation
Pitch names	Step	Consonant	Staff notation
Sharp, flat	Leap	Dissonant	Treble and bass
Octave	Scalic	Major	Stave (staff)
Intervals	Interval	Minor	Bar/double bar lines
Range	Chromatic	Modal	Key and time signatures
Register	Glissando	Atonal	Note values
Diatonic key		Cadences	Phrase
Tonic		Modulation	Articulation mark
Subdominant		Transpose	Dynamic signs
Dominant		Pedal	Ornament signs
Pentatonic		Drone	Graphic score
Raga		Chord pattern	Non-standard notation
Note row		Arpeggio/broken chords	Three-line staves
			Oral tradition

Duration

This refers to the length of musical sounds. You need to know the following terms:

◆ note values – for example, crotchets, semiquavers and so on
◆ pulse/beat
◆ triplet
◆ dotted rhythm
◆ phrase length and shape
◆ phrase structure.

Dynamics

In your exams, you will be asked to comment on the dynamics in an extract and to describe how dynamics change, including crescendos and diminuendos. The articulation of the music (how it is played) is often linked to dynamics.

Dynamics		Articulation
Fortissimo	Crescendo	Legato (smooth)
Forte	Diminuendo	Staccato (short and detached)
Mezzo forte	Subito (suddenly)	
Mezzo piano	Accent/sforzando	Tremolo (wavering)
Piano/pianissimo		Pizzicato (plucked)

Tempo

The speed or **tempo** of the music is expressed mainly in Italian terms and you need to know the following basic terms:

Tempo	Tempo changes
Adagio – slow	Accelerando – getting faster
Largo – slow and broad	Ritardando/rallentando – slowing down
Andante – at a walking pace (medium tempo)	Allargando – broadening out
	Rubato – 'robbed' time, not in strict tempo
Allegro – fast	Silence
Vivace – fast and lively	Pause
Presto – very fast	

Glossary

tempo speed of the music

Timbre

The **timbre** of music means the tone quality of the sound and the difference between sounds – for example, the timbre of a trumpet is quite different from the timbre of a flute.

You will need to be able to identify changes in musical timbre and also to be able to recognise the sounds of individual orchestral instruments, as well as the sounds of various instrumental ensembles.

Glossary

timbre particular tone colour of an instrument or voice

Vocal sounds	Instrumental sounds	Ensembles
Soprano/treble	Brass instruments	Orchestra
Alto	Percussion	Chamber orchestra
Tenor	Strings	Wind band
Bass	Woodwind	Brass band
Falsetto	Electric instruments	Pop band, rock band
Choir	Keyboard instruments	Indian/African ensemble
Chorus	Indian instruments:	Quintets/quartets/trios/duets
A cappella	sitar/sarod/sarangai/	
Backing vocals	tambura/tabla	
	African instruments:	
	djembe/talking drums/agogo	
	bells/master drummer/kora/	
	mbira	

Texture

Texture describes *two* different but related elements of music.

1 The number and movement of musical parts and how this can vary during the course of a piece or extract. Words to describe this aspect of texture include the following:

◆ number of parts – for example, two-, three-, four-part texture and so on
◆ tutti – all playing
◆ solo line – one part (called **monophonic**)

Glossary

texture the number of parts in a piece of music and how they relate to one another. There are several distinct types of texture: homophony, polyphony, monophony and heterophony

- descant/counter melody – a second melody added to the texture
- sparse texture – just a few musical parts or lines present – for example, a solo flute accompanied by a cello
- dense texture – a texture that is 'busy' and is characterised by many instruments or different parts
- varied texture – most musical textures will fall into this category and will change frequently during a piece of music in order to provide both variety and interest.

2 A particular type of established and recognised texture.

- **Monophonic** – literally means just 'one sound'. A single musical line, but can be sung or played by many people.

- **Homophonic** – literally 'same sounds'. Melody and accompaniment style. Parts move roughly together. This is the most common type of musical texture.

- **Polyphonic** – literally 'many sounds'. Two or more parts playing a melody and entering the texture individually to create a contrapuntal texture. Common in Renaissance vocal music.

- **Heterophonic** – literally a 'difference of sounds'. Two or more parts play a melody together but with some slight differences in pitch. This is common in Eastern musical traditions where music is learnt and played by ear (oral tradition).

Structure

All the musical elements discussed so far can be found within the musical structure or form. The structures that you will need to know are the structures that you have studied in your set works from the four Areas of Study. This section also includes common musical devices that occur within musical structures.

Structure	Musical devices
Ground bass and variations	Repetition/sequence
Rondo/ritornello	Ostinato/riffs
Sonata form	Imitation/canon
Binary form	Motific development
Ternary form	Introduction
Minuet and trio	Coda
Song verse/chorus structure	Link
Indian raga structure	
Call and response	
Aleatoric/chance	

Glossary

acciaccatura an ornament – literally 'a crushed note' – played as quickly as possible before the main note

affection the mood of a piece of music. It was customary in Baroque music for a single mood to prevail in a movement

alap the opening unmetred and improvised section of a raga

altered chord a chord in which one of the notes has been sharpened or flattened to become a chromatic note

alto C clef the clef used mainly by the viola

aria a solo vocal piece with instrumental accompaniment

arpeggio the notes of a chord played one after the other rather than together, e.g. C–E–G–C

atonal absence of tonality (key)

augmentation doubling (or more) of the original note values

augmented chord any chord which contains an augmented interval – that is, a chord where the length of the notes is prolonged by a semitone

augmented made larger by a semitone, as in an augmented interval

bandish the last section of a vocal raga – a 'fixed composition' in the form of a song

bansuri Indian flute without keys

bass (or F clef) clef that fixes the note F on the fourth line of the stave

bebop a jazz style requiring virtuosic technique, including fast tempos and complex harmonies

big band a jazz style popular in the 1920s and 1930s in which the pieces were generally written for a large ensemble to be played in dance halls

blue note a 'bent' note between the minor and major third

bols in a tala, these are the independent rhythm parts that go against the main beat of the cycle creating exciting syncopations

breve a long note of eight crotchet beats duration

bridge passage a linking passage often used to change the key of the music (modulate) in preparation for the second subject

burlesque a parody or humorous piece

cadence two chords at the end of a musical phrase. There are four main types of cadence: perfect, imperfect, interrupted and plagal

cantabile instruction for music to be performed 'in a singing style'

cells short musical ideas

changes the chord sequence in a jazz song

chord substitution replacing one chord with another

chord the simultaneous sounding together of two or more notes

chromatic music in which notes are used that are not in the key of the piece

chromatically moving by semitones up or down

chromaticism notes used that are foreign to the key of the music. For example, sharps and flats in the key of C major would be chromatic notes

clef French for key, clefs fix a particular note on the stave

comic opera see **opéra-bouffe**

comping an abbreviation of 'accompanying'

complement the six semitones not used in the first hexachord

compound interval an interval larger than an octave – for example a ninth is also a compound second

compound time signature a time signature where the beat is dotted and subdivides into groups of three, as in 6/8 which has two dotted crotchet beats, each of which comprises three quavers

cross-rhythms rhythms that literally cross the usual pattern of accented and unaccented beats, creating irregular accents and syncopated effects

delay repetition(s) of a sound after a set time interval, usually at a lower volume and with less high frequency content than the original

diatonic notes or chords belonging to or literally 'of the key'

diminished made smaller by a semitone

diminished 7th a chord made up of superimposed minor third intervals (e.g. B, D, F, A♭)

djembe goblet-shaped drum from West Africa

dominant fifth note of the scale or key – the strongest note after the tonic

dominant 13th chord V (dominant) with the added 13th note

dominant pedal a sustained (or repeated) note(s) on the dominant note of the key

donno hourglass-shaped 'talking drum', held under the arm and played with the hand

drone a note repeated or sustained across chord changes, often creating a dissonance

dundun double-headed drum (in several different sizes) played with sticks

enharmonic different ways of 'spelling' the same pitch, for example B♭ and A♯

EQ abbreviation of equalisation – electronically cutting or boosting specific frequencies in a sound

extended chord a chord in which diatonic notes other than the seventh have been added to the original triad

extravaganzas stage shows containing a variety of acts

first inversion a chord with the third in the bass. A chord of C major (C-E-G) in first inversion would be E-G-C

first subject the first theme or melody

flanger a studio effect ranging from subtle 'swirling' sounds to 'jet plane' effects

four-to-the-floor a strong reinforcement of a 4/4 beat by a bass drum

frontline the solo instruments in a jazz ensemble

fugue a musical texture involving polyphonic writing for instruments/voices. It is also known as a structure in which voice parts enter one after the other in imitation. The fugue has three sections: exposition – middle entries – final entries

fusion a mingling, or blending together, of more than one musical style or culture to create a new 'fused' sound

gat the final section of an instrumental raga – a 'fixed composition' with some improvised embellishments

gharana Indian system of master–pupil teaching

harmonic relates to the harmony parts

harmonic rhythm the number of times the chords change per bar

head the main melody of a jazz song, generally played at the beginning of the song

hemiola in triple time, this is a rhythmic device often used towards a cadence point, in which notes are grouped in two beat units, e.g.

heterophonic two or more parts playing the same melodic line simultaneously with small variations between the parts

hexachord a group of six notes selected from the 12 available pitches that are used as a musical motif or chord

homophonic common musical texture comprising a melody part and accompaniment

imitative literally separate parts copying or imitating each other. If the imitation is note for note the same, this will then be a canon

imperfect cadence a cadence ending on chord V which sounds incomplete. Usually preceded by chord I, II or IV

impressionist a style of music that seeks to describe a feeling or experience rather than achieve accurate depiction

inner pedal a sustained (or repeated) note(s) in the middle of a musical texture

interrupted cadence most commonly comprises chord V followed by chord VI. So-called because the expected perfect cadence V–I has been interrupted by the unexpected chord VI

interval distance between any two notes

inversion a method of developing a series by turning all the intervals upside down so as to create a mirror image of the original series

inverted dominant pedal a sustained (or repeated) note(s) as the highest part in a musical texture

inverted pedal a sustained note at the top of the musical texture

jhalla the third section of a raga and the climax of the whole piece. A lively tempo and virtuoso display of improvisatory skills

johr the second section of a raga – a medium tempo with improvisation

klangfarbenmelodie literally 'tone colour melody', a word used to describe how timbre contributes to melody in addition to pitch and rhythm

libretto the text/words of a musical work such as an opera or oratorio

loop a section of a piece of music which is edited so that it can be repeated seamlessly by electronic means

major Western tonal music in bright sounding keys. A major key has four semitones between the first and third notes (C–E)

matras individual beats in a rhythmic cycle

meend/mind the sliding effects between notes

melodic refers to the melody line

melodramas dramas in which spoken lines are punctuated by music

membranophones category of instruments that have a drum skin (membrane)

minor Western tonal music in solemn sounding keys. A minor key has three semitones between the first and third notes (C–E♭)

minstrelsy form of entertainment, popular in the 1800s, in which white actors would be made up in 'blackface' to imitate black slaves and poke fun at the rich and powerful

minuet and trio a ternary form structure, performed as minuet–trio–minuet. The minuet is a stately dance in triple time and the contrasting middle section (trio) usually features a reduction in instrumental parts. Often used as the third movement in a Classical symphony

modal jazz a jazz style in which the soloists base their solos on modes instead of the chord changes

modal referring to modes – the precursors of modern scales

modes precursors of modern scales. There are seven different modes, each with a different series of tones and semitones

modulating when the music changes key

monophonic musical texture of a single melodic line with no accompaniment

mordent ornament in which the written note is played, followed by the note above and the written note again

MTV A TV channel dedicated to playing music videos

neopolitan 6th chord of the flattened supertonic (second degree) in first inversion

New Orleans Jazz one of the first recognised jazz styles, originating in New Orleans

note addition a method of developing cells in minimalist music by gradually adding notes to the original cell

note subtraction as for note addition, but taking notes away

octave the interval of eight notes – for example, C to C eight notes higher

opéra-bouffe a light opera, often with spoken dialogue and some comical content

operetta light opera

oral tradition music that is learnt by listening and repeating, and passed on orally from generation to generation (without being written down in traditional notation)

oratorio large-scale musical setting for chorus, soloists and orchestra of a biblical text, designed for concert performance

overdubs the use of a multi-track recording device to layer recorded parts

pathétique literally 'pathetic', refers to a melancholy mood

pedal a sustained note usually in the lowest bass part. In the middle of a musical texture it is called an inner pedal and if at the top, an inverted pedal

pentatonic scale a scale built on five notes (penta=5) of the scale on the first, second, third, fifth and sixth degrees of the scale. In C major, these are C, D, E, G and A

perfect (i) a perfect interval, such as the fourth, fifth and eighth; (ii) a type of cadence – chord V followed by chord

perfect cadence chord V followed by chord I

phasing when two or more versions of a sound or musical motif are played simultaneously but slightly out of synchronisation, with the two parts gradually coming back in sync after a number of repetitions

pitch how high or low a note sounds

pivot note a note common to both keys and used to pivot between two different keys, i.e. A♭ (of D♭ major) is also G♯ (in C♯ minor)

pizzicato playing a string instrument by plucking the strings

plagal cadence chord IV followed by chord I – the 'Amen cadence'

polyphonic a musical texture featuring two or more parts, each having a melody line and sounding together

polyrhythmic texture a texture made up of many different rhythms

power chords a chord commonly played on the guitar consisting of the root note and the perfect fifth

prime row the musical material on which a piece of serial music is based, normally consisting of the 12 notes of the chromatic scale in an order set by the composer

principal voice the main melodic line

protest songs folk songs with political lyrics

raga improvised music in several contrasting sections, based on a series of notes from a particular rag

ragtime music characterized by a syncopated melodic line and regularly accented accompaniment

rasa mood created by the sounds of the pitches in a particular rag

recitative a style used in operas, oratorios and cantatas in which the text is 'declaimed' (told) in the rhythm of natural speech

resultant melody a new melody produced when a variety of parts each play their melodies at the same time

retrograde a method of developing a series by reversing the order in which the pitches are heard

retrograde inversion a method of developing a series by reversing the order in which the pitches of the inverted series are heard

reverb the reflection of sound off surfaces to give the impression of space – may be natural or electronically applied to a sound

Romanticism an artistic movement in Europe, between c. 1800–1900, in which the artist was more concerned with feelings and emotions than with form

rondo Classical form comprising a series of rondo sections interspersed with contrasting episodes. The simple rondo was structured as ABACA, where A is the rondo theme, and B and C are the episodes

root position chord with the root in the bass. In the case of a chord of C major, this would be C-E-G

sam the first beat of the rhythmic cycle

second inversion chord with the fifth in the bass. A chord of C major (C-E-G) in second inversion would be G-C-E

second subject the second theme or melody

secondary voice the next most importance melodic line after the principal voice

semibreve long note lasting for four crotchet beats

semitone half a tone – the distance between a white note and an adjacent black note on a keyboard

serialism a compositional technique invented by Schoenberg and used by many composers of the 20th century

shehnai a double reed Indian instrument, similar to the Western oboe

simple time signature a time signature where the beat can be divided into two, such as 2/4 which has two crotchet beats, each made up of two quavers

sinfonia an Italian form in origin, these were works in three sections for strings and continuo.

slide a playing technique on string instruments by sliding the finger from one note to another or a metal/glass device used to slide form one note to another on guitars

soft pedal pedal on a piano that, when pressed, softens the tone of the music

sonata form a large-scale form invented in the Classical era comprising three sections – exposition, development and recapitulation

soundscapes music concentrating on the manipulation of timbre and texture to create a musical 'landscape' or atmosphere rather than the statement and development of musical themes

staff/stave the five parallel lines upon which music notation is written

sus2 chord a triad with the major or minor third replaced by the second degree of the scale

sus4 chord a triad with the major or minor third replaced by the fourth degree of the scale

sustaining pedal a pedal that, when pressed, sustains all the strings on the piano by removing the dampers from all strings and allowing them to vibrate freely

swing a development of big band jazz. The term is also used to describe a particular type of rhythmic 'groove' desirable in jazz music

symphony a large-scale genre for orchestra in three or four movements. Sonata form was often used for the first and last movements in symphonies

syncopations notes accented off the beat. The weak part of the beat is often emphasised

tan the rapid scalic flourishes on the sitar, sarod or sarangai

teental (or tintal) common 16-beat (4+4+4+4) rhythmic cycle

tempo rubato literally means 'robbed' time – this is a technique where the player can pull back (or speed up) the tempo for expressive effect

tempo speed of the music

tenor C clef used in conjunction with the bass clef for high notes on the bassoon, trombone, cello and double bass

ternary a three-part structure in ABA form in which the opening section is repeated and section B provides contrast

texture the number of parts in a piece of music and how they relate to one another. There are several distinct types of texture: homophony, polyphony, monophony and heterophony

theme and variations a theme (melody) followed by a series of variation on the original theme

timbre particular tone colour of an instrument or voice

time signature the two numbers at the beginning of a piece of music. The top number refers to the number of beats per bar and the bottom figure indicates the type of beat

tonal ambiguity when the key of a piece is uncertain

tone interval of two semitones – for example, F to G is made up of F to F♯ (a semitone) and F♯ to G (a semitone)

tone languages in African music, languages made up of only a few pitches, called tone languages. The pitch level determines the meaning of the words

tonic the first degree of a scale, the keynote, e.g. in C major the note C is the tonic note

Treaty of Versailles the peace settlement signed after World War I had ended in 1918

treble (or G clef) this fixes the note G on the second line of the stave. The treble clef is used for high-pitched instruments and voices

triad a three-note chord ('tri' means three)

trill rapidly alternating between two notes

turnaround a short chord pattern at the end of a sequence signalling the return to the beginning of the sequence

V7c dominant 7th chord (V7) in second inversion (c)

vaudeville a form of entertainment, popular in the 1700s, in which popular songs were performed with alternative words

Vb dominant chord (V) in first inversion (b)

virtuoso performer a person – in music or the arts in general – who has mastered the skills and techniques of their art form

vocables effects made by the voice, using vowel sounds such as 'eh', 'ah', 'oh'

voicings a term used to describe various ways of ordering the notes in a chord from lowest to highest

Index